Praise for THE BLOOD COUNTESS

"Shelley Puhak skillfully reveals the layers of deception and fear surrounding Countess Elizabeth Bathory, portraying her as a complex and misunderstood figure: commanding, powerful, and punished for defying the limits imposed on women. A new image emerges—a formidable woman fighting against men eager to seize her property and power. *The Blood Countess* reveals how influential women are often vilified and underscores the significant role myths play in shaping our understanding of history."
—LYDIA REEDER, author of *The Cure for Women: Dr. Mary Putnam Jacobi and the Challenge to Victorian Medicine That Changed Women's Lives Forever*

"Shelley Puhak leaves no stone unturned in her thorough debunking of the myths surrounding Elizabeth Bathory . . . [Bathory's] only crime was being a woman who would not cede her power . . . This tale, though set in the seventeenth century, strikes so many notes with contemporary resonances . . . Exciting, revealing, and often enraging, the life of the powerful Elizabeth Bathory finally gets the treatment it has long deserved."
—CATHERINE PRENDERGAST, author of *The Gilded Edge: Two Audacious Women and the Cyanide Love Triangle That Shook America*

"A feminist debunking of the myth of a monstrous Renaissance noblewoman . . . Through close reading of Bathory's many letters and various contemporary accounts, poet and writer Puhak uncovers a thoroughly premodern Renaissance woman, well bred and well read, from a distinguished ancient family . . . Admirably clear-eyed history related in crystalline prose."
—*KIRKUS REVIEWS* (starred review)

"This striking account from poet and historian Puhak separates the true story of Hungarian noblewoman Elizabeth Bathory from her blood-soaked mythology . . . It's a stunning feminist reconsideration of one of history's most reviled villainesses."
—*PUBLISHERS WEEKLY* (starred review)

"With vivid scenes and astonishing detail, Puhak takes us on an enthralling journey into the life of the notorious Elizabeth Bathory. In this deeply researched, essential historical corrective, we finally . . . meet the woman behind the myth."
—OLIVIA CAMPBELL, *New York Times* bestselling author of *Women in White Coats*

"A brilliant reappraisal of the life and legend of Elizabeth, Countess of Bathory... Employing an engaging style and meticulous research, Puhak slices through four hundred years of superstition and smears with the ease of a Renaissance knight on a noble quest for truth and justice. Both an invaluable contribution to scholarship and a compelling true crime mystery, *The Blood Countess* makes for a fascinating read."
—NANCY GOLDSTONE, author of *The Rebel Empresses: Elisabeth of Austria and Eugénie of France, Power and Glamour in the Struggle for Europe*

"In a remarkable feat of research, Shelley Puhak untangles the four-century-old mystery of the Blood Countess, a tale long tainted by misinformation in a society determined to sink a powerful woman. Puhak's fine writing brings the notorious countess to life with clarity and passion."
—BECKY AIKMAN, author of *Spitfires: The American Women Who Flew in the Face of Danger During World War II*

"I greatly enjoyed this pacy, compulsive investigation, with its persuasive unpicking of many claims made against Elizabeth Bathory. We think we know about this witchlike, vampiric murderess—but Puhak tells us a whole new story of intrigue and injustice."
—MARION GIBSON, author of *Witchcraft: A History in Thirteen Trials*

Praise for THE DARK QUEENS

"Powerful feminist history... sweeping and detailed."
—*USA TODAY*

"Medieval history at its most fun. *Game of Thrones*, eat your heart out!"
—*NAPA VALLEY REGISTER*

"A deeply fascinating portrait of the early Middle Ages that vigorously reclaims two powerhouse women from obscurity."
—*PUBLISHERS WEEKLY* (starred review)

"A well-researched and well-told epic history. *The Dark Queens* brings these courageous, flawed, and ruthless rulers and their distant times back to life."
—MARGOT LEE SHETTERLY, *New York Times* bestselling author of *Hidden Figures*

The
BLOOD
COUNTESS

BY THE SAME AUTHOR

The Dark Queens: The Bloody Rivalry That Forged the Medieval World

Harbinger: Poems

Guinevere in Baltimore: Poems

Stalin in Aruba: Poems

The
BLOOD COUNTESS

MURDER, BETRAYAL,
and the MAKING of a
MONSTER

SHELLEY PUHAK

BLOOMSBURY PUBLISHING
NEW YORK · LONDON · OXFORD · NEW DELHI · SYDNEY

BLOOMSBURY PUBLISHING
Bloomsbury Publishing Inc.
1359 Broadway, New York, NY 10018, USA
50 Bedford Square, London, WC1B 3DP, UK
Bloomsbury Publishing Ireland Limited,
29 Earlsfort Terrace, Dublin 2, D02 AY28, Ireland

BLOOMSBURY, BLOOMSBURY PUBLISHING, and the Diana logo
are trademarks of Bloomsbury Publishing Plc

First published in the United States 2026

Copyright © Shelley Puhak, 2026
Maps created by Ortelius Design

All rights reserved. No part of this publication may be: i) reproduced or transmitted in any form, electronic or mechanical, including photocopying, recording, or by means of any information storage or retrieval system without prior permission in writing from the publishers; or ii) used or reproduced in any way for the training, development, or operation of artificial intelligence (AI) technologies, including generative AI technologies. The rights holders expressly reserve this publication from the text and data mining exception as per Article 4(3) of the Digital Single Market Directive (EU) 2019/790.

Bloomsbury Publishing Plc does not have any control over, or responsibility for, any third-party websites referred to or in this book. All internet addresses given in this book were correct at the time of going to press. The author and publisher regret any inconvenience caused if addresses have changed or sites have ceased to exist, but can accept no responsibility for any such changes.

ISBN: HB: 978-1-63973-215-9; EBOOK: 978-1-63973-216-6

Library of Congress Control Number: 2026930796

2 4 6 8 10 9 7 5 3

Typesetting by Six Red Marbles India
Printed in the United States by Lakeside Book Company

To find out more about our authors and books visit www.bloomsbury.com
and sign up for our newsletters.

Bloomsbury books may be purchased for business or promotional use. For information on bulk purchases please contact Macmillan Corporate and Premium Sales Department at specialmarkets@macmillan.com.
For product safety–related questions contact productsafety@bloomsbury.com.

CONTENTS

Author's Note ix
Maps 2
Dramatis Personae 5

Prologue 9

PART ONE: 1603–1609

CHAPTER ONE: A Long, Terrible Year 19
CHAPTER TWO: The First Clue 31
CHAPTER THREE: A Wedding and a Rebellion 45
CHAPTER FOUR: The Curious Case of Miss Modl 63
CHAPTER FIVE: See You in Court 77
CHAPTER SIX: The Dose Makes the Poison 91

PART TWO: 1610–1614

CHAPTER SEVEN: Strained Relations 105
CHAPTER EIGHT: The Preacher of Čachtice 121
CHAPTER NINE: The Mysterious Will 137
CHAPTER TEN: The Raid 149
CHAPTER ELEVEN: The Servants' Trial 161
CHAPTER TWELVE: Her Day in Court 177
CHAPTER THIRTEEN: The Last Bathory 189

Epilogue 199

Acknowledgments 211
Bibliography 213

Notes	239
Image Credits	273
Index	275
A Note on the Author	288
Elizabeth Bathory: Fact vs. Fiction	289

AUTHOR'S NOTE

This is a work of nonfiction. Anything between quotation marks comes from a letter, diary, deposition, or other historical document. For further information on these and all other sources, please see the bibliography and endnotes at the back of this book. Many of these primary sources are in Hungarian, while others are in Latin, German, or Slovak; they are all, because of their age, difficult to decipher. To ensure accuracy and clarity, I have commissioned transcriptions and translations by experts who specialize in documents from this period. Translating contemporary Hungarian to English is difficult enough; translating sixteenth- and seventeenth-century Hungarian idioms and grammar is an even more complex task. Because the words of Elizabeth Bathory and her contemporaries have been subjected to so many mistranslations and misunderstandings, I have kept all translations as faithful to the original texts as possible, preserving archaic phrases and even clumsy grammar. The one alteration I have made is to place names. Because many towns in Central Europe have changed names multiple times, and to better enable readers to walk the Blood Countess's footsteps if they so wish, I have updated all quotations to indicate the most current or common place names.

The
BLOOD
COUNTESS

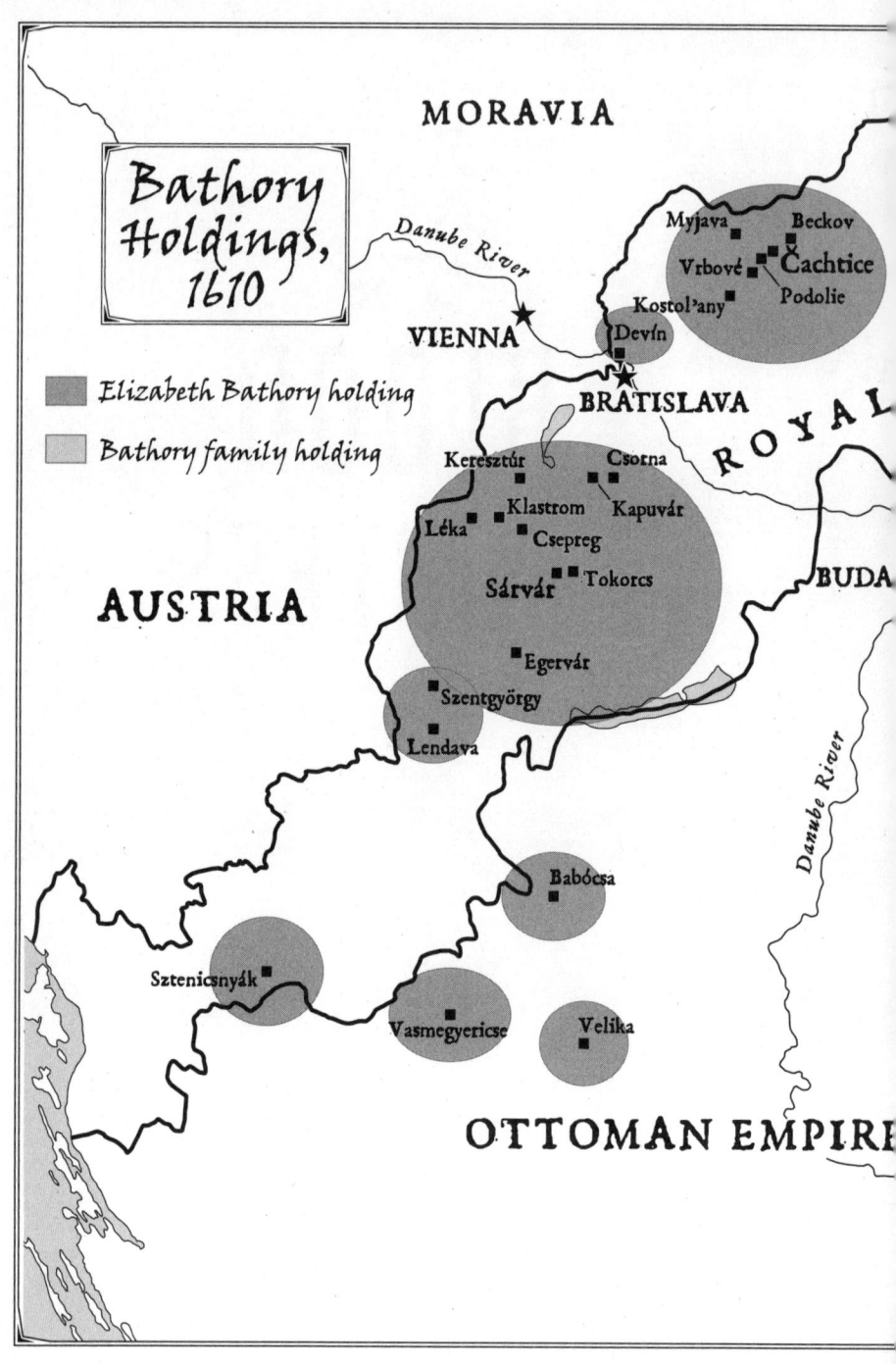

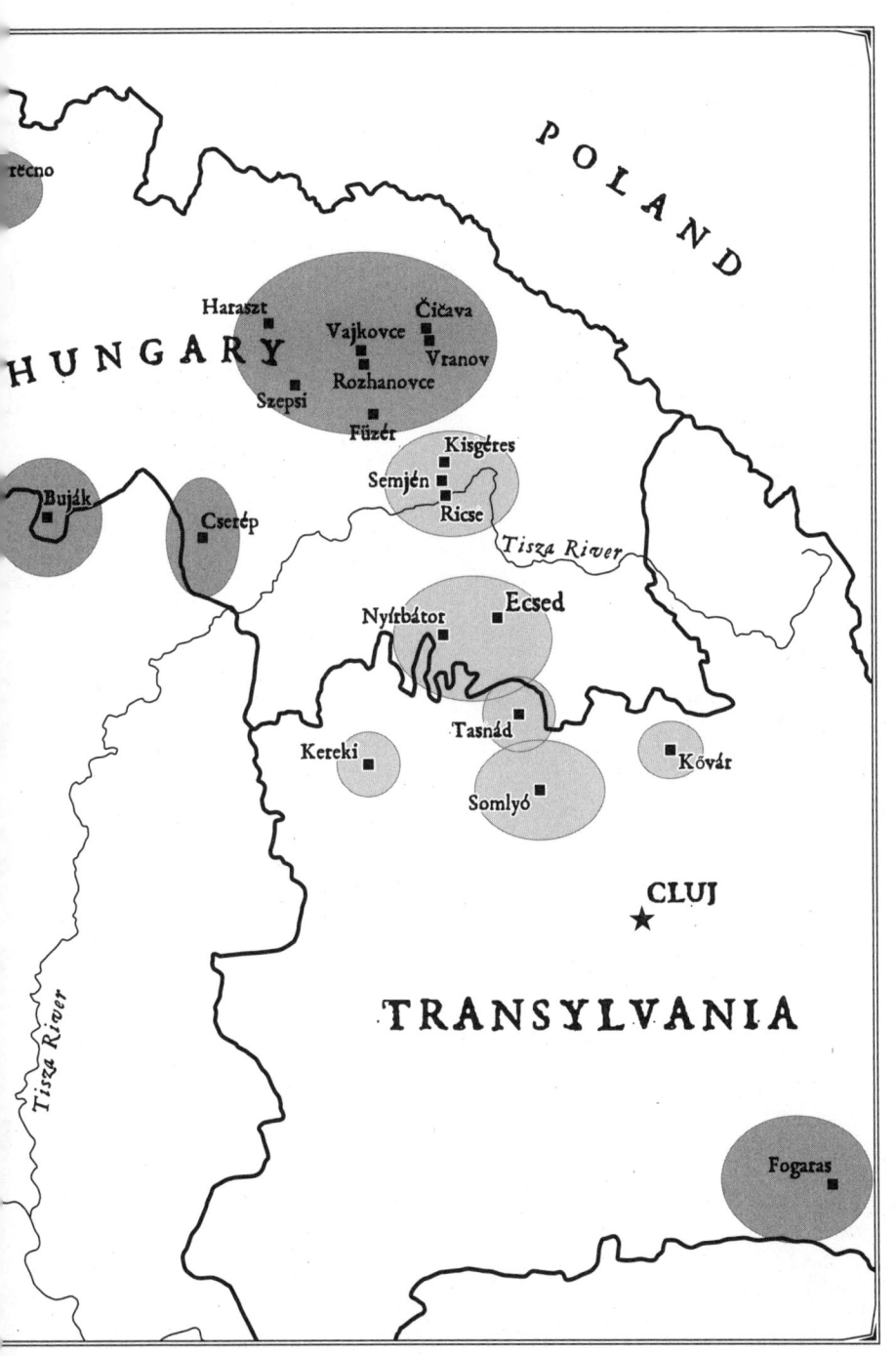

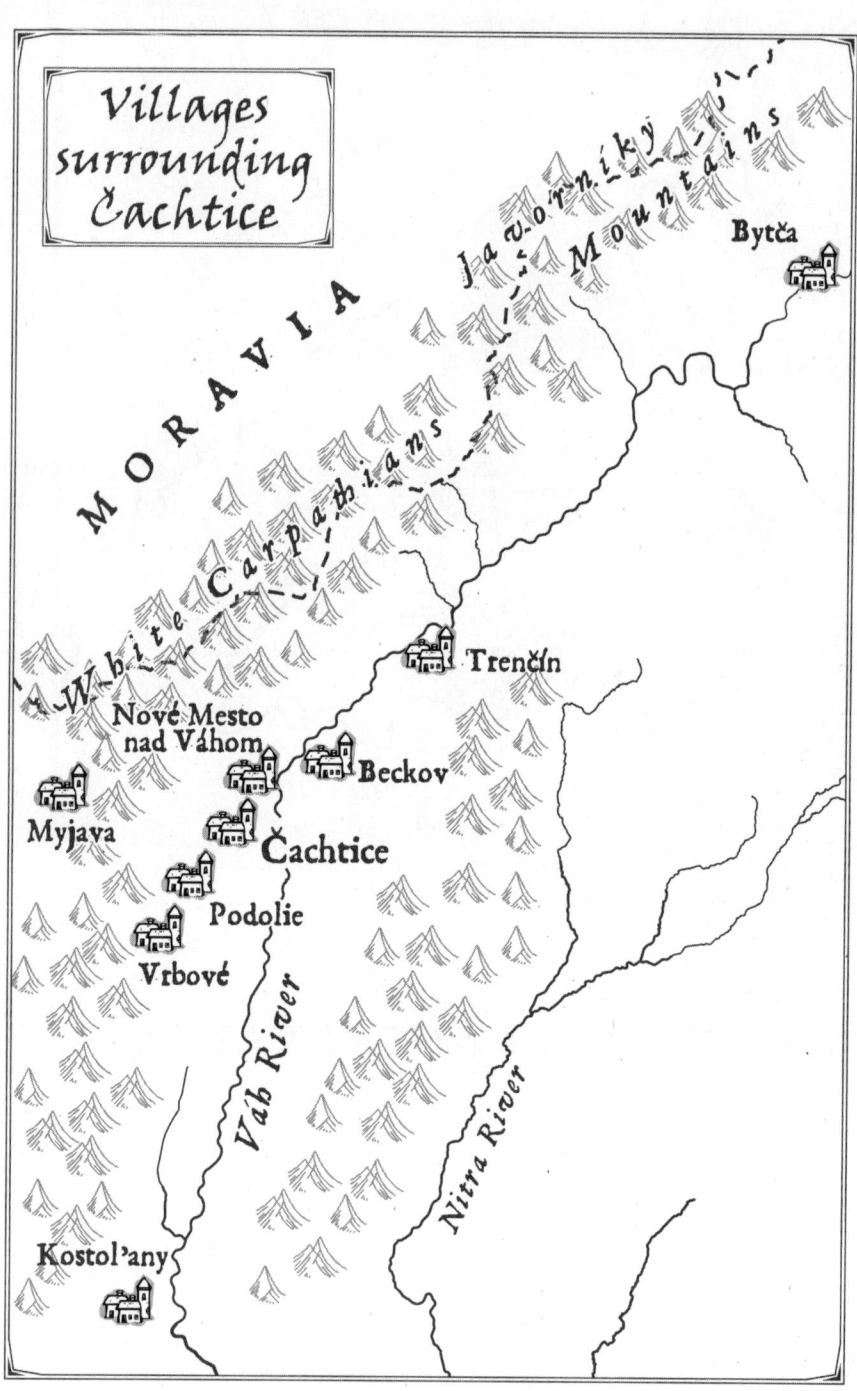

DRAMATIS PERSONAE

Most of the men in this book are named Stephen, after the patron saint of Hungary. Quite a lot of the women are named Anna (or Kate, or Elizabeth). Reader, I am sorry.

I have anglicized names and titles in an effort to make a case that is frequently cast as dark and mysterious more accessible. These spellings would not be entirely unfamiliar to the characters themselves; while they signed some letters and documents in Hungarian, they also frequently used the Latin or German versions of their names. So while the Countess is "Báthory Erzsébet" in Hungarian (which always lists last names first), she also signed her name as "Elizabetth de Batthory" and "Elisabeth comitissa de Bathor." I have also standardized spelling, which, in this era, was rather flexible: The Countess spelled her last name at least four different ways.

Note, too, that Hungarian women retained their family names and titles after marriage. While women were sometimes referred to as extensions of their husbands (Mrs. Francis Nadasdy, for example), it was more common for them to keep their maiden names. Whenever a woman's first name is used, the last name that follows is her family's name, not her husband's.

DRAMATIS PERSONAE

THE COUNTESS'S FAMILY

Elizabeth Bathory (1560–1614)

Her husband, **Francis Nadasdy** (1555–1604), the Black Lord, Count of Nádasd and Fogarasföld, military hero in the war against the Ottoman Turks

    Her (surviving) children
        Anna Nadasdy
            Count **Nicolas Zrinyi** (m. 1604)
        Katalin (Kate) Nadasdy
            Count **George Drugeth of Humenne** (m. 1610)
        Paul Nadasdy

Her older brother, **Stephen Bathory (XIII)** (1555–1605), Chief Justice of Hungary

    His adopted children
        Gabriel Bathory (1589–1613), Prince of Transylvania
        Anna Bathory, Gabriel's younger sister

Her aunt **Klara Bathory** (1525?–after 1578)

Her Transylvanian cousins **Kate Torok**, the largest landowner in the principality, and **Kate Iffiu**, the wife of a top politician

HER SERVANTS AND RETAINERS

Emery "Red" Megyery, flame-haired real estate mogul and guardian of Paul Nadasdy

Lady Helen Hernath, noblewoman in Elizabeth Bathory's court

Lady Anna Velikey, noblewoman in Elizabeth Bathory's court

John Ujvary, aka Ficzko, orphaned boy raised to be one of Elizabeth Bathory's footmen

Helena Jo, the children's nanny

Anna Darvulia, court midwife and healer

DRAMATIS PERSONAE

Dorothy Szentes, court midwife and healer, Anna Darvulia's replacement

Katherine Beneczky, washerwoman

Mistress of Myjava, herbalist and trusted companion of the Countess, wife of a prominent farm administrator, overseer of livestock and cheesemaking in Čachtice region

"Woman Scientist" of Tokorcs, village healer and foster mother near Sárvár

THE HAPSBURGS

Ferdinand I, Holy Roman Emperor, 1556–1563, brother-in-law of Hungarian king Louis II

Rudolf II, Holy Roman Emperor, 1576–1612, patron of alchemists and artists

Matthias II, younger brother of Rudolf II, king of Hungary 1608–1619, Holy Roman Emperor 1612–1619

THE NOBLES

Stephen Bocskai, Protestant lord, rebel leader, then prince of Transylvania

Francis Batthyany, Elizabeth Bathory's neighbor, son of one of Francis Nadasdy's best friends

George Thurzo, ambitious new-money aristocrat and Hapsburg loyalist, palatine of Hungary

    his wife, **Elizabeth Czobor**, effusive and often sickly

George Banffy, ruthless aristocrat known for poaching properties

    Mrs. Caspar Banffy, his widowed sister-in-law, mother of eight, a Nadasdy relation

Valentine Drugeth of Humenne, rival of Gabriel Bathory for the Transylvanian throne, cousin of George Drugeth

Gabriel Bethlen, adviser to Transylvanian princes, future prince

THE CLERGY

Stephen Beythe, Protestant bishop for Nadasdy lands until his resignation in 1591; progressive scholar and botanist

John Reczes, Lutheran hard-liner who opposed Beythe and initiated the split between Calvinists and Lutherans on Nadasdy lands

    Stephen Magyari, former army camp chaplain to Francis Nadasdy, then chief pastor at Sárvár, committed Lutheran

    Michael Zvonarics, "the Shoemaker of Sárvár," Magyari's replacement, chief pastor of Sárvár beginning in 1605

    Elias Lany, Lutheran bishop and mentor to Ponikenus, personal pastor of Thurzo

    John Ponikenus, Lutheran pastor of Čachtice

    Zachary Gasparides, Lutheran pastor of Podolie

    Nicolas Baroseus, Lutheran pastor of Vrbové

Prologue

In the foothills of the Little Carpathian mountains lie many threats: yellow-eyed wolves prowling the dark woods, brigands waiting in copses of birch. But there is no threat so great as what waits inside the old manor house.

Above the manor, a grand castle looms, perched on a limestone peak. Below the manor, the village's wooden houses huddle around a wide square. Inside, Gothic stone angels dance across brightly tiled walls. Underneath, a warren of damp passageways leads out into the dark woods.

There have long been whispers. No one can say when these rumors started circulating, exactly—months? Years? But everyone, it seems, has heard something from someone about the great lady's black heart.

This great lady is a countess, from one of Europe's oldest families. It is an extraordinary privilege to serve at her manor, whether as a scullery maid or a noble attendant. There is rich food, good wine, fine clothes, the promise of respectable connections and future opportunities. But there are also the screams coming from the underground tunnels. There are the somber-eyed girls, seen climbing into the great lady's carriage and scurrying across the manor yard with bruised cheeks or bandaged hands. And then there are the carts, bringing out one plain pine coffin after the other, always at night.

The protests of peasant families go ignored, but then nobles begin reporting their daughters missing too. After the complaints have accumulated before the king, year after year, he finally opens an investigation.

The countess is warned, but she cannot rein in her dark appetites. At first the rumors were of rough treatment, the constant crack of her whip. But her tortures have become ever more cruel and deranged. Now the great lady, to preserve her beauty and outwit time itself, regularly bathes in virgin blood. When the locals refuse her their daughters, she sends her envoys and scouts farther afield, to lure girls from distant reaches of the kingdom.

The night they finally come for her, December 29, 1610, the moon is high in the sky, bright and nearly full, reflecting off the heavy snow. When the king's men force their way into the manor house, they catch the Countess with literal blood on her hands, surprised in the very act of murdering yet another of her maids. This poor girl is saved, but it is too late for her companion, whose naked, bruised body is sprawled on the floor. In the tunnels under the manor house, other battered girls are discovered, bound and hanging from the ceilings or chained up in corners, next in line to be viciously tortured and bled.

Witnesses begin to come forward. At first, there are just a few, but once the word is out that the great lady has been imprisoned, unable to inflict any more harm, more and more people speak up, accusing the countess of kidnapping and killing their daughters and sisters. At first there are around fifty victims. Later, as even more people stream in to testify against her, that number rises to three hundred. Later still, the body count doubles, with her victims numbering more than six hundred.

Four servants confess to helping their mistress torture and kill innocent girls in the most gruesome ways. Given such evidence, any other woman would be beheaded or sentenced to burn. But this countess is no ordinary woman, not even an ordinary noble. Her powerful family colludes with the prosecutor, who agrees to hush up the scandal. In exchange, the great lady is walled up within the tower of her own castle, with only a small slit for food and water. She is never seen again, except in silhouette in the tower's uppermost barred window, brooding over the countryside, cursing all those who dared speak up against her.

PROLOGUE

This is the legend of Elizabeth Bathory. And nearly none of it is true.

. . .

When *The Guinness Book of World Records* first appeared, in 1956, its most gruesome distinctions fell in the Crime and Punishment section. Here H. H. Holmes was named "Most Prolific Murderer," having "disposed of some 150 young women 'paying guests' in his 'Castle' on 63rd Street, Chicago."

But over a decade later, by the time the 1968 edition appeared, H. H. Holmes had been demoted to "the most prolific murderer known in recent criminal history," and his former title was bestowed upon a woman, a sixteenth-century Hungarian aristocrat with an actual castle:

> The greatest number of victims ascribed to anyone has been 610 in the case of Countess Erszebet Bathory (1560–1614) of Hungary . . . a witness testified to seeing a list of her victims in her own handwriting totaling this number. All were alleged to be young girls from the neighborhood of her castle . . . [When] she died on 21 August 1614 . . . [s]he had been walled up in her room for 3½ years, after being found guilty.

Countess Bathory was later demoted to "Most prolific female murderer," her body count being surpassed by that of a man, but Guinness would continue to claim that she had dispatched more than six hundred victims.

As one of the world's cruelest and most notorious serial killers, and a *female* serial killer to boot, the Countess has long been an object of dark fascination. Today Bathory enjoys a dedicated cult following. She is the namesake of a Swedish death metal band and the subject of novels, poems, films, and an opera; she even garnered a TV portrayal by Lady Gaga in *American Horror Story*. The ruins of the castle where she was imprisoned are a popular tourist site; thousands flock there every year. One can buy Elizabeth Bathory mugs, T-shirts, Halloween costumes, and miniature figurines. Her story has influenced everything from fairy tales and vampire legends to the development of modern psychiatry and criminology. The claim that Bathory bathed in the blood of virgins has morphed into the contemporary trope of the "blood bath," featured in everything from *Batman* comic books to an Eminem music video and episodes of *The X-Files* and *Buffy the Vampire Slayer*.

Yet there are serious flaws in a story long propped up by horror fans and true-crime enthusiasts. The original Guinness account, for example, contains several inaccuracies. Bathory was never found guilty in a trial, and she was never walled into her tower room. And as for that witness who testified to seeing a list of over 600 victims? She was a young servant girl named Susanna, the only one of the 303 witnesses who did not provide a last name. She repeated a story she had heard about a man who worked a hundred miles away. This man, one of the Countess's estate administrators, had supposedly "found a written document or a register in the captive Lady's trunk listing the dead girls, numbering up to 650, a number that was authenticated by the very own signature of the Lady." At the time, the scribe recording this tale marked it as something only "know[n] from hearsay." Yet in the centuries since, Susanna's shocking claim became an established fact.

Six hundred and fifty victims would be an enormous number even today, but in 1611, when Susanna testified, there were only 1.8 million people in the entire country of Hungary; most villages had only twenty to twenty-five houses and a total population of 150 to 170 people. Susanna was accusing the Countess of killing enough girls to fill four entire villages. How could this be true? Was it creative license, a way to express the enormity of the trauma Elizabeth Bathory had inflicted upon the community? Or was it completely invented?

After all, at this time, girls like Susanna testified to all manner of things—that they saw their neighbors fly, that their mothers brought down the hail, that their siblings spoiled the cow's milk. In England around this time, a nine-year-old girl denounced her mother, her brother, and her neighbor as witches, leading to their execution. (That girl would, decades later, be accused of similar crimes by a ten-year-old boy.)

Perhaps Susanna's testimony can be attributed to the overactive imagination of an illiterate servant. But what do we do with all the other testimonies? They claim that the Countess brutally tortured her victims, not just by beating them, sometimes for hours, but also by dunking them in ice water, pricking them with needles, and burning and branding them. Some witnesses also claimed that Elizabeth Bathory not only killed girls, but also cooked and ate them; that she attempted to assassinate the king and other government officials; and that she once conjured demonic cats and dogs to harass a local pastor.

The most chilling accusations, however, are those that declare that Elizabeth Bathory was the head of a child trafficking ring, assisted by "dedicated girl catchers," a ring that included other noblewomen, servants, and even one of her own daughters. Was Elizabeth a criminal mastermind, coordinating a vast network across a dark and foreboding landscape? Or are these testimonies just as problematic as Susanna's?

If Elizabeth Bathory did even *some* of the things she was accused of, she challenges most of our conventional wisdom about serial killers. And if she didn't do any of them, then she is the victim of a remarkably successful disinformation campaign, one that has lasted more than four hundred years.

· · ·

Elizabeth Bathory lived a life of extreme privilege. Her bodices were beaded with pearls, her skirts embroidered with gold thread. By the age of twelve, she had enough jewelry that it required its own inventory. She also possessed enough gold florins to purchase her own manor house or even half a castle; the gold she kept on hand weighed over two hundred pounds and today would be worth over nine million dollars. She came from the uppermost echelon of society and so held the lives of tens of thousands of serfs in her hands. Her detractors insist that her crimes are evidence of aristocratic privilege taken to its most logical, horrific extreme.

This is not an unreasonable assumption. We know all too well what can happen when certain groups of people—whether star athletes, dynastic politicians, or blue-blooded nobles—feel themselves entitled, untouchable. We know how often the poor, the disabled, the female are preyed upon. We know how rich families cover up for their own and backroom deals are struck to keep favored children out of prison.

But we also know witnesses can be bought, evidence can be manufactured, verdicts can be decided in advance. We know that this is a story of nobles behaving badly. The question becomes: Which ones?

Bathory's defenders point to the other nobles entangled in her case: a prosecutor eager to clear his son's path into politics, aristocratic neighbors eyeing her land, ambitious sons-in-law, and a king who owed her money. They point to the volatile political backdrop: two wars, several plots, and one daring coup. Mixed up in this case are also, for good measure, a witch-hunting pastor and a second alleged female serial killer.

The more one digs, the more mysteries there are. One of the Countess's main detractors was a Hungarian archivist whose 1908 biography cemented her reputation as the mentally ill and sadistic scion of a depraved old family. But even he recanted his claims at the end of his life. At the age of ninety-two, he made a special trip to inform his former editor that the Countess had been framed; unfortunately, he died before he could publish his new evidence. Even *The Guinness Book of World Records* has recently expressed some doubts. While I was writing this book, Guinness put out an online article, "Was Elizabeth Báthory Truly the Most Prolific Female Serial Killer Ever?," that entertains the possibility that the Countess may have just been "an unfortunate victim of the patriarchy."

I have been struck, over and over, by how invested many scholars, historians, and true-crime aficionados are in the gory legend despite the very real doubts about Elizabeth Bathory's guilt. Some take disconcerting delight in describing trembling young women chained up in underground tunnels, decomposing bodies stacked up in cellars, and a vicious mistress bathing in blood. But they struggle to provide a clear motive. Why would the Countess savage the women and girls in her care? Many have shoehorned Elizabeth Bathory into the prevailing understanding of child predators or serial killers of their era, adjusting the facts to fit the narrative. Her alleged crimes have been blamed, in turn, on female vanity, a lack of religion, and even menopause. There have been allegations that she was insane, whether because of aristocratic inbreeding or epileptic fits (both claims are demonstrably false, stemming from misreadings of primary sources). More recently, there have been claims that Elizabeth was scarred by childhood trauma, either from witnessing a peasant's brutal execution (supposedly by being sewn into a horse, which is exceedingly implausible, given the astronomically high value of horses at the time) or from enduring a seduction or rape that led to an illegitimate pregnancy (a grievous mistranslation). In fact, most accounts of Bathory's case are plagued with translation errors, sloppy genealogical work, and lack of historical context.

When Elizabeth Bathory was born, Elizabeth I was the brand-new queen of England, Ivan the Terrible was the czar of Russia, Michelangelo and Titian were still painting, and the Protestant Reformation was not yet fifty years old. Bathory was the contemporary of Bacon, Galileo, Marlowe, and Shakespeare. During her lifetime, the compound microscope and the telescope would be invented; Earth's magnetic field and the human circulatory system would be discovered.

Her case unfolded at a singular inflection point in history, at the intersection of the Age of Queens and the Great Hunt—a surge of female rule in Europe and an explosion in witchcraft accusations and trials. Elizabeth Bathory lived in an era in thrall to conspiracy theories, thanks in part to a new and unregulated technology. There were now many local printing presses, each with its own owner and agenda, and there were no fact-checkers, no copyright, and no universally acknowledged impartial sources of information. Imaginary executions were illustrated, deathbed scenes were scripted, letters were forged. Kings were declared to be dead while they feasted in their banquet halls, very much alive, and princes were declared to be winning battles while they lay wrapped in funeral shrouds. Rumors and disinformation now spread faster and farther than ever before. And curiously, Elizabeth Bathory's case parallels a conspiracy theory that has appeared in many iterations over the centuries, a theory that persists in chat rooms and on social media even today—that there is a shadowy group of elites abducting large numbers of children for nefarious purposes.

Elizabeth Bathory never confessed and always claimed she was innocent. After she was imprisoned without a trial, supposedly for her own good and that of her family's reputation, the Countess fought back. She demanded, over and over, to be tried in open court, even though a conviction could have meant the loss of her head, or worse, being burned alive.

So Bathory, the so-called Blood Countess, has become one of history's most horrific, and intriguing, cold cases. Which parts of her story are true, which are exaggerated, which are fabricated, and which are, still, willfully misunderstood? Is this a story about how an educated, intelligent, and seemingly compassionate mother ends up brutalizing other people's children? Or is this a story about how educated, intelligent, and seemingly compassionate people can be made to believe the most monstrous things about their neighbors, family, and friends?

This book draws upon archival evidence in four different countries, as well as the talents of old-handwriting experts and several translators and historians, in order to reassess old documents, uncover new evidence, and see if we can finally, once and for all, settle the question of Bathory's guilt.

This is the story of history's most dangerous woman, and a reckoning with how we got her all wrong.

PART ONE

1603–1609

CHAPTER I

A Long, Terrible Year

December 31, 1603

The tables in the great hall were crowded with platters of stuffed capons and colossal roasts whose thick dark sauces congealed in the cold. The hosts were still able to afford the rich holiday dishes, but they had not been able to afford a physician at court for many years. So one had to be sent for, and he traveled through the deep snowdrifts by horse-drawn sleigh.

His patient was one of the most celebrated warriors in Europe, toasted even by his staunchest enemies as "a man who has no match in the court of the emperor or the sultan, whose sword is the mightiest sword, who goes everywhere and wins everywhere." Count Francis Nadasdy had always been preternaturally lucky—an only child conceived after twenty barren years; a toddler who triumphed over horrible fevers; and a soldier who evaded injury, capture, and, amid the stink and muck of the camps, consumption and dysentery too. He had even outfoxed the plague: Last year it had swept through Paris and then London, delaying James I's coronation before making its way east across the Danube into the army camps, where it felled thousands of troops in a single week. Francis was a study in defiance. Tall, dark, and sturdily built, he glowers in all of his portraits, looking like a contemporary cartoon villain: widow's peak, curling

Francis Nadasdy, the Black Lord

mustache, and a nose like a dagger. He had the sort of face, and fearsome reputation, that could inspire immediate surrender.

The woman sweeping in and out of his sickroom—drawing the bed-curtains, ordering servants to bring more furs and wine, and to stoke the fire—was no less impressive a figure. Her husband was a battlefield legend and the fourth-most-powerful aristocrat in the entire realm. But even he was outranked by her family, a family more than five hundred years old, with a name as renowned as that of Medici or Hapsburg. She had no real need for her husband's title; she had one of her own. She signed her letters in a firm, clear hand: "Elizabetha comitissa de Bathor," Elizabeth, Countess Bathory.

She was forty-three years old, dark-haired, and in full possession of the big doleful brown eyes that were her family's hallmark. She was considered attractive, although she was not the era's most celebrated beauty. Perhaps her ears were a touch too big—or this may have simply been the fault of one clumsy portrait artist. But she had the fashionably high forehead, the pale skin, and the thin eyebrows that were de rigueur for her station. Her natural charms were only enhanced by her sumptuous attire—one of the newly fashionable velvet waistcoats, laced up with silk ribbon or gold cord, slimmed her waist; clusters of sapphires, rubies, or pearls encircled her white neck.

But even the most richly embroidered skirts and a five-hundred-year-old name could not spare one the tribulations of the age. It had been a long, terrible year.

First, their older son and heir, the beloved six-year-old Andras, had died. Next, their estates had been raided by the Turks. And then, in the middle of November 1603, with the campaigning season over for the year, Francis was packing up to head home for the holidays when, as he wrote to one friend, "in the last days in the camp . . . [God] threw a sudden illness upon me." And now, as the moat froze over and the snow piled higher, lucky, lauded Francis grew progressively weaker, unable to ride, then to walk, then to stand.

When the moon was full, its light, reflected back by the snow, played on the pale arches of their grand castle and the low, undulating hills beyond. But on this night, even the moon turned its face. As the new year of 1604 began, they were plunged into darkness.

. . .

Given the plague, the dark, and the cold, it was said the Devil himself walked among them. Many had seen him: a tall, dark-skinned man, dressed just like a damned Turk, slinking through the fields just before the grapes turned on the vine, the cow's udders went dry, the master took ill.

Of course, it had not always been so. Just a few generations previously, the kingdom had sprawled across the heart of Europe, from ports on the Adriatic coast up to hills in lower Saxony. It comprised modern-day Hungary, the Czech Republic, and Slovakia; most of Romania; large portions of Austria, Croatia, Serbia, and Slovenia; and even parts of Germany and Poland. Its populace was composed not just of ethnic Hungarians, but also, as a royal secretary detailed, "Germans, Czechs, Slavs, Croats, Saxons, Székelys, Oláchs, Rák, Kuns, Jász, Ruthenians and finally Turks," living more or less in harmony. Hungary was not only bathed in light, but casting it: One noble declared their kingdom was "the star of Europe."

During this period, it wasn't the Devil but their own king who walked among the people, learning of their hardships and planning his reforms. That stranger warming himself in the tavern? The peddler with the borrowed cart? Perhaps that was him—Matthias the Just, Matthias the Raven King, disguised as a commoner, hiding his flowing auburn hair and resolute chin under a borrowed cloak.

As their great king strolled the cobbled streets, their queen was busy with reforms of her own. She had packed the ships that brought her from Naples not just with silks and servants, but with architects, engineers, cooks, and artists. It was not long before the palace had a new loggia and her ladies-in-waiting sported slashed sleeves. Italian cooks introduced the marvels of onions, garlic, and pasta; over dinners of tagliatelle the court now debated theology and listened to poetry recitations. Leonardo da Vinci was commissioned to paint a Madonna, Verrocchio to chisel a relief of Alexander the Great, and Dalmata to render the royal pair's likenesses in Carrara marble. Forts were renovated to mimic Sforza castles, country residences to resemble Medici villas, and during banquets the fountains dispensed sparkling wine instead of water.

There was plenty of wine to spare. The royal secretary noted: "It often happens that favorable weather and a good season produce such a large amount of wine that it is difficult to find enough barrels in which to store it." In fact, there was plenty of everything:

> The fields, once or twice shallowly plowed and sown, yield abundant crops of wheat . . . There are so many forests, and they are so big . . . There is an abundance of bees and honey . . . there are so many herds of cattle, goats and sheep, and such an abundance of all kinds of game . . . If someone has a net, there is no shortage of fish, and what's more, they are free.

There was light, there was beauty, there was abundance. In the streets of the capital, Florentine merchants hawked their exquisite silks. Broadsides and books were even for sale—Hungarian artisans had secured several of the new Gutenberg presses before the Dutch or Flemish or English possessed a single machine. Scientific demonstrations were held before Parliament, while the Raven King's library organized all the scientific knowledge of the Western world, from "elementary things to the pinnacle of the sciences . . . in bookcases and racks . . . marked with the branch of science and discipline." The rare and ancient texts within were bound in leather, silk, and bright velvets; some had silver buckles, others clasped shut with a little copper leaf. This library filled two vaulted rooms and was second in size only to that of the Vatican.

When King Matthias needed counsel on which volumes of Cicero to procure, he sought out a bishop—a Bathory, educated in Florence and in possession of a very enviable library himself. When Matthias's formidable Black Army marched out to conquer more territory, a Bathory commander rode at its head. Elizabeth Bathory's ancestors were ubiquitous at the luminous Hungarian court: clerics and cupbearers, generals and royal governors.

After the great Raven King's death, shadows crept over the court. But the Hungarian empire would not truly be tested until the summer of 1526, when the messengers first came galloping back. The Hungarians had long traded and coexisted with the Turks. But now the Ottoman Empire, to the south, had a new young sultan, Suleiman the Magnificent. He had begun advancing north, first taking Belgrade, then Petrovaradin, Ilok, and Osijek, directly south of Buda itself. The vaulted halls emptied as most of the nobles and bishops—including Elizabeth's grandfather and uncle and cousins and neighbors—rode out to meet the invaders with the new king.

That was the last time many of them were ever seen. At the end of August, the twenty-year-old King Louis II, outnumbered and outgunned, met the Ottoman forces in an open field at Mohács. Within ninety minutes, fourteen thousand Hungarians were dead. During the uphill retreat, the young king slipped off his horse into a rain-swollen stream, where he drowned under the weight of his armor. The Ottoman sultan decreed he would take no prisoners; as torrential rains fell, from the cover of his tent, he watched as the two thousand survivors, most of Hungary's elite among them, were executed.

Soon after, the capital that had once been the rival of Paris, Naples, and Prague was set on fire. Even the palace library was breached—the copper-leaf clasps on the silk-bound books forced open, the rare and precious volumes carted off. The survivors found themselves bewildered, blinking at the sudden extinguishing of their light.

Overnight, Hungary lost its status as a European powerhouse. The battle was also a turning point for the rest of the continent, which would be consumed, obsessed even, with battling the infidel threat for the next 150 years. Terror permeated Europe's most exclusive drawing rooms and lowliest public taverns. As the Turks marched north, reaching the Danube and besieging Vienna, people sang of the sultan's advance:

From Hungary he's soon away,
In Austria by break of day,
Bavaria is just at hand,
From there he'll reach another land,
Soon to the Rhine perhaps he'll come.

There was good reason to fear the Turks' arrival. It was not just what they would do to unarmed farmers or their defenseless wives, but also to their *children*. The Turks' wartime atrocities (some real, most imagined) were illustrated in gory detail in pamphlets and broadsheets. One leaflet described what the "Turkish tyrant" did to Christian infants:

Splitted the babies into two parts
They bursted and steaked [*sic*] them
Put them on top of sharpened poles

Every battle of the sultan's armies was covered by the proto-newspapers of the day, the handwritten Italian *avvisi* and German *zeitungen*, each troop movement carefully tracked by everyone from the Medici family to Cardinal Richelieu. Eventually, kingdoms as far away as England became involved. Elizabeth I would order her people to pray three times a week for Hungary, "which has been the strongest bulwark of Christendom for a long time." Idealists and adventurers rushed to the front lines to join the fight, including the poet Sir Philip Sidney, who served as a war reporter, and John Smith, of Pocahontas fame, who fought as a mercenary.

Within Hungary, the devastating defeat at Mohács in 1526 was a psychic wound from which the nation never fully recovered. The anniversary is still commemorated today, with memorials, wreath-laying ceremonies, and mournful newspaper commentaries. Hungarians even have the idiom *Több is veszett Mohácsnál*, which roughly translates to "even more was lost at Mohács." A figurative approximation would be "This isn't going to be your Waterloo," a dark consolation that no death and hardship, whether from revolutions, world wars, or Communist dictators, could come close to matching the losses of this one battle.

With its capital city lost and its central lands occupied, Hungary descended into chaos. King Louis II died before he had the chance to have children, so there was no heir to rally around. Instead, two contenders emerged for the crown: his brother-in-law and his top surviving general.

The brother-in-law, Ferdinand, was a foreigner, born in Castile and unable to speak a word of Hungarian. But he also happened to be the younger brother of the Holy Roman Emperor. They were Hapsburgs, a clan that controlled Austria and Germany, but also Spain and its colonial conquests, the Netherlands and the Kingdom of Naples. The rich Hungarian lands would make an excellent addition to the family's vast empire.

The second claimant, John Zápolya, was a native Hungarian and the former commander of the eastern region known as Transylvania. These lands were much different from the agricultural plains—rugged and wild, with snowy Carpathian peaks and thick old-growth forests. Because of this, they would be difficult for any outsider to conquer.

In towns a hundred miles apart, dueling parliaments crowned both men, in near simultaneous elections. Hungarians now had to decide which powers they feared most. Many backed King Ferdinand, seeing the powerful Hapsburgs as their best chance for vengeance upon the Ottoman Turks. Others feared the interference of this foreign king and his mercenary armies even more; at least King John was a native Hungarian, with real battlefield experience to boot. Families quarreled and the plentiful fields were set on fire. Then, a civil war broke out.

The Bathory family was more fortunate than most. Many of the old families had died out at Mohács, losing both father and son, or the family heir and the spare, on the same day. Elizabeth Bathory's paternal grandfather and great-uncle were both commanders on the field that day, but somehow they survived and, even more miraculously, escaped. Almost immediately, they threw their support behind the Hapsburg king, Ferdinand. In exchange, they were both granted plum positions at his court in Vienna; Elizabeth Bathory's grandfather even became the master of the treasury.

The Bathory family, though, was a large and sprawling one. Elizabeth's grandfather and great-uncle belonged to the western branch of the family, which had its base in the Ecsed swamp of the Great Hungarian Plain, wetlands bigger than the entire city of Philadelphia today. Elizabeth was raised there, surrounded by the shallow and treacherous waters, in one of the era's "water castles," a complex erected on an elaborate system of platforms and bridges, its stone walls built on piles driven into the swamp. But there was an even older branch of the family, perched high in the Transylvanian hills in their ancestral castle of Somlyó. These eastern Bathorys threw their support behind their fellow Transylvanian noble, King John, and rose to prominence in his court too. This meant that during any clash between the rival kings, one Bathory ended up pitted against another.

Sometimes even immediate family members found themselves at odds: In one instance, Elizabeth Bathory's father found himself besieged by his older brother. This was, however, not nearly as dramatic an occurrence as it might seem. While some Bathorys were ardent supporters of one king or the other, most approached the civil war more strategically. Elizabeth's father and uncle, along with other aristocratic families, were party to a secret treaty that aimed to circumvent the dueling kings entirely. They agreed that if those supporting King John had their land

A seventeenth-century engraving of the water-castle complex of Ecsed

seized, those supporting King Ferdinand would return it back to them, and vice versa. When one Bathory attacked another, their land, while ostensibly switching hands, always stayed in the family.

Another instance of one Bathory besieging another involved Elizabeth's aunt Klara, a bold, even headstrong woman who favored the color red: Her jewelry was inlaid with rubies, red carnelian, red balas, any and all kinds of red stones. Klara was from the water-bound Ecsed branch, the indulged only daughter in a family of boys. Her father and most of her brothers occupied prominent positions in the Hapsburg court. But she ended up married to a prominent supporter of King John and living in another "water castle," an Italian-style hexagonal fort plopped down in a Transylvanian swamp.

When King John died, the Hapsburgs went on the offensive, invading the lands of his supporters. Klara, newly widowed at the time with two young daughters, could have easily welcomed the imperial forces, whose commanders included her brothers and cousins. But Klara was one of the true believers, willing to risk her fortune and her daughters' inheritance by joining the resistance. In the fighting that followed, she was captured, separated from her girls, and imprisoned in a remote Gothic tower. The imperial army commandeered Klara's swamp castle and the rest of her lands. Still, being a Bathory, even the rebel Klara was eventually released into the custody of one of her Hapsburg-supporting brothers, who then restored to her most of her property.

The civil war was continued by the kings' heirs, and what was left of the Hungarian kingdom was formally divided into imperial Royal Hungary in the west and a Transylvanian state in the east. The Bathory family straddled this border, amassing lands and titles, its members serving as generals, royal judges, counts, and princes. They even exercised power outside the Hungarian lands: One Bathory became a Catholic cardinal in Rome, another became king of Poland and grand duke of Lithuania.

And Elizabeth Bathory was related to all of them. Elizabeth's mother and father both carried the Bathory name. Her father was from the western Hapsburg-supporting Ecsed branch, while her mother was an eastern Somlyó Bathory. This fact has led to claims of incest, but the two branches of the ancient clan were separated by two hundred miles and more than two hundred years. Elizabeth's parents were distant sixth cousins. By comparison, the U.S. founding fathers John Adams and Thomas Jefferson both married their third cousins, and England's Queen Elizabeth II and Prince Philip were even more closely related, being second cousins once removed. The House of Hapsburg, for its part, was plagued with epilepsy, insanity, and distinctive jaw deformities, thanks to frequent marriages between first cousins.

Elizabeth Bathory was spared any such legacy, although she did inherit a tangled web of family alliances. Born a generation after Mohács, she managed to be related to both the Hapsburgs' most trusted advisers and their fiercest adversaries. Elizabeth had only ever known her homeland, and her own family, to be divided. Her Hungary was no star, but a waning crescent moon, its center carved out.

· · ·

As 1604 dawned, western Royal Hungary, where Elizabeth Bathory resided on her husband's estates, was still firmly under Hapsburg control. Submitting to imperial rule was supposed to protect the region from further incursions from the Ottoman Turks. But a decade prior, the Turks had launched a new campaign in an attempt to move into western Europe.

Francis Nadasdy had spent the better part of that time attempting to beat them back. The Turks had conveyed their grudging respect for his efforts by giving him a nickname, the Strong Black Bey. "Black" was a reference to Francis's thick dark hair and beard, and "Bey" was their honorific for ruler; a close approximation in English would be "Black Lord." They had also singled Francis out as a target of their increasingly audacious raids. While Francis was off fighting to free the former capital, Buda, the Turks had besieged three of his castles, set eight hundred villages on fire, and enslaved ten thousand local people in retribution.

Any hope Elizabeth Bathory may have had that this new year would be better than the last were soon dashed. The famed Black Lord, Elizabeth's ever-fortunate Francis, was now too weak to leave his bed. Despite the fervent prayers of his pastor, wife, and three surviving children, Francis found himself convinced that God was calling him home.

The Black Lord's holdings comprised a third of Royal Hungary, with most of his estates nestled in the rolling countryside that today straddles the Austrian-Hungarian border. Distant relatives would make claims on his lands; neighbors would encroach. The Turks would surely be back, and soon.

Whenever one of Elizabeth's many uncles had died, their estates were neatly, and quickly, absorbed by other Bathory uncles. But Francis had no siblings who could step in and helm the Nadasdy estates. He had no adult sons or sons-in-law ready to defend his lands. Instead, he would be leaving behind two unmarried daughters, Anna and Katalin, and a five-year-old boy, Paul. Everything depended upon his wife.

On the evening of January 3, 1604, as her husband felt his strength waning, Elizabeth called for the secretary so Francis might dictate his last letters. The next morning, he was dead.

CHAPTER 2

The First Clue

Francis's first letter was a farewell to a neighbor. "After my death," he implored young Lord Batthyany, "[ensure] my poor orphaned wife and our dear children will continue to be protected and cared for." Francis expressed his gratitude for the long "alliance and brotherly friendship" between their two families—Batthyany's late father had been one of Francis's best friends. The two men had run the Turks off their adjoining lands many times before, and the families even shared a townhome in Vienna.

The second letter was an insurance policy of sorts. Francis Nadasdy had spent much of his childhood as the playmate of the Hapsburg archdukes. He had accumulated public honors at their court: imperial pallbearer, Master of the Horse, and Knight of the Golden Spur. And at the time of his death, he held the title of lord-lieutenant over two populous counties of Royal Hungary—responsible for serving in the upper house of Parliament as well as implementing the Hapsburgs' laws, collecting their taxes and fines, heading up the local courts and militias, and arranging for the region's defense.

But even he could not be certain of the Hapsburgs' loyalty in turn. And so he wrote to Lord George Thurzo, a rising star who had fought alongside Francis on several campaigns. Mindful of Thurzo's grand ambitions, Francis flattered him as one of his "most trusted lords and relatives." He asked Thurzo to be "my poor orphans' warden, guardian and protector" at the Hapsburg court. With Batthyany providing support closer to home, Francis hoped Thurzo would advocate for his children at the center of the Holy Roman Empire. Before long, Paul Nadasdy would be coming up in court alongside Thurzo's son. Francis hoped they might be allies rather than competitors.

Within hours of her husband's death, Elizabeth was busy dictating letters of her own. The first we know of was to a German merchant at the Hapsburg court in Vienna. "Only the true-hearted God knows what pain my heart is suffering, alas, because of my beloved husband's death, who was taken by the Almighty this night," she grieved. Then she reverted to her usual brisk and authoritative style—one at odds with the flowery and meandering missives of other aristocratic women (and men!) of her age: "Next, how many things I need for his funeral."

Although the war with the Turks raged on, the world had to believe that the Nadasdy family, and by extension the Bathory family, was unshaken, immune to the rationing and privations of the age. There would be a days-long funeral, then a forty-mile march through the snow to Francis's family crypt. There would be wine and meat for thousands of guests and hay for their hundreds of horses. The new widow could not be seen to flinch at the expense.

The money would have to be borrowed. While Elizabeth owned fistfuls of jewels and vast tracts of land, at the moment she was cash poor. Francis had been a successful general, gaining land and treasure for the Hapsburgs, but he had not been paid his promised salary for close to a decade. His back wages totaled over 17,000 gold florins, close to $5 million today. But Elizabeth, a trusted customer, was allowed to shop on credit; the merchant sent her all that she asked for, 456 thalers and some odd pfennigs' worth, the equivalent of $12,000's worth of goods.

Next she dispatched her representatives to the imperial court with petitions for her five-year-old son, Paul, to be appointed his father's political successor. If her request were granted, she would serve as regent. And why not? In the aftermath of Mohács, given the deaths of so many men and the absence of so many others on long military campaigns, women had been forced to take on many new roles—farmer, merchant, printer, and even, sometimes, soldier.

During the 1552 siege of Eger, women had helped a ragtag force of twenty-five hundred repel an Ottoman army of thirty thousand. They set fire to anything they could get their hands on—oil, lard, or shit—and continuously dumped it on invaders attempting to scale the castle walls. In another, smaller skirmish, one woman was said to have used a scythe to behead two enemy soldiers with a single swing. During another battle when Elizabeth was six years old, women even dressed in armor and fought alongside their husbands; she grew up seeing and hearing their bravery lauded in print and in song.

Elizabeth would not be attempting anything as audacious as that. All over the Hungarian lands, wives and widows were overseeing family estates on their own. Elizabeth had done this for the past decade while Francis was away on the front lines. She had capably supervised the harvests and the animal husbandry, paid the bills, arranged the repairs of the roads and the health care for her court and serfs, and mustered the local militias to fend off the Turks. In assuming even greater political powers—sitting in Parliament, collecting taxes, implementing laws—Elizabeth would be following in the footsteps of her own mother and mother-in-law, who, after the deaths of their husbands, served as lord-lieutenants until their sons came of age.

Still, Elizabeth Bathory's position was far from secure. Would the other nobles in the region consent to being governed by a woman, especially during a time of war? They might not believe that a grieving widow with three dependent children would be able to manage it all: administering her own estates while enforcing the laws, convening the courts, and seeing to the defense of *all* of their lands.

Soon the castle yard was crowded with people solemnly processing past the elevated bier behind the guard tower, where Francis's body lay in state. The military brass, entire cavalry units, and rank-and-file soldiers began showing up to pay their respects, then the local gentry and her fellow aristocrats. Some were there to grieve, some to gawp. Many others were there simply to size up the new widow.

For Elizabeth, it was now a matter of waiting to see who would step out from the shadows and strike first.

. . .

We have no record of Elizabeth's reaction while she listened to Francis's eulogy from her seat of honor, but she must have been alarmed or at least annoyed. It was not only the Turks or rival nobles she needed to be worried about: Of more immediate concern were the clergy purporting to console her. The pastor upbraided her guests about their "errors" in faith. He went on to insult her husband's memory as he described a Francis she hardly knew.

Francis, like many men of the era, had been a study in contradictions. Despite his many long absences, he tried to be an involved father and husband, asking for regular reports on the children's health and declining important invitations so he could nurse Elizabeth when she took ill. Upon the recent death of their son Andras, the fierce general had broken down in a letter to one of his friends. But Francis had also witnessed, and wrought, unimaginable violence. He had stabbed, slashed, and beheaded any number of enemy soldiers; he had once, in a retaliatory rage, had three Ottoman officers impaled. These violent anecdotes would not have made his eulogy, of course. Rather, Elizabeth would have expected Francis's loyal service to the Hapsburg empire to be memorialized, or his prowess on the battlefield to be mentioned, at the very least. Even Francis's love for his family was ignored. Instead, the focus was solely on religion: The Black Lord was merely a "good spiritual warrior" whose accomplishments were listening to his pastor, being "moderate in food and drink," and, most importantly, "suffer[ing] no foul language."

Swearing was the sin Pastor Stephen Magyari was currently obsessed with. A month before Francis's death, Magyari had held a church council on the Nadasdy estates. It was bitterly cold, there were wartime food shortages, the plague was running rampant, and many commoners had just lost their homes in the Turkish raids. Today, we might expect churches to provide humanitarian aid—organize temporary shelter or collect and distribute food, for example. But these practical solutions were left to the secular authorities. Instead, Pastor Magyari and the council decided to institute hefty fines for cursing. Any cleric caught swearing on Saturdays, Sundays, or during certain holy seasons would be punished (presumably, cursing on a Tuesday in the middle of summer was still acceptable). The fine was three golden florins, three times the cost of a calf and equivalent to 20 percent of most people's annual salary.

Elizabeth was well acquainted with Pastor Magyari's eccentricities: Before he became a church dignitary, Magyari had been the family's personal pastor, and before that, Francis's army chaplain. She may have even been somewhat sympathetic: The pedantic pastor had been, like so many others, traumatized by the long war with the Turks. Ministering in the camps, he had seen all manner of gruesome injuries and mass slaughter: He bemoaned that he once had so many corpses to bury that "the fields and waters [were] running with blood."

Pastor Magyari was further bewildered when the Turkish soldiers he encountered were more disciplined, sober, and humane than the European troops sent to defend Christendom. While most in Europe thought Hungary was doing God's work vanquishing the infidels, Pastor Magyari was no longer so sure. Magyari preached that the Turks were not devils, but agents of God himself, sent to punish the Hungarian people for their immorality. The anti-swearing commission was the opening salvo of a crusade to save their souls.

. . .

Pastor Magyari's efforts were but one part of a broader battle over salvation and how to achieve it.

At the start of the sixteenth century, Europeans were ushered from cradle to grave by the Catholic Church—baptism, weekly mass, last rites. After someone died, their family often tried to ensure their entry into heaven by paying the church to say masses on their behalf and making sizable donations. Then the monk Martin Luther, a professor at the German University of Wittenberg, began preaching that salvation could not be bought or sold. His call for reform might have circulated only among religious scholars and administrators were it not for Gutenberg's new presses, which made Luther a literary superstar. By the middle of the century, his most ardent fans were looting Catholic churches, smashing statues of the Virgin Mary, and whitewashing the murals on cathedral walls.

At first, Luther's ideas had been vigorously opposed in Hungary. His followers were burned at the stake as heretics. But the defeat at Mohács was taken as evidence that Luther preached the truth: A Catholic archbishop had led Hungarian forces into battle, wearing golden armor and carrying a cross, yet they were still defeated by infidels. God must have turned his face, disgusted by the corruption of the Catholic Church.

Priests struggled to combat the new *contagium hoc Lutheranorum* afflicting their parishioners. In one Hungarian town, they complained to their bishop that, upon hearing Luther's message, "There are now many who are infected with itchy ears." These infected parishioners then "seduced" and "corrupted" others, spreading the heretical "pestilence" near and far. Protestantism quickly gained a foothold in the Hungarian lands.

Noblewomen were crucial early supporters of what has come to be known as the Reformation. German and French countesses and duchesses, as well as a French princess and two queens of Navarre, sheltered Protestant preachers, financed their religious tracts, and introduced their ideas to their subjects. All over Europe, they put their own reputations and lives at risk. Bathory women led the charge in Hungary. Elizabeth's fierce aunt Klara, swept up in the tide of idol-smashing, drove Franciscan monks off her husband's lands. And Elizabeth's formidable mother, Anna, as an acting lord-lieutenant, had convened one of the first Protestant assemblies in the kingdom. Elizabeth's father had found the young widow's ministry so convincing that he broke with his Catholic family to become her next husband.

These women leaders had no way of knowing whether the fledgling Reformation would prevail or if the Catholic Church would manage to squash the movement, as it had so many others before. At the same time that Aunt Klara closed down a monastery and Elizabeth's mother called her assembly, other wellborn Protestant women were being arrested and executed. The noble von Beckum sisters-in-law burned at the stake, one after the other, in a Dutch town square, and Anne Askew was brutally tortured in the Tower of London before her own immolation.

The Catholic Church had swiftly regrouped and mounted a Counter-Reformation. But there were few clerics left to organize these efforts in Hungary; most of the Catholic leadership had perished at Mohács. Protestantism prevailed. Some historians estimate that as much as 80 to 90 percent of the population had converted by the time Elizabeth was born. Under her mother's patronage, Hungarians declared their independence from the authority of the Catholic Church: "We are free from all human traditions (which are not based on Scripture), rites, and orders of bishops which serve to mislead souls." But what did it mean, exactly, to be Protestant?

Martin Luther wanted to allow priests to marry and make the Bible the final authority in theological matters, but he saw no reason to abolish every Catholic tradition and custom. He wanted to do away with unnecessarily ornate priestly garb, for example, but he did not want clergy to abandon vestments entirely. Some of his followers took a more extreme view. One preacher, in addition to substituting a plain wooden table for an altar, had scandalized his colleagues when he began "wearing his everyday clothes, performing the sacred service in those."

Some feared the reforms were in danger of going much too far, while others thought they had not yet gone far enough. If Mass could be celebrated by a plainclothes priest at a kitchen table, could people ignore the old conventions about weddings and funerals too? Could women—women like Elizabeth's mother—play a greater role in this new church? The most liberal reformers saw no reason why not. Rituals were radically simplified, and a few parishes began allowing women to conduct baptisms and funerals in emergency situations; some even ordained women as preachers.

As Protestants debated everything from what they should wear to how they should pray, they began splitting into factions. Smaller sects emerged, like the Anabaptists, the precursors to today's Amish. But there were two main Protestant factions: Lutheranism—the original German, based on the teachings of Martin Luther himself—and Calvinism, the Swiss, based on the teachings of the younger Frenchman John Calvin, who embraced more radical reforms.* The power struggle between these two main Protestant sects inflamed tensions throughout all of Europe.

Elizabeth Bathory, however, grew up among the reeds and the geese in the literal and figurative safety of an island. She and her older brother, Stephen, were raised in the Calvinist faith by their reformer mother, but the family was not fanatical in their beliefs—they remained close with their Catholic Bathory relatives, including one who was a cardinal in Rome.

When Elizabeth was orphaned at the age of twelve, she was forced to leave the safety of Ecsed to travel more than three hundred miles east. She would live at the home of her seventeen-year-old fiancé. Though lacking the vast, murky waters that surrounded the water castle where she grew up, her new residence had similarly progressive residents. The Nadasdy family was, like her own, an intellectual one. They prided themselves on being patrons of Renaissance learning and science.

Her new home of Sárvár Castle was a marvel of light and symmetry and precision. This was no rambling and drafty knight's castle. The pentagonal fortress was newly renovated—airy and vaulted and freshly plastered white. Sárvár had its own mills, beehives, vineyards, and large medicinal herb gardens, as well as a garden pond with goldfish and swans. Almonds and figs were cultivated on the estate, as well as peaches, pears, melons, and apricots; there was even, rather extravagantly, an orchard with orange and lemon trees imported from Venice. Sárvár hummed with activity: It had its own hospital and almshouse, its own school and scholars, and even a printing press, renowned throughout the kingdom for having printed the very first book in the Hungarian language.

Sárvár was the Nadasdy family's seat of power, but within a day's ride, there were four other significant estates. Léka, Keresztúr, and Kapuvár each had its own castle and agricultural fields, and a fourth estate,

---

* Denomination was often dictated by language. Hungarians who went to Wittenberg University to study the new theology found that Martin Luther lectured exclusively in German. Hungarians from the north and west, closest to the German lands, could listen to Luther in his native tongue. Others from the central and eastern lands had to attend the Latin lectures given by other faculty, which happened to favor Calvin's more radical ideas.

Csepreg, was the largest market town in the region, with a college for schoolteachers and preachers. There was also a holiday home farther north, Čachtice, which Francis would gift to Elizabeth as her *morgengabe*, her morning gift, once their marriage was consummated.

The young couple appeared well matched. Francis would be able to provide Elizabeth with all of the comforts, and culture, to which she was accustomed. There was just one major difference between the two—Francis was a Lutheran. It is often assumed that Elizabeth must have converted when she married Francis right around her fifteenth birthday. However, "mixed" religious marriages were common, especially among the nobility. If anyone converted, it was far more typical for the groom to convert to the bride's religion, as Elizabeth's father had done, than vice versa. In this instance, no conversion would have been necessary.

Though they were Lutherans, Francis's mother quoted Calvin in her letters, and his father had protected a Calvinist-leaning preacher whom Martin Luther personally denounced. They also employed carpenters and cabinetmakers from the fledgling Amish community—outcasts almost everywhere else—for renovation projects, and counted Catholics among their friends and neighbors. In the villages surrounding all of the Nadasdy estates, Lutherans and Calvinists attended the same service, in a single, unified church district.

Even the region's Protestant bishop modeled tolerance. Stephen Beythe, a close friend of the family, was a scholar more concerned with discovering new species of plant than uncovering heretics. He studied botany in his spare time, using the Nadasdy estates' extensive medicinal herb garden as his classroom. He collaborated with the Dutch botanist Carolus Clusius (the man responsible for popularizing both the tulip and the potato in Europe) on a compendium of native flora, and, once elected bishop, had published a renowned Latin-Hungarian botanical catalog, in addition to religious tracts and hymns.

Bishop Beythe's broad-mindedness was likely part temperament, part pragmatism. Many of his rural villagers were unabashedly ignorant about the most basic tenets of their religion. Beythe still had congregants who spent the spring equinox not only making Easter preparations, but also drowning an effigy of the old pagan goddess of death in the nearest river.

And despite the Reformation doing away with the Catholic cult of the saints, icons of the Virgin Mary and others kept turning up in Protestant churches, adorned with lit candles and offerings. Some local churches cheerfully accommodated the doctrinal confusion, performing Catholic exorcisms, Lutheran churching ceremonies, and Calvinist public confessions for their followers.

This companionable coexistence was threatened by a theological dispute hundreds of miles away. At Wittenberg University, where Martin Luther had taught until his death, professors in dark woolen robes had long debated concepts that now sound like New Age buzzwords: *synergy* and *essence* and *destiny*. By the 1580s, their most impassioned battles, though, were over the Lord's Supper, known as the sacrament of communion: Did the bread and wine consumed during church services literally or figuratively become the body and blood of Jesus Christ?

The official Lutheran position hewed closely to old Catholic traditions, although professors had long been free to challenge this doctrine. Soon, though, a debate over theological technicalities developed into a power struggle over who would control the direction of the young church. The more liberal professors at Wittenberg were sidelined by a rumor that they were secret Calvinists, intent on indoctrinating impressionable students. A moral panic ensued, and matters quickly spiraled out of control. Four professors were arrested (two of whom died in prison); other professors and advisers were banished, and a university chancellor was beheaded.

If Calvinists had infiltrated the Lutheran bastion of Wittenberg University, where else might they be found? Word of the conspiracy wound its way south along the trade routes. On the Nadasdy estates, a fiery and combative Lutheran pastor named John Reczes took up the cause, preaching that secret Calvinists walked among them too. They must be unmasked and driven out.

But, villagers countered, to what end? Why borrow trouble?

They still grumbled about the damned Turks, prayed for the liberation of the occupied lands, and kept careful watch for raiders. However, there had been no major campaigns for two decades; a tentative peace had been reached with the Ottoman Empire. The old rhythms had been restored—harvests, feast days, market fairs. Many felt secure enough to invest in the future, planting new vineyards and expanding their orchards. Surely they now enjoyed God's favor.

Their confidence was shaken by two new developments. There was a renewed threat from the Turks: A new Ottoman pasha began moving troops north. Skirmishes along the border became more frequent, and there was talk that a large-scale campaign was imminent. Even worse, the world entered the worst phase of the Little Ice Age: The cold, wet weather that had characterized the past decades became increasingly vicious. A terrible frost was followed by a poor harvest; even the most tolerant pastor became short-tempered when his livestock froze and his children went hungry. Pastor Reczes, who blamed these misfortunes on the Calvinists, began attracting more followers.

These followers became increasingly boisterous, denouncing pastors and heckling local administrators. In June 1591, Francis Nadasdy attempted to head off the rising acrimony by asking his former childhood teacher Bishop Beythe to meet with Reczes and his coalition. This assembly of Protestant preachers, held at the college in Csepreg, was an unmitigated disaster. Reczes publicly accused his bishop of being part of a secret Calvinist conspiracy to destroy the church. Bishop Beythe, now on the cusp of sixty, was so offended that he stormed out. After upbraiding Reczes and his faction as "thieves, fornicators, and murderers," Beythe resigned.

Francis cajoled Beythe and Reczes into agreeing to meet once more. But the printing press, the very technology that had made the Reformation possible, now encouraged further division. In the lead-up to the new assembly, rival Lutheran and Calvinist presses traded insults and accused one another of fabricating "fake news." Pastors dueled one another from their pulpits, and their increasingly pitched rhetoric led to crackdowns on previously tolerated behaviors. Common people found themselves unsure which tenets of faith they were supposed to profess on any given day and which of their daily practices and superstitions were now outlawed.

Elizabeth, now a thirty-three-year-old mother of two, had to manage this escalating religious conflict on her own. The dire prognostications about the Turks had turned out to be true. The Ottomans had launched a major new campaign, and Francis was called away to fight at the front. In Sárvár, the tension was racheted up when an anonymous satirical poem made the rounds, mocking several of the hard-line ministers like Reczes by name. Despite his public denials, Beythe was assumed to be its author. Outraged and offended, Reczes and his followers withdrew from the upcoming assembly.

When the Black Lord learned of the roiling conflict, he wrote to Reczes directly, commanding the pastor to wait to take any further action until he had returned home. The fractious pastor ignored him: Reczes demanded all clergy in the region sign a public declaration of faith. Those who refused would no longer be considered Lutherans. The long-unified Protestant church district was dismantled, divided into four Lutheran dioceses and five Calvinist ones.

This split was not neat and tidy—the two denominations had worshipped side by side for so long that the new Lutheran dioceses were filled with Calvinist pastors and vice versa. To purify their churches from the blasphemies of the other sect, parishioners were encouraged to keep close watch upon their pastors and report any unorthodoxy they might observe. Church authorities also began organizing "visitations," sending unannounced inspectors into parishes to monitor how services were conducted and which hymns were sung. These visitations were conducted with great enthusiasm and thoroughness; one pastor complained to his inspectors: "You even broke into my closet after I went home so you could see what books I had!" The former bishop Beythe complained that he was threatened, cursed, and slandered, repeatedly and publicly. He worried that false criminal charges might soon be leveled against him.

It was within this new atmosphere of suspicion and denunciation, in which clergy regularly branded one another murderers and tyrants, that the very first clue in the case of Elizabeth Bathory turns up.

. . .

When Reczes, the leader of the hard-line Lutheran faction, died, in 1599, the Sárvár court pastor Stephen Magyari was selected as his successor. By

1602, the pastor seemed to be unraveling. He published his own book, *On the Causes of the Decay of Our Country*, a tome that railed against the war, leveling ethnic slurs at the foreign mercenaries in Hungary and expressing the treasonous sentiment that the kingdom should simply surrender. His increasingly fiery sermons declared that an evil had taken hold in the region. The war would not end until every last bit of rot had been hacked off.

That spring, less than two weeks before the big Easter holiday, Magyari sought advice from two other Lutheran pastors about how to best discipline a "certain wicked woman." Their exchange, all in Latin, revolved around whether this unnamed member of his congregation, an employee of Elizabeth Bathory, should be able to receive communion during the upcoming services. The pastors called this female servant a *carnifex*, from *caro*, for "flesh." Translated literally, *carnifex* means "butcher." In ancient Rome, this term was used as a nickname for soldiers, later taking on the meaning of "executioner"; because executioners also conducted torture sessions, the word then took on the meaning of "torturer." Some translations of the pastors' letters have, rather understandably, cast the *carnifex* servant as "that executioner woman" or "that torturer woman." One version: "through . . . the tyranny of the noble Lady herself, there is a certain wicked woman and the Lady has her work in that torturer's chamber."

In their exchange, the pastors reference a censure or "rebuke" that they are drafting, in which they will formally establish punishments for their congregants' various sins. But this sinful woman would "want to come to the holy Mass during the upcoming feast days, and that will be before the rebuke will be decided." So, in the meantime, what should they do?

"I would like her not to take communion, except if she did penance," the first pastor offered. The second pastor agreed and proposed the woman ought to be excluded from communion for three months, until St. Paul's Day.

Some interpretations deem the pastors' letters the first mention of Elizabeth Bathory as a killer. The pastors viewed "that butcher woman['s]" penalty as relatively harsh, designed to "stimulate the acceleration of serious penance" in others. Yet it seems curious that the same pastors who had their inspectors breaking into private libraries to check for forbidden texts would simply deny Elizabeth Bathory's accomplice her communion for a few months. Even more curious, they made no mention of reporting this woman to any sort of secular authority.

If they were not talking about murder, what sin could this "wicked woman" have committed?

This letter was written during Lent, when eating meat was forbidden to Christians. The word *carnifex* likely referred to someone who was not fasting properly. When a monk in a nearby city ate meat on a fast day, he was publicly punished and similarly berated as a *carnifex sanguinarius*, "a bloodthirsty butcher." The area around Sárvár had a long tradition of overwrought reactions to unsanctioned meat-eating: Another local preacher who ate meat on a feast day was labeled not just a butcher, but a child-killing werewolf. These instances of meat-eating were deliberate acts of nonobservance. While Lutherans had maintained many of the Catholic traditions surrounding fasting, the more radical Calvinists had advocated for defying them altogether.

Elizabeth stood accused of harboring heretical, Calvinist views for tolerating one of her servants ignoring the Lenten fast. The pastors even referred to the Countess as a "tyrant," a common slur for a religious opponent, the same insult their faction had leveled against Bishop Beythe.

Elizabeth was said to be so upset that she summoned Francis home to help mediate the dispute. Fortunately, the Black Lord and his pastor were able to talk the matter through; one official reported that "it was not very long before the pastor and the Lord reconciled." Accusations have a long half-life, though. Though it was likely not his intent, Pastor Magyari's letter had conflated those who crossed church authorities with actual monsters, amid a drive to monitor, to surveil, to inform upon the foibles and moral failings of one's neighbors.

Hungarians hadn't burned a witch in their capital city of Bratislava for over twenty-five years. But in the spring of 1602, they burned two.

CHAPTER 3

A Wedding and a Rebellion

In the intervening two years, Magyari and the Countess had moved past the unpleasantness over the *carnifex* servant and were on good terms—the pastor publicly praised her as a devout and "loving wife." But Francis's funeral presented Magyari with an opportunity he could not pass up. Gathered before him were not just the locals who regularly filled his pews, but entire infantry and calvary regiments as well as dignitaries and nobles from farther afield. After his portrayal of the Black Lord diligently reading his Bible and forgoing all swearing, Pastor Magyari launched into a lecture about the superiority of Lutheran doctrine. He scolded the Calvinists and Catholics in attendance—and there were many—for their errant beliefs. Pastor Magyari even accused the pope of having tried to bribe his deceased master, claiming the pontiff had offered the Black Lord the equivalent of eighteen million dollars to convert. (While the pope may have indeed reached out to Francis, the cash-strapped Vatican simply did not have that kind of money.)

Pastor Magyari undoubtedly hoped to convert as many Hungarians as possible, but his eulogy was also a very public and pointed reminder to the new widow of the commitments her late husband had made to the Lutheran church. Magyari lived quite comfortably thanks to Francis and Elizabeth's generosity, supported not just by the usual tithe and the income from the grain mills. The pastor was a new landlord; he had been granted special permission to rent out church land. Beythe had sneered at Magyari for this cushy arrangement, pointing out that even he, when a bishop, had "neither ten nor twenty serfs in the parish, like you do."

If Elizabeth openly embraced Calvinism, all of the Lutheran pastors stood to lose their power and influence, and quite a lot of money. Pastor Magyari reminded Elizabeth from the pulpit that when her deceased husband "had any difficulty . . . he communicated it to his pastor, and received testimony and consolation from him." The subtext: Elizabeth would be wise to defer to her pastor too.

With a war raging, Elizabeth was in no position to directly challenge her local clergy. She needed her people to be unified against the invading Turks. She agreed to support, or at least not impede, Magyari's pet projects. The pastor's anti-swearing campaign had not been embraced by the local populace. Now the Countess, adopting the "royal we" as the embodiment of the local law, informed her subjects that "if someone should say such [curses] from now on, we will inflict upon that person a strict punishment, be sure of that." She also allowed the Lutheran "visitations" to continue, writing passes that guaranteed the church examiners safe conduct through her lands and ordering her subjects to cooperate fully: "If you assault them or do not answer every question, we will not endure it without [leveling] punishment, believe that."

While she made some concessions to Magyari, Elizabeth would not openly declare herself a Lutheran. Instead, she embraced a moderate position: The Nadasdy estates could remain formally Lutheran, but Calvinist churches must be allowed to continue operating. The Lutherans would not get their wish to drive out the Calvinists entirely, but neither would they have to fear being driven off themselves. Both churches would be permitted to operate with relative autonomy. The Countess could have exercised her rights of patronage, which gave her a say in the appointment of local clerics. Elizabeth was proud of her tolerant stance, later declaring, "I was the patron and mother of all ministers; I never used my rights, not against the smallest or the biggest."

. . .

Elizabeth's tone in these early decrees and other documents is abrupt and clipped, leading to charges that she was haughty or cold. But it also happens that much more of her legal and business correspondence has survived than her personal letters. With her intimates, though, there are signs of warmth. There is Elizabeth the dog lover, having a servant report back on whether a new puppy misses its mother, or writing to her neighbor Batthyany about prize greyhounds. There is Elizabeth the benevolent mistress: At least some of her employees felt comfortable enough to write informal requests for everything from medical advice to help turning "a little bit of profit." She counted among her friends both an heiress to the Fugger banking fortune and a peasant village healer. She maintained relationships with zealous Lutherans like Magyari while, at the same time, a Catholic bishop called himself her "most devoted friend." While she was never effusive, the Countess could not have been entirely devoid of charm.

Having brokered a religious détente, and relying on the public goodwill accorded the new widow of the revered Black Lord, Elizabeth assumed the role of lord-lieutenant of the two counties of Vas and Sopron. The day Francis's long funeral concluded, she had received an invitation to the upcoming Parliament, a courtesy extended to only two other prominent widows.

In happier times, Elizabeth and Francis had often traveled to Parliament together. The aristocracy spent so much time on their isolated rural estates or off fighting the Turks that, aside from weddings and funerals, Parliament was the one occasion when they could all socialize together. They gathered in Bratislava, whose distinctive four-cornered castle perched above the Danube River a mere thirty nautical miles downstream from Vienna. From its turrets, on a clear day one could see all the way to the Austrian Alps. Crowded into the walled city just beneath, nobles passed the time calling on one another and organizing hunts and dinners, horse races and theater productions, gambling and shopping excursions. Despite her famous reserve, Elizabeth had always figured at the center of these events, commanding great respect. When the rising political star George Thurzo listed the wives in this elite coterie whom he most admired, Elizabeth came first.

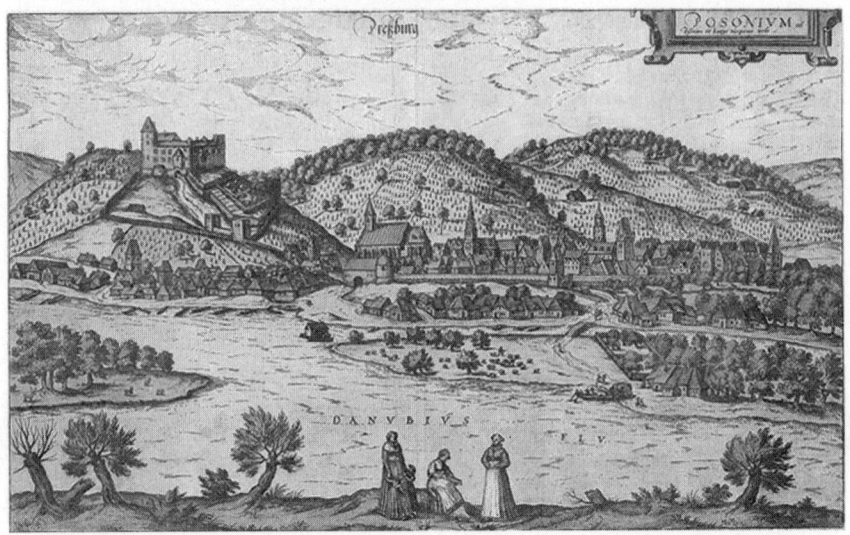

A 1588 sketch of Bratislava (then known as Pressburg or Pozsony) with its distinctive hilltop castle (Collection of Bratislava City Gallery, photo © archive GMB)

But now the Countess was exhausted.

The day she received her invitation, she wrote to another family friend, a Catholic archbishop. Francis's position as imperial Master of the Horse entailed additional responsibilities whenever Parliament convened. There were a limited number of lodgings in Bratislava, and the Master of the Horse oversaw their distribution. This was the perfect position for someone who enjoyed lording their power over others—one could upgrade a favorite to roomier quarters, slight a rival with a drafty room, and move their peers closer or farther from that season's most fashionable hostess.

Elizabeth's response is especially telling: "I do not want to get involved in this at all."

Instead, she begged her family friend to handle the matter for her. She mailed off "the kingdom's register of the lodgings" and the accompanying list of names and asked the archbishop to use his "wise judgment to decide what should happen about this."

For George Thurzo, giving up such a court honor would have been unthinkable.

A WEDDING AND A REBELLION

The Thurzo family had clawed their way into the nobility only fifty years earlier, thanks to their staggering wealth. The Thurzo patriarch had been a mining engineer who bought flooded copper mines at a steep discount and installed new pumps to make them functional again. He had convinced the powerful Fugger banking family to fund his enterprise, and the resulting Thurzo-Fugger company is often regarded as the first modern corporation in Europe.

Stocky, florid-faced, and with a thick, dark beard, Thurzo was only thirty-six years old but already the royal cupbearer, pouring and serving the Hapsburgs their wine—a position of great trust given the constant threat of poisoning. But he saw the position as a mere stepping stone and had been lobbying hard for an advancement to the post of Lord High Steward.

Money had brought George Thurzo recognition and social status, but it could not buy his acceptance into the closed circles of the most ancient families. He had a new Renaissance manor ready and waiting to entertain them, and he was desperate for his young wife to make the Countess's acquaintance. Once, learning that Elizabeth would be traveling back to Ecsed to visit her brother, Thurzo ordered his wife to "go ahead of her," intercept Elizabeth on the road, and invite her to dinner. "Get to know her," he implored.

His wife, however, was unable to race across the countryside in pursuit of the Countess. She was home sick yet again, unable to keep food down. Before she reached her twenty-sixth birthday, Elizabeth Czobor would give birth nine times, and the pace of her pregnancies only exacerbated her chronic health issues. But even if they had managed to meet, the two women would not have had much in common. In an era where it was assumed an upper-class girl would be taught to read "from her

George Thurzo in a 1607 engraving

earliest childhood," Elizabeth Czobor had been, on her wedding day, illiterate.

Thurzo eventually taught his young wife to read and write. He also carefully, patiently instructed her how to properly administer his vast estates, but supervised her from afar, sending lists of whom she ought to invite to dinner or instructions on how to prepare guest rooms (including the rather obvious reminder that rooms ought to have beds and candleholders). While Elizabeth Bathory had been trusted to negotiate with imperial and estate officials, and freely expressed her opinions to Francis, Elizabeth Czobor seemingly had no opinions. In a single short letter—a breathless run-on sentence, crookedly lettered, curiously spaced, and clearly written with great effort—Elizabeth Czobor called Thurzo "my beloved soul," "my beloved Lord," "my beautiful beloved soul," and "my beloved only heart and husband as long as I live, as dear as my own life" and reassured him, again, that she loved him more than her own "heart, soul and life." Elizabeth Bathory had called Francis simply "my beloved husband."

Thurzo would go to the 1604 Parliament on his own, as usual. Even when Elizabeth Czobor was healthy and eager to accompany her husband, Thurzo kept her at home. Elizabeth Bathory stayed home too, sorting through her late husband's papers and her "many troubles." What she missed was a raucous assembly. It seemed cursed from the start: First a fire broke out in Bratislava, requiring further reshuffling of the nobles' lodgings. Then, amid the drinking and dining, there was talk of armed revolt.

The long war with the Turks was draining the imperial coffers, along with the Holy Roman Emperor's generous patronage of the arts and sciences. Rudolf II's vast collections included bright minds and silver tongues—painters, poets, artisans, philosophers, mathematicians, and scientists of every ilk. Obsessive, secretive, and syphilitic, he shut himself away in Prague, surrounded with every bright and shiny thing imaginable, from winking gemstones the size of a fist to a clockwork peacock that strutted about, fanning a tail of real feathers. He was reported to sit for hours in absolute silence contemplating his latest paintings by Dürer or Brueghel, turning away his advisers. Money troubles could be solved easily enough. He commanded his alchemists to work ever longer hours in their castle laboratory so they might turn lead or tin into gold. He also began shaking down the Hungarian aristocracy.

Criminal cases were usually settled between the involved parties; a noble who harmed another would pay restitution to the victim's family. If one hot-headed young lord ambushed or dueled another, the imperial crown had no right to get involved. But if an aristocrat was convicted of *nota infidelitatis*, or disloyalty to the kingdom itself, the emperor gained the right to seize his lands. Rudolf discovered that any crimes that harmed the kingdom's noble bloodlines could, technically, qualify as treason. If one scans the imperial records, it appears a rash of nobles became exceedingly depraved almost overnight. They suddenly began murdering, mutilating, and sleeping with family members.

Elizabeth had already watched a series of her friends and relatives be accused of such crimes. One of her late husband's relations who married a cousin found himself charged with polluting his bloodline through incest, even though the Hapsburgs frequently married cousins, and first cousins at that. When another noble injured a friend in an altercation, he found himself accused of deliberate castration, a charge he vigorously denied. Still, he was tried for disloyalty, too, accused of committing bodily mutilation. Some charges were even applied retroactively: A third noble was charged with treason because he had not prevented his stepmother from marrying a Polish prince a year earlier; the man could not answer the charges against him because he was already dead.

Threatening the nobility was a lucrative practice for the Hapsburgs, even if many criminal charges didn't ultimately stick. Often, the accused would maintain their innocence but, faced with the prospect of a lengthy legal battle, offer the emperor a choice estate to make the charges go away. One teenage lord was accused of usurpation; he managed to keep his head and his title only after forfeiting a castle the emperor had long coveted.

During this period, courts were trusted to, in their own winding way, approximate something resembling justice. With the first few cases, there was the sense that there must be some truth behind the outrageous charges. But as these shakedowns continued with increasing frequency and regularity, the Hungarian Parliament filed formal protests in 1599 and 1603. By the time they gathered for the Parliament of 1604, nobles were openly feuding with their emperor. Rather than working to ease tensions, Rudolf II chose to magnify them.

The Catholic Hapsburgs had long acknowledged the reality that Hungary was a Protestant nation and focused their efforts on unifying all Christians against the Turks. There was enough religious strife in Hungary as it was, with Lutherans and Calvinists "visiting" each other's churches and scuffling in the streets. But Rudolf had become increasingly delusional, certain that he was on the cusp of discovering the philosopher's stone, obliterating the Turkish infidels, and converting all of his subjects back to Catholicism. He chose this tumultuous moment to aggressively champion the Catholic Counter-Reformation.

The emperor ordered a Catholic prelate to begin seizing some Protestant church property. Days later, the Gothic cathedral in Košice— one of the grandest in all of Hungary—was raided by a Hapsburg general, who forcibly ejected all Protestant clergy. One letter of condolence Elizabeth received included an update on both the rumor that the emperor was drafting orders that "those who are not Catholic will lose all of their goods" and the aristocracy's defiant response: "If he [the emperor] does not leave them to their faith . . . they will not even pay their taxes anymore." Nobles attending Parliament formally petitioned that they be allowed to keep both their Protestant beliefs and their lands.

The emperor only tightened the screws. Rudolf informed the aristocracy that entire regiments of Catholic mercenaries would soon be arriving on their estates. Ostensibly, they were meant to protect the populace from the Turks, but they could also serve a secondary purpose: keeping a close eye on nobles contemplating revolt. Elizabeth learned that her northern properties would host a regiment from Alsace, and Sárvár's countryside was expected to support an Italian regiment.

The timing was poor, to say the least.

The imperial court had given her two villages as a partial contribution to Francis's back pay. But the emperor still owed her the equivalent of $1.5 million. She now had thousands of Catholic mercenaries to feed, and bills were coming due for another affair: an engagement party. A husband had been secured for her older daughter, Anna.

The match had been formalized just before Francis's death. A union between the families of two of Hungary's greatest warriors, it had all the makings of a seventeenth-century celebrity wedding. The bride was the daughter of the renowned Black Lord, and the groom's grandfather was still celebrated as the hero of Szigetvár. With less than twenty-five hundred men, he had held off an Ottoman force of a hundred thousand for over a month before leading a final suicidal cavalry charge. His actions halted the Ottoman Turks' otherwise unchecked advance to Vienna and on through the rest of western Europe. France's Cardinal Richelieu later called this "the battle that saved civilization."

The bride would be fifteen or sixteen, while the groom, Nicolas Zrinyi, was at least twenty-four, but may have even been older, in his thirties. This was not ideal—the expected age difference in a first marriage was less than ten years—but in every other respect, the match was an excellent one. The families were longtime allies, and the Zrinyi family estates adjoined Nadasdy property and stretched all the way to the Adriatic. This alliance would strengthen the security of both families and give Elizabeth access to trading ports.

In May, less than two weeks before Anna's engagement party, scuffles erupted between Elizabeth's people and the new Catholic regiments. Some of the soldiers had been raiding and harassing the locals; when Elizabeth's people fought back, the mercenaries imprisoned some of her serfs. While overseeing preparation of food and arranging lodgings for her guests, she began petitioning for her people's release and dispatched an envoy to Vienna to protest the many "calamities and difficulties" caused by these foreign soldiers.

At the last minute, Elizabeth even changed venues. Instead of Sárvár, whose countryside now swarmed with soldiers, the party was held thirty-five miles north, at the castle in Keresztúr. A select group of aristocrats, having just left the contentious Parliament, gathered to watch young Anna Nadasdy exchange gifts and ceremonially hold hands with her future groom. Thurzo was pleased to be counted among them.

. . .

A hajduk, with his characteristic feather-topped cap, in a 1600 woodcut

In the weeks that followed the engagement party, discontent with Rudolf II and the Hapsburg empire reached fever pitch. Facing imminent arrest for treason, a disillusioned former general named Stephen Bocskai decided to fight back. The troops from his own estates, and those of sympathetic nobles, could not hope to match the numbers of the Hapsburgs' mercenary coalition. However, throughout Transylvania and Hungary there were bands of outlaws called *hajduks*, who roamed the countryside in distinctive feather-topped caps.

When hajduks ambushed Ottoman raiders, they were celebrated as folk heroes. But when they stole livestock from Hungarian villages, they were derided as common criminals. Some were refugees who had resorted to banditry to survive, but most were peasant soldiers who had deserted once the Hapsburgs stopped paying their wages. Bocskai promised these hajduks that if they fought for him, they would be paid regularly, and, if he was victorious, each would be granted a plot of land of their own. In a rigid feudalist system, this was a once-in-a-lifetime opportunity to advance.

By the fall of 1604, Bocskai had launched an uprising in the east. At the same time, Rudolf's court astronomers were stunned by a luminary blazing in the night sky, "a silver comet star." They debated what this marvel could mean. A harbinger of great calamity, some declared. But others were certain that this was the biblical Star of Bethlehem, portending a new savior. Bocskai seized the moment to ambush one of the emperor's armies, liberate the Košice cathedral, and send his envoys to major cities, trumpeting, "We have rebelled and taken arms for the Christian [Protestant] religion, for Our Lord Jesus Christ, and for Hungary, our dear homeland!" Then he began marching west.

Thurzo, a Hapsburg loyalist, was alarmed by the news and took refuge in his most secure mountaintop castle. He began checking his gunpowder stores, repairing the fortifications, and "stocking the castle to the brim with food and other necessities."

Elizabeth had to make preparations of a much different kind. A momentous choice loomed over her. Her late husband had faithfully served the Hapsburgs, whose paid mercenaries now surrounded her estates. But for any Bathory, kinship was stronger than political allegiances. The leader of the rebellion was not just an old family friend—he was, in fact, family. Stephen Bocskai had come to power through his service to Elizabeth's mother's family, the hilltop Somlyó clan. One of Elizabeth's uncles had even married Bocskai's sister, and when the couple died, Bocskai stepped in, serving as the guardian for his young Bathory nephew. Bedeviling matters further, Elizabeth's own brother, Stephen, was suspected of being involved in, or at least sympathetic to, the rebellion.

Stephen Bathory was the last male member of the Ecsed branch of the Bathory family. The lord-lieutenant of three counties of his own and also the chief justice of Hungary, he was the second-most-powerful man in the entire kingdom. Had he been born in a different family or era, he would have made an excellent monk. Although he had distinguished himself in battle against the Turks, sustaining serious injuries, he was, at heart, neither a warrior nor a politician. In an age of aspiring Machiavellis, he was sincere to a fault. He had inherited his mother's devout nature and liked to spend his leisure time painstakingly writing out religious tracts by hand. Over the past twenty-six years, Stephen had been working on a meditative memoir in which he agonized over the meaning of existence.

His position as chief justice of Hungary proved a good match for his temperament; he enjoyed both the intricacies of arcane laws and philosophical debates. His judgments were sought out, and he was trusted as a negotiator and peacemaker. He had, for example, been able to do what Francis Nadasdy had not—prevent a split between Protestant factions on his estates.

Emperor Rudolf was worried that support from the straitlaced Stephen Bathory might further legitimize the rebellion. Stephen had refused his invitation to attend the contentious 1604 Parliament, quipping that he would only feel safe if he could bring his entire fortress along with him. He hunkered down at his Ecsed water castle, surrounded at all times by a personal bodyguard of 150 men.

The Hapsburgs' suspicions were, at least in this case, not unfounded—Bocskai was actively courting Stephen Bathory. Elizabeth was known to be quite close with her brother, a longtime companion as well as crucial male ally for a woman newly in power. It is not clear how involved Elizabeth was in her brother's decision-making; none of Stephen's correspondence with his sister has survived. Stephen Bathory ordered all of his personal letters burned after his death, and he rarely committed anything but the most mundane discussions to paper. We cannot know what the siblings discussed through trusted intermediaries, but it strains credulity to think Elizabeth was entirely ignorant. She *was* already accustomed to being at the periphery of her family's many political intrigues; surviving letters show that earlier, she had assisted another Bathory relative in hiding a secret Venetian courier on her estates.

Together, the Bathory siblings presented an existential threat to the Hapsburgs. They commanded five of the twenty-seven counties under Hapsburg control, and their specific counties were of immense strategic value. Stephen's three counties bordered Transylvania in the east, which could give rebel troops a clear path into Royal Hungary. Elizabeth's two counties in the west were within striking distance of Vienna itself. And both of the Bathory siblings had new cause to be incensed with their emperor: During a recent rampage, one of his commanders had burned down both a school and a church that Stephen Bathory had built. Worse, during another rampage, their parents' coffins had been broken open and desecrated.

By January 1605, a year after her husband's death, Elizabeth was in a precarious political situation. She was short of money, her people were harassed by foreign soldiers, and now she was under a cloud of suspicion: The Hapsburgs assumed she shared her brother's sympathy for the rebellion. One of her late husband's advisers was concerned enough to pen a warning: "The estate was hoarded up over many centuries, but by not taking care of it, it can be lost in one hour." If she were not careful, the Countess might be the next aristocrat charged with disloyalty.

As spring approached, it was time for Parliament yet again. This assembly was poised to be even more contentious than the last—but much more sparsely attended. In support of the rebellion, aristocrats were declining their invitations and county assemblies were refusing to send their representatives. Rudolf, furious at their defiance, was threatening to punish any noble who dared stay home.

Elizabeth had been invited but was slow to respond. The previous year, in the aftermath of Francis's death, she had sent her adviser Emery Megyery as her representative. This year, he wrote, that would not be an option. Given such high stakes, he was "not inclined to take part." Her adviser had, however, strong feelings about how she should proceed: "A widow and her orphans must show obedience, i.e., also on account of your brother, against whom there are great suspicions, which could be interpreted evilly, so all of these [suspicions] have to be eliminated." He warned her to accept the invitation at once and to begin making public preparations by sending "food and wood, hay and fodder to Bratislava." He also begged her to get her affairs in order: She should obtain "an official document certifying her son's age and a power of attorney [for] herself and her two daughters, and send those to me." If she were detained, he would be able to act in her stead.

In his alarm, Emery Megyery, known as "Red" on account of his distinctive hair, adopted a frankness above his station. While Elizabeth had a solid handle on the running of the estates, Red Megyery worried she might be missing the bigger picture: "I urge Your Ladyship, for the sake of Your Ladyship's children, . . . to value the external affairs concerning the estate, like the country's public business and matters to be brought before the monarchs, higher than Your Ladyship's internal affairs."

Elizabeth had been busy outfitting an entire bridal party and preparing a generous trousseau for her daughter's send-off. A receipt (from the same German merchant who helped provision Francis's funeral) details purchases of velvets of every color and pattern—green, green dotted, blue, black floral, "cuticolor," red, crimson, mulberry, and mulberry floral—along with damasks, furs, and Spanish silks. Also listed are such basics as combs and scissors, bolts of fabric for tables and bed linens, along with "2 ells satin for the young master" Paul and, for the bride and her twenty-four attendants, golden rings for their fingers and matching wreaths for their hair. The same receipt, totaling over nine hundred thousand dollars, would later be used to tell another story: of a heap of indulgences for a vain, middle-aged widow on a shopping spree just months after her husband's death.

Other rumors worked to Elizabeth's advantage. What Red Megyery took to be feminine dithering or inexperience seems to have been a deliberate, tactical delay. On the same day as Anna Nadasdy's wedding to Nicolas Zrinyi, a parliament was convened at a Calvinist church in the east. As the two warrior-families danced and dined, their guests stamping their feet and raising their glasses, a group of Hungarian nobles proclaimed Bocskai the rightful king of Hungary. He was the "Moses of the Hungarians," sent to liberate his people from Hapsburg tyranny. In support of his candidacy, the Ottoman Turks sent Bocskai a gem-encrusted crown. Elizabeth's brother resigned his position as chief justice of Hungary and threw his support behind the rebellion.

The retribution from Vienna was swift. First, the Hapsburgs went after Elizabeth's family titles. Her late husband had ruled over two counties. Her son, Paul, had already been officially installed as lord-lieutenant of one county, allowing Elizabeth to act as regent. The title to the other county had not yet been granted, although records show Elizabeth was unofficially functioning there in the same capacity. Now, overriding the wishes of the local people, the emperor snatched that title away. He bestowed it, instead, upon Elizabeth's neighbor Lord Batthyany, who had no holdings in that county, had not petitioned to be considered, and only reluctantly accepted the appointment. This was intended as a very public snub.

Worse, that summer, as rebels surged into the area, Hapsburg troops invaded her lands, swarming the castle where a year before Elizabeth had hosted her daughter's engagement party. She wrote to Lord Batthyany:

> Yesterday the Germans came out . . . to my house in Keresztúr. They brought cannons, they burned down completely my town and my farms . . . They also occupied my castle. I don't know why they had to do this to me, because I can prove before the living God that I was devoted to my gracious Lord [the emperor] and will be until I die.

Elizabeth's protestations that her loyalties remained with the emperor were met with increasing skepticism as more men in her family threw their support behind the rebels. The Nadasdy relative who'd been charged with disloyalty for marrying a cousin was the army captain of a nearby town. Rather than defending the town against the rebels, Thomas Nadasdy surrendered to Bocskai before a single shot had been fired. Then a male Bathory publicly humiliated the emperor: An army captain sent on a mission to negotiate with the rebels for the Hapsburgs instead switched sides and joined the siege of an important city.

What happened to Elizabeth's Keresztúr estate was only a taste of things to come. A message darkly warned that the destruction would have been worse except that "we kept in mind and kept count of the merits of your distinguished Ladyship's pious late husband." The note's author was General Giorgio Basta, one of the highest-ranking Hapsburg mercenaries, who had led the destruction of her brother's schools and desecrated their parents' graves. Basta ordered, "Declare your mind, which you have left vague until now with this neutrality (I will not have this anymore)." To prove her loyalty to the emperor, Elizabeth must allow him to garrison his army inside the walls of Sárvár Castle. For her own good, of course.

Elizabeth knew all too well the potential price of refusing. A generation earlier, Aunt Klara had refused to turn over her property to the Hapsburgs' armies; this had cost her two years' imprisonment. But unlike her aunt, Elizabeth had no brothers in the emperor's favor who could negotiate on her behalf. Frightened and unsure, she again wrote to Lord Batthyany asking for his advice. But in the end, she stood up to Basta, rejecting his demands: "The castle is my main residence, as Your Grace knows; we are 'squeezed' here with my court, with whom I cannot settle in the city." She suggested, diplomatically, that the imperial army would be more comfortable in another town entirely, and for some reason, Basta complied. Still, Elizabeth had to have been shaken by the encounter. In less than two years, she had gone from being the respected widow of a revered war hero whose biggest headache was her local clergy, to becoming a suspected traitor suffering the loss of a title, the devastation of one estate, and direct threats by a notorious general.

Other nobles in the region, even if they were in less immediate danger, watched nervously as imperial mercenaries and rebel hajduks clashed on their estates. Like Elizabeth, George Thurzo worked carefully to play both sides. Thurzo had just achieved his coveted position as lord high steward at the Hapsburg court. He publicly declared unwavering support for the emperor but privately negotiated with Bocskai. Thurzo secured a letter of protection for his property, signed by the rebel leader himself, which he warned his wife to keep a secret: "It is not good to show this letter to anyone ahead of time . . . because it says in it that I have sworn allegiance to Bocskai, which is not true and never will be true. This letter is only needed if the hajduks were to invade, but if other lords saw it, it would be very bad, they would condemn my action."

Elizabeth also negotiated to have her property protected. When rebel troops ravaged the area around her northern holiday home of Čachtice, they left her castle and manor untouched. But while nobles like Thurzo had no intention of joining the rebellion, Elizabeth seems to have been seriously contemplating joining forces with her brother. A letter to Elizabeth from her deputy that appears to be dated a few weeks after the destruction of her Keresztúr estate references an uprising multiple times. It also mentions contact with one of her husband's cousins who had joined the rebels and the possibility of organizing some type of gathering at his behest. Elizabeth had already reached out to other lords in her region, and she and her deputy were waiting to "see what answer we will get from the Lords Batthyany and other Lords, and from that Your Ladyship will know their minds." The deputy warned her, though, that if these lords were not willing to join her, "Your Ladyship cannot undertake anything on her own."

Whatever Elizabeth may have been plotting, it was all upended just a week later. On July 25, 1605, at nine o'clock at night, her brother, Stephen, after a sudden fit of "writhing," died.

Given the timing of his death—just as he had joined the rebellion—there were rumors the former chief justice had been poisoned. Such rumors followed many unexpected deaths, but in this instance, there were other odd circumstances. A family servant claimed that Stephen's wife had become violently ill at the exact same time, although she recovered. Another story circulated that the water castle of Ecsed was now haunted; a ghost had taken to tossing stones at people and rearranging items. Thurzo rather dramatically relayed this gossip to his wife, certain this was some kind of demonic mischief; another interpretation was that these were the acts of a spirit crying out for vengeance.

After her brother's death, in addition to a gold chalice, various tapestries, and gem-encrusted golden reins, Elizabeth inherited several properties in eastern and southern Royal Hungary. Stephen left her the imposing mountaintop fortresses of Füzér and Buják, as well as the castles and the manors of Szentgyörgy and Babócsa. She also jointly inherited ten other properties with other Bathory women (primarily Aunt Klara's granddaughter and great-granddaughter). Elizabeth had under her control at least seventeen castles and reinforced manor houses, with access through her family to many more. Her lands now spanned about five hundred miles; together, their combined acreage overshadowed entire kingdoms and duchies. Without the protection of any male relative—father, husband, brother, or adult son—she made for a very attractive target.

CHAPTER 4

The Curious Case of Miss Modl

Every time Elizabeth Bathory's serfs awoke to a scream in the night and stumbled into their doorways, armed with daggers or scythes, they could never be sure whom they might encounter. The Ottoman Turks were taking full advantage of the political upheaval, slipping over the Hungarian border to harry the locals. Everyone, even those sympathetic to Bocskai's rebellion, feared his outlaw hajduks, "who prey, kill, rob and lurk in many places." And the Hapsburgs' mercenary armies seemingly answered to no authority.

Elizabeth's neighbor and family friend Lord Batthyany had been given command over the foreign troops in their region, but he could not bring them to heel. The Countess reminded him sharply that the armies "were not sent here by our gracious Lord to harm us, but to protect us." Yet half-starved soldiers seized her serfs' livestock; they also looted villages, broke into nobles' manors, and destroyed valuable grazing land. The minutes of one county council meeting read: "Mrs. Nadasdy [Elizabeth] and the whole county protest against the abuses of the soldiers . . . If Captain Batthyany does not remove them from the county, they will rise up against them." In addition to threatening to revolt, many people refused to pay their taxes, not wanting to fund their own harassment.

Public opinion was on the verge of turning against the Hapsburgs entirely. Bocskai made special overtures to the emperor's most loyal subjects—ethnic Germans and Slovaks in western and northern Royal Hungary—by circulating an open letter written in German. These minorities identified with the Holy Roman Empire, but most were Lutheran, not Catholic like their emperor. So Bocskai carefully framed the rebellion in religious terms, as "a just defense against the disturbers of our Christian [Protestant] faith and freedoms." Bocskai also disseminated a different manifesto throughout western Europe, an appeal to all lovers of liberty. Rudolf II had controverted the ancient privileges of the nobility and defied both natural and divine law, Bocskai declared. His rebellion was an act of "self-defense" against an unlawful tyrant.

This message tapped into a growing belief that monarchies should not be absolute. The Hapsburgs, with their deformed jaws and inherited insanities, had only helped the argument along. Clearly, no clan was perfect, and no kingdom should be at the mercy of a monarch unwilling or unable to govern. The right to resist an unjust ruler had become particularly popular in Calvinist circles across Europe, adopted by French Huguenots in the French Wars of Religion, the Scots in their struggle for independence, and the Dutch in their own battle against the Hapsburgs, known as the Eighty Years' War. The concept presaged the English Civil Wars between the king and his Parliament and the writings of John Locke that would figure into the American Revolution.

Alarmed, the Hapsburgs unleashed their own propaganda campaign. It was not the Hungarians who were unjustly subjugated: It was the Germans, whom Bocskai himself had been courting. From their pulpits, German pastors warned their parishioners that they might soon find themselves evicted by their Hungarian landlords or forced to convert at sword point to heretical Calvinist beliefs. In tandem, German-language newspapers reported that Bocskai and his hajduks had made a deal with the Turks to allow them to conquer Europe:

> There is great terror in Vienna
> For all the rumors say
> that the Turkish sultan will personally come out here

and will occupy this city
and Bocskai and his followers will clear the [mountain] pass for him

Everyone had been raised on tales of what the Turks would do once they arrived: dishonor their wives and daughters, butcher their babies.

The dueling propaganda campaigns encouraged Hungarians and Germans to fear one another even more fiercely than they feared the mercenaries. Where once the kingdom's diversity had been a point of pride, now it was a source of contention. Before, the Devil walked among them in the guise of a dark-skinned Turk. Now, he shifted form, becoming a handsome peasant man. In German villages, he wore ethnic Hungarian dress; in Hungarian ones, he wore German garb. As he traipsed from one village to the next, swapping out his cap or embroidered overcoat, all saw that he filled out his doublet, well fed.

It was through this divided landscape that Elizabeth was forced to travel in the autumn of 1605. To claim her inheritance and bury her brother, Elizabeth needed to return to the swamps of her childhood. Even in the best of times, this was a harrowing undertaking on rutted dirt roads. George Thurzo recounted the hazards he encountered on one ordinary 40-mile journey: First, four of his horses slipped off a bridge into the rain-swollen river, and later, his carriage overturned, leaving two of his companions with bruised and bandaged hands. Elizabeth's trip would be 430 miles each way, in unpredictable autumn weather, and involve the transport of dozens of people—guards, groomsmen, cooks, attendants—through an active war zone, during a raging plague epidemic. She would be traveling north and then east, through areas heavily populated with Germans and Slovaks. These ethnic groups had once lived on the outskirts of the Hungarian empire. When the Turks invaded, the aristocracy fled north, encroaching into their enclaves. Once, their overlords had visited their far-flung estates occasionally; now, they had set up house, employing the German and Slovak locals as their cooks, nannies, and gardeners.

The minorities on the Countess's main estates, even if they disapproved of her close relations with rebels, still knew her as the feudal mistress who took in their orphans and made sure disabled widowers had enough grain to feed their children. Elizabeth paid for the brightest boys to go off to German and Italian universities and donated butter, chicken, and one goose for each of their wedding feasts. When the rivers froze over, she posted guards to keep bandits from sneaking across the ice; when the foreign soldiers continued their harassment, she issued impassioned pleas on their behalf: "Please, Your Lordship, don't let the poor be oppressed and ruined so freely again."

But in these more northern regions, Elizabeth had accrued no such goodwill. As her retinue hurried from one fortress to the next, spending as little time as possible out on perilous dirt roads, Elizabeth's visit made quite an impression. With her large entourage, ornate carriage, and fine attire, the Countess was an object of great curiosity, and of suspicion. Would she soon betray her emperor, just as her late brother had? Would she return with an escort of rebel troops, or worse, Turkish ones? German villagers' fears only intensified when they learned that, during Stephen Bathory's funeral, Bocskai showed up at the cemetery with a large contingent of his troops and Elizabeth personally met with the rebel leader.

It was during this long trip that the curious case of Miss Modl unfolded—the earliest and most enduring allegation against Elizabeth. In a sea of testimonies about nameless, faceless victims, there are several that mention Miss Modl by name★ or recall some other identifying detail about her. She was ethnically German, she was from Bratislava, she was young and newly married, and she was tall. The tales about her, no matter how inflated, seem to be rooted in *something* that happened to a real person.

The outline of the story, as it appeared in multiple witness testimonies years later, went something like this: During her long trip east, the great lady found herself shorthanded at a dinner she was hosting. At the time, it was customary for only unmarried young girls to serve at the lady's table. The Countess asked her German housekeeper to help out, but Miss

---

★ "Modl" is suspiciously close to the German "Moidli," a diminutive of "Mädel," or "young lady." This was an affectionate nickname bestowed upon ladies at other neighboring courts, including that of the Batthyanys next door.

Modl protested—she was a grown woman with a son. Furious at her insolence, Countess Bathory crafted a creative public humiliation. Since Miss Modl had bragged about her baby son, she was given a log and forced her to walk around pretending to nurse it, as if it were her child. Later, two men who claimed to be eyewitnesses both recalled the Countess angrily calling Miss Modl a "whore." One swore the punishment happened in Vranov, an estate the Countess inherited from her brother in the east, while another said he saw Miss Modl's humiliation unfold over two hundred miles away, back on the estate of Čachtice.

The story of Miss Modl circulated at the same time as German folktales about other log babies. By guttering candlelight, old women told of healthy babies snatched by forest spirits and the "changeling logs" left in their place. Or of the desperate, infertile couple who brought home a little log and dressed and suckled and sang to it until, one day, it transformed into a flesh-and-blood baby (a precursor to the fairy tale of Pinocchio). It's impossible to sort out whether the German mother's punishment was inspired by these stories, or if these folktales seeped into retellings of Miss Modl's fate.

The only testimony by a lady in Elizabeth's personal circle was decidedly more banal. Miss Modl had not been forced to suckle a log; she had simply been flogged. Her reported defiance occurred during one of any number of feasts held in honor of Stephen Bathory; a German servant's refusal to honor a rebel Hungarian noble would have been both a political statement and a personal affront. Even if Miss Modl had banal reasons for refusing to serve at that dinner, Elizabeth could not let other German servants get the idea that they could disrespect her brother's memory in this way.

A flogging was uncharacteristically harsh, not for the era, but for Elizabeth, who had a reputation for being generous with her servants. Once she turned down a large grain sale in part because "my poor serfs have quite much to do anyway, I cannot compel them to go everywhere." And when Red Megyery wrote to Elizabeth, panicked that she did not comprehend the political climate, he also chided her for being overly concerned with "internal affairs" like "securing the servants' salaries." Elizabeth was known for her lavish bonuses to trusted staff: To reward her children's longtime nanny, she paid for the weddings of both her daughters and gifted the girls "beautiful skirts" for their trousseau.

It wasn't just her people's work hours and compensation she worried about. When one of Elizabeth's maids, named Justine, took ill, the local doctor was sent for twice and it was discussed whether the expensive Italian physician who treated the Hungarian elite should be brought down from Bratislava to give his opinion. Elizabeth, away at the time, wrote to the ailing maid herself; that letter has not survived, but from Justine's response, it is clear that Elizabeth spared no expense for her care. Justine assured her mistress that "nothing is forbidden to me that could be beneficial."

Miss Modl's defiance was an isolated incident; there are no indications that other servants followed suit. By all accounts, Elizabeth's trip was a success. Her brother, Stephen, was laid to rest in the family crypt—on solid ground close to Ecsed—with all the ceremony befitting his station. Bocskai himself issued a decree recognizing Elizabeth's claims to her newly inherited lands, ordering the hajduks to offer their assistance.

But, proving herself a resourceful diplomat and negotiator, Elizabeth never openly declared herself a supporter of Bocksai's rebellion. She kept up the appearance—in public, at least—of remaining loyal to the Hapsburg emperor, Rudolf II. Whether he believed her or not was another question, but legally, a woman could not be charged with treason. If women are not by nature political creatures, how can you punish them for meddling in politics?

Often a whisper campaign could accomplish what a legal case, or brute force, could not. The story of a cruel and haughty Hungarian mistress oppressing a young German mother fit in well with the Hapsburg's current propaganda offensive. The rumors about Miss Modl spread like wildfire.

Five more witnesses—eight in total—would, years later, offer bloodier versions of the German servant's punishment. Four claimed Miss Modl had not been humiliated, but killed. A servant of Elizabeth's made no mention of the log baby, but said that Miss Modl had been secretly murdered at Keresztúr—a difficult undertaking given that at the time, the castle was occupied by Hapsburg troops. Others reported hearing that Miss Modl had been subjected to grievous tortures—one person heard she had flesh sliced off her backside, a second that she was burned on her abdomen with a hot iron, a third that the poor woman had her breasts cut off.

The villagers seem to have been conflating two rumors that they had heard, one about Miss Modl being publicly humiliated and another about barbarous medical practices on the Countess's estates.

. . .

Everyone was sick nearly all of the time. The elites of the day exchanged letters replete with the failings of their mortal bodies: infections and infertility, gout and arthritis. During the political unrest, this was one topic it was perfectly safe to write to one another about, but it was also an indication of the near constant levels of infection and infirmity. Foreign troops brought with them heresies and vices, but also bubonic plague, typhoid fever, smallpox, and influenza (not to mention syphilis). There was also the specifically named *morbus hungaricus*, or Hungarian disease— spawned in the crowded army camps.*

Even in spacious quarters, with access to plenty of fresh air and clean water, the Countess was not able to entirely escape the epidemics sweeping through her estates. She once wrote to Francis about the "vile illness . . . spreading in the region" that had felled her too. "Last night was wicked again for me," she complained. But generally, Elizabeth's letters speak of ailments that were, at least at first, minor and commonplace: in her twenties, digestive troubles and lower back pain; in her thirties, a bad bout of headaches, and later, sore eyes. The Countess could even be considered lucky: She managed to survive childbirth six times. But in addition to whatever new epidemics the soldiers brought through the region, there were the usual childhood killers in constant circulation: measles, scarlet fever, diphtheria, and dysentery. Only three of her children would reach adulthood; the era's finest nutrition and medical care could not circumvent a 50 percent child mortality rate.

---

* This was likely a form of typhus. It is worth noting that this term was resuscitated in the nineteenth century for an entirely different disease: tuberculosis.

George Thurzo's wife defied these odds. The very petite Elizabeth Czobor (she was not quite four foot nine) experienced nine difficult pregnancies, but had five girls and one boy survive to adulthood. But she was also usually bedbound by headaches, the source of much concern for her husband. Thurzo brought in multiple prominent physicians, including the personal doctor of a Hapsburg archduke, to examine her. Today, archaeologists and forensic scientists have been able to piece together what the doctors could not. Elizabeth Czobor's headaches were the consequence of a genetic condition called *hyperostosis frontalis interna*: She had an abnormally thick cranial bone constantly weighing down on her forehead. Given this, her reported menstrual disorders, and other symptoms, some have hypothesized that she suffered from the endocrine disorder now known as Morgagni-Stewart-Morel syndrome.

Elizabeth Czobor's extensive and well-documented care gives us a glimpse of the different types of healers employed on an aristocratic estate. The doctors, educated abroad, developed a narrative of the illness, explaining the patient's symptoms in terms of the interplay of blood, phlegm, and yellow and black bile. In Elizabeth Czobor's case, for example, they decided her headaches stemmed from an imbalance of blood: Her irregular periods meant her body could not cleanse itself properly.

The "barber-surgeon" at Thurzo's court was then called in to administer any prescribed bloodlettings or purgatives. He traveled with his little chest or leather bag, containing his pliers, scissors, razors, saw, scalpel, and "hot iron." He was prepared to do everything from trimming a beard to performing basic dentistry and minor surgery.

The third kind of healer at Thurzo's court was the "woman scientist." He employed the famous Mrs. Zavis, a commoner with a deep knowledge of herbal remedies. Her drafts and tinctures gave Elizabeth Czobor considerable relief. Mrs. Zavis was so well respected that when consulting doctors visited, they did not question her efforts but rather tried to supplement them. There were similar "women scientists" or "old women" to be found in almost every court. Some even hailed from the nobility: A Hungarian lady-in-waiting served as a court healer, a German princess helped run a pharmacy, and a Danish princess treated the Holy Roman Emperor himself. Elizabeth's neighbor, Lord Batthyany's young wife, brewed tinctures for the elite, including the Thurzo family. Whatever their social class, these women all practiced a noninvasive, plant-based medicine, and many of their traditional remedies are still in use today: marshmallow and mint teas for upset stomachs, calendula creams for skin rashes, and salves and tinctures containing willow bark, the precursor to synthetic aspirin, for aches and pains.

Each of the three types of healers had their distinct role to play in a patient's treatment plan: The doctor was the brains, the barber-surgeon the brawn, and the "old woman" the voice of practical experience.

Elizabeth's court at Sárvár was organized in much the same way. Her mother-in-law had once administered an entire hospital on the estates, but the privations of the war years had made that difficult to sustain. Now, Elizabeth brought in elite foreign-trained doctors to consult on certain cases. She hired a barber-surgeon for minor surgical procedures. The Countess also frequented two female herbalists: a "woman scientist" on the Sárvár estates and another on her northern Čachtice estates. And she had her own counterpart to Mrs. Zavis residing at court: Anna Darvulia. Unlike Mrs. Zavis, though, Darvulia was not a local commoner; her origins are murky. Her surname is not Hungarian or Slovak, so some have theorized that she may have hailed from farther east, in Transylvania. Darvulia had arrived at the Sárvár court sometime before Francis's death, perhaps as early as 1595.

Even in a time of relative peace and prosperity, the common people were suspicious of foreign female healers. When Elizabeth's mother-in-law had gone into labor with Francis, along with the local Hungarian midwife, a German woman had been called in. The staff were skeptical of her strange methods and unwilling to follow her instructions; the German midwife berated them for their ignorance. Even though the labor was long and difficult, it was ultimately successful, thanks to the outsider's efforts. One Nadasdy servant was gracious enough to admit to his master, "Your Excellency, although we all disliked the German midwife . . . if she had not been here, I do not think that either my lady or the child would be well." Had the labor not resulted in a healthy, long-awaited heir, the German midwife could have easily ended up a scapegoat.

Anna Darvulia was not only foreign, she was rumored to have expanded her practice beyond herbal salves and ointments, midwifery and pediatrics. She would not have been the only woman to assume responsibilities usually reserved for male practitioners. Women were banned from serving as doctors and barber-surgeons in places such as France and Italy. In England, though, women had the legal right to practice medicine, and there were female barber-surgeons working in Belgium and the Netherlands too. In the Hungarian lands, there were also women doctors, but reactions to them varied greatly. When Elizabeth was a child, a particular "Jewish woman doctor" had been very much in vogue among the aristocracy; some would only consult the Hapsburgs' male physicians if she were not available. Yet in 1599, two female doctors were arrested and charged with witchcraft, and one of their male mentors was charged with the crime of educating a woman in "medical science."

Perhaps Elizabeth, never one to be bound by convention, employed a female barber-surgeon outright. Or, finding herself as shorthanded in her sickrooms as she was in her dining hall, the Countess authorized her "old woman" to attempt emergency surgeries. Either way, even though female barber-surgeons were not illegal in Hungary, they still would have inspired suspicion and fear. Working with herbs or treating children was within their proper sphere. Church authorities and conservative villagers may have even tolerated a woman stitching a wound or lancing a small boil. But Anna Darvulia would later be named as someone who caused great pain to the girls at Elizabeth's court, a "torturer" who taught other servants how to burn and cut the girls.

A female barber-surgeon and her assistant cupping a patient's foot in a seventeenth-century engraving

Much of what a barber-surgeon did was bloody and gruesome. In one instance, Elizabeth called in a (male) barber-surgeon to treat an abscess in her younger daughter Kate's mouth. She wrote to Francis that the infection was stopped through cautery: "the barber-surgeon went in with his iron up to the middle of her tooth." How frightening this must have been for a wriggling child, held down while a strange man forced a red-hot iron inside her small mouth. Such a procedure would have been no less terrifying to undergo as an adult. It could seem a dreadful punishment, torture even, if one did not know or believe their untreated tooth abscess could kill them. And in addition to cauterizing infections and "needling" cataracts,* barber-surgeons sometimes attempted more ambitious procedures: repairing fistulas, removing bladder and kidney stones, amputating limbs, or, when a pregnant woman died, performing a cesarean section to see if her baby might be saved.

People were wise to be wary. Quacks and charlatans abounded, often harming more than they healed. In one instance, an illustrious noble suffering from "malaise" came to George Thurzo's court seeking treatment. During his prescribed bloodletting, the barber-surgeon cut the wrong vein, and the noble bled to death. Another surgeon was charged by a city council after a patient "had his head drilled open" and then an infection set in. And amid the ongoing trauma of war, barber-surgeons had gained additional dark associations with the battlefield. The new cannons and muskets had created an entirely different sort of war injuries from swords and axes. Now terrifying stories spread of screaming men tied or held down as legs were sawn off, pieces of shrapnel yanked out, wounds scraped clean and cauterized. The shrieks, the copious blood and burning flesh—for many villagers, the barber-surgeon was a living embodiment of one of their pastor's fire-and-brimstone sermons. It was the Devil's work these men undertook, in their bloodstained aprons with their crude metal tools. But a woman who did the same—she must be a literal demon.

. . .

---

* Barber-surgeons would try to improve their patients' vision by using a small needle to slice up the clouded lens.

Anna Darvulia's presence at Elizabeth's court casts new light on the Countess's 1602 clash with her pastors over her *carnifex* servant. This servant might have not just been eating meat during Lent, but also providing medical care. The Latin word *carnifex*—one who cuts flesh—was also linked to the field of medicine. The first recorded use in this context was by Pliny the Elder in the first century C.E., bemoaning the practices of Greek doctors who eschewed traditional Roman herbs for more aggressive methods such as surgery. Pliny said one such doctor initially had a good reputation as a "wound healer," but then became known as a *carnifex* because of his cutting and cautery. The term was also the title of a twelfth-century satire against doctors and, in the sixteenth century, an insult leveled against the great Erasmus by an Italian physician. A female medical practitioner—like Anna Darvulia herself—who cut and cauterized could easily earn a reputation as a butcher too. The pastors' letters are worded in such a way that the "butchery" might not be a reference to the woman's sin, but to her *profession*:

> Some wicked woman—about whom everyone knows, that the Lady has her work very much in *that butcher's chamber*—is surely known to want to come to the holy Mass during the upcoming feast days . . .
> When he will have approached *that butcher woman* . . .
> Concerning *that butcher woman*, about whose exclusion from the communion my opinion was asked . . .

In late 1605, Anna Darvulia's reputation could have also colored many villagers' understanding of whispers they heard about tragic happenings on Elizabeth's trip east. In addition to the tales that Miss Modl had been cut into or cauterized, there was a report of a girl being submerged in ice-cold water with her clothes on. Ice-water baths were a common way to quickly bring down a dangerously high fever. They were also recommended to revive plague patients, whom doctors commanded should not be allowed to sleep and, given their relentless diarrhea, be kept clean. But some wondered if this girl was another servant creatively punished by a cruel Hungarian mistress.

Then there were the reports that someone—maybe the unfortunate Miss Modl, maybe the girl dunked in ice water, maybe another servant entirely—had died. One witness later insisted the death of this servant girl occurred on the journey east to Stephen Bathory's funeral; another testified it occurred on the way back home. One witness thought two girls had died, another just one. There was no way to check because the deceased had been buried somewhere along the road. Maybe this was in accordance with the order to bury plague victims immediately, before they could spread their illness to others. Or maybe the hasty burial was a way for the Countess to hide the butchery of her old woman, Anna Darvulia.

And then there were the two young servant girls. When villagers were later pressed to recall any instances of Elizabeth's cruelty, they remembered something they saw when the Countess stopped in Trenčín, twenty miles north of her estate in Čachtice. There were two girls in her entourage with bandaged hands. A tax official remembered that "they could not grip anything with their hands, they would not even get onto a carriage using their hands, they needed help from others." The tax official said he was told that their hands had been burned. Maybe the girls had injured their hands in one of the usual ways—a cooking fire, an overturned kettle. But he was certain their mistress was somehow at fault. Another citizen of a different town reported that his relative had also seen the two girls in Trenčín. This witness had heard the girls' hands were not burned but rather had been "pierced," much like a martyr's might be.

The Turks were coming. The rebels were coming. The emperor's mercenaries were coming. The Devil was already among them. The commoners lived in constant fear for their lives and their immortal souls. When they next heard of a girl gone missing, they had to wonder: Had she been carried off and ravished by soldiers? Enslaved by the Turks? Or had she fallen victim to a danger much closer to home? When they heard the screams at night, echoing in the hollow or flying across the plain, when they could not blame their emperor, the Turks, or God, they could not help but think of the Countess and her old woman.

CHAPTER 5

See You in Court

By the end of 1605, the cornerstones of the grotesque Bathory legend had been established: from the Lutheran preachers, that Elizabeth was not entirely pious, and perhaps in league with the Devil; and from her German subjects, that she was harsh with her servants and allowed her old woman to torture the girls in her care.

There is no indication that Elizabeth herself was aware of these rumors. Even if she had heard some passing mentions, the gossip of commoners would have interested her much less than the threat of regiments of soldiers and men like General Basta. The Countess no longer felt safe in Sárvár, even within its pentagonal walls, with five sturdy Italian bastions and a four-story gate tower where guards kept watch. Her neighbor Lord Batthyany suggested she hire some of the foreign mercenaries who were now in plentiful supply. But Elizabeth was skeptical that any of these men could be trusted, writing back: "I can't see anyone's heart. I will not transfer any of these troublemakers to my town."

Instead, she hired a private security force of "good persons" who owed her their loyalty. Her late brother had kept himself surrounded at all times by a bodyguard of 150 men; Elizabeth was not able to secure such a large force, but she did hire "fifty paid infantrymen, a commander, an ensign and a drummer to stay in Sárvár continuously." This much-needed security had a high price tag. Elizabeth wrote to the Hapsburgs, pleading yet again for the money owed her: "I have reached—oh, how painful!—a state of intolerable scarcity of all things and especially money . . . and I hardly will be able to feed the soldiers either, whom I enlisted because of the situation's exigency and to save this place from danger." She claimed that she needed these soldiers to protect her estates from the rebels, and so they were "proof of my due loyalty to my most merciful Lord." The Hapsburgs officially directed the court chamber to pay the Countess the remainder of what she was owed. But, true to form, they delayed actually disbursing the funds.

While Elizabeth was struggling to pay her bills and preoccupied with the defense of her property, one of her fellow aristocrats saw an opportunity. In January 1606, George Banffy and a group of armed men occupied one of her estates in what is now northeastern Slovenia. Lendava was a market town whose houses and terraced vineyards ran up a hill crowned with a looming castle. A relatively recent acquisition of the Nadasdy family, Lendava had become a favorite target of Ottoman raiders. It was at Lendava, coincidentally, that the famous Captain John Smith, before heading off to Jamestown, earned his army title. Smith was part of the mercenary army that arrived to break the Ottoman siege of the castle. Smith later claimed to have earned his promotion with his ingenuity, first by using torches to send messages to the men trapped inside the castle, and then with a novel use of explosives to misdirect the Turkish forces.

The Ottomans listed Lendava as a Nadasdy property at the time of that siege, in 1603, but it is unclear how long the Nadasdys had possessed the property prior to that and exactly how they had acquired it. Banffy may have been convinced that he was only taking back what was rightfully his; Lendava had been in his family since 1192. But Elizabeth was not the least bit sympathetic. In a letter to Banffy, she thundered:

> Why did you have to act like this? . . . I won't be silent about this case at all. I will certainly not let anyone possess what is mine . . . If nothing else is possible, I will have your house torn down above your head, because you occupied my estate by force like this. Now, I only wanted to let Your Grace know this much. May God keep Your Grace in good health.

She added a taunting postscript:

> I know, my good Lord Banffy, that only your poverty moved you to this, to long for my small property, not your wealth, but do believe me, you've met your equal. I certainly won't let you possess it for long.

Then, Elizabeth Bathory—granddaughter and niece of royal judges, sister of the late chief justice—took George Banffy to court.

She did not adopt the more traditional tactics of Thurzo's wife, the long-suffering Elizabeth Czobor. She was not accommodating or, for lack of a better word, *nice*. She gave voice to her incredulousness and displeasure, quickly and loudly. Here is a glimpse of the Countess Bathory of legend: enraged, imperious, and maddeningly stubborn.

It is possible these traits inspired admiration just as often as fear. Elizabeth was approached by Mrs. Caspar Banffy, a newly widowed Nadasdy relation who was being bullied by her Banffy in-laws. George Banffy had taken her land too, and she also wished to file a suit against him. He was her nephew by marriage, and she was a new widow with eight children to support. Rather than offer his assistance, Banffy had teamed up with his brother to attack her while she was most vulnerable.

This is just one of the many instances of widows, intimidated or strong-armed by the men around them, turning to Elizabeth for help. Elizabeth was perceived to have great political acumen; in the widow Banffy's words, "Your Ladyship herself knows and understands these times' situation." The widow wanted Elizabeth to advocate on her behalf: "As Your Ladyship understands the common law, please do aim at His Majesty and the counselors for my rights not to be suffocated." This could be translated into contemporary English as a request to "strive in front of His Majesty and the counselors . . . to defend my rights." But it is significant that the widow Banffy never asks Elizabeth to beg or plead, but rather chooses verbs drawn from the battlefields around them, asking the Countess to "aim" her influence and intellect at specific targets.

Just as significant is the Hungarian word the widow Banffy selects to refer to both the common law and her property rights: *igazság*. This refers to truth and justice in the broadest sense. Elizabeth was considered someone who knew her way around the law, as one might expect from a woman who had grown up with prominent judges in the family. But the widow's choice of words also demonstrates that in a society rife with bribery, corruption, and quid pro quo, Mrs. Caspar Banffy believed Elizabeth to be someone with a strong ethical sense, someone who would fight for what was morally right and not just politically expedient. This request also shows that, despite the rumors beginning to circulate, Elizabeth was still perceived to have considerable political clout and influence at the imperial court.

Another noblewoman asked the Countess to intervene in hostage negotiations. Her husband had been taken captive by the Ottoman Turks during the war, she could not afford the demanded ransom, and the Hapsburgs were dragging their feet (as usual) about becoming involved. This woman had been resourceful enough to find and purchase herself a Turkish prisoner of war, and she wanted to arrange a prisoner exchange. She asked Elizabeth to help her secure an influential male sponsor to help with the swap, and Elizabeth managed to convince her neighbor, young Batthyany, to become involved.

Even commoners sought the Countess's help. In one instance, a woman healer from Tokorcs, a village just outside of Sárvár, came to Elizabeth seeking protection. Elizabeth referred to her with the utmost respect, with the same address used for the famous Mrs. Zavis at Thurzo's court—as a "woman scientist." This "woman scientist" had raised a young woman from childhood, likely one of the many war orphans in the village. This girl had become pregnant and named three village men as the possible father (it is unclear if these were all consensual relationships). One of these potential fathers had reacted with great anger, vandalizing their home. The healer begged Elizabeth for help. Elizabeth directed her second-in-command, her deputy Blaise Kisfaludy, to investigate the case thoroughly and see to it that the "woman scientist" and her foster daughter were protected and that justice was served. All of these women saw Elizabeth as an ally and advocate, someone who could be counted on to fight for them, fiercely.

Mrs. Caspar Banffy offered to do some fact-finding for Elizabeth in exchange for her help. The villages outside of Lendava were deserted, having been decimated by the Hapsburg forces sent to protect and surveil them. The widow reported on the living conditions of the Countess's subjects: "Your Ladyship's poor serfs . . . are hiding on the Mura River's other side . . . Many lost their houses to the fire last year because of the Germans, also their livestock was taken, so they had to flee across the Mura into their vineyards." The serfs may have fled, but they were willing to return and rebuild: "None of them left not wanting to come back again, if only Your Ladyship would free them from the hands of the Lords Banffy." The widow promised to serve as a go-between with the serfs still in hiding, to offer them support or to help entice them to relocate to another of the Countess's estates.

The Banffy brothers certainly did not want Elizabeth's serfs to remain in hiding or to resettle on one of her other properties. They needed those serfs tilling the fields in order for the estate to be profitable. So while men like the Banffy brothers may not have started the rumors about the Countess, they were certainly not above taking advantage of the distrust they might create. Elizabeth's piety and political loyalty had already been questioned, and the latest rumors about her treatment of servants called into question her ability to administer her lands and people. The Banffys could only benefit if Elizabeth's serfs became convinced that Elizabeth was an unjust mistress and they'd be better off shifting their allegiance to new overlords. Those embroiled in court battles with the Countess had little incentive to speak in Elizabeth's defense, and every reason to let the poisonous speculation spread unchecked.

. . .

At the end of March 1606, people marveled as the moon turned scarlet, blotted out by the earth during a lunar eclipse. The intent of this divine communication soon became clear: God was calling for an end to the bloodshed. As summer approached, instead of bracing for another brutal campaign season, Elizabeth learned peace negotiations were underway. The citizens of Royal Hungary and Transylvania held their collective breath. While talks had been attempted before, they had always been stymied by the emperor's stubborn delusions. But this time something was different.

Emperor Rudolf II had been confronted with another revolt, this time within his family. The increasingly morose emperor would not communicate with his ministers and refused to grant even his own family members an audience. Finally, alarmed by a depleted treasury, plummeting public approval, and mounting military defeats, three of Rudolf's brothers secretly met with some of the Hapsburg cousins. Together they decided that the Hapsburg empire could not fight two separate wars indefinitely. Rudolf was strong-armed into allowing his younger brother, Archduke Matthias, to negotiate a peace with Bocskai and the Ottoman Turks.

On June 23, 1606, Bocskai and Archduke Matthias signed the Peace of Vienna. The rebels had, by almost every measure, succeeded, forcing the Hapsburgs to address their complaints of religious and political repression. The treaty permitted all Hungarians (or, at least, all free and land-owning Hungarians), whether they resided in Royal Hungary or Transylvania, the "free practice and pursuit of their religion." Hungarians were also granted additional political freedoms. Transylvania would remain an independent principality, with Bocskai as its prince. In Royal Hungary, citizens would still be subject to a Hapsburg king, but they would have an elected royal governor, or palatine, to serve as their advocate.

The rebels were also assured there would be no more sham trials to seize aristocrats' lands. The treaty granted amnesty to nobles who had previously been targeted. It also restored due process: "No one shall be punished who has not been properly cited before a court and prosecuted."

Together, Archduke Matthias and Bocskai then negotiated a separate treaty with the Turks. That agreement, signed months later in November, guaranteed a twenty-year ceasefire between the Hapsburg and Ottoman Empires. The "Long War" was over. As the news was delivered in letters and broadsheets and announced from pulpits, the celebrations were giddy, nearly delirious.

But even after the treaties were signed and ratified, neither the Hapsburgs nor the rebels considered the conflict truly resolved. The Hapsburgs had not abandoned their plans to bring the Transylvanian lands under their dominion; they would merely have to wait for a more favorable time to try again. Bocskai, well aware of this fact, saw the Transylvanian nation as a necessary check on Hapsburg power: "As long as the Germans, a more powerful nation, have possession of the Hungarian Crown, and the Hungarian Kingdom is dependent on them, it will remain necessary and useful to have a Hungarian prince in Transylvania, for he may be able to offer help and protection." Bocskai dreamed of the day that the people of Royal Hungary would rise up again to expel their foreign overlords with assistance from their "blood brothers" in Transylvania. Soon, they might be reunited under the rule of a Hungarian king.

After the flush of celebrations had subsided, the inhabitants of both regions were unsettled too. After fifteen years of war, they were at a loss. So much of their daily routine and their personal identities were crafted around defense—against religious opponents, ethnic outsiders, nighttime raiders. The war had impacted everything from career and marriage choices to farming methods to fort construction. It had also forced everyone to look at their neighbors in a new light. Few people were ready, or willing, to set aside their suspicions, as Elizabeth soon discovered.

She traveled to the outskirts of Bratislava to survey a property that she had not been able to reach during the war. Most of the land Elizabeth had inherited from her brother lay in the east, near their childhood home, but this choice property lay where the Danube and Morava Rivers meet, less than fifty nautical miles downstream from Vienna. Perched atop a seven-hundred-foot cliff, the sprawling Devín Castle complex is now a popular tourist attraction, but in Elizabeth's day, it was a fortress of great strategic importance, marking the western border of the Hungarian kingdom.

It was also a symbol of the old alliance between the water-dwelling Ecsed Bathorys and the Hapsburg empire. When Elizabeth's grandfather had thrown in his lot with the Hapsburgs after the disaster at Mohács, this castle had been his reward; Devín Castle had stayed in the Bathory family since. Stephen Bathory left the property to Elizabeth and his niece and great-niece (Aunt Klara's granddaughter and great-granddaughter); he made the captain who managed the property swear an oath to assist in the handover to the Bathory women.

From the banks of the Danube, a ferry was the only way to reach Devín Castle: one trip to a small island in the middle of the river, and then a second the rest of the way across. Elizabeth made it all the way across the Danube with two of her stewards, three of her wagons, and four other servants. The rest of her party—a large group of "servants, horsemen, and footmen"—made it to the island and then onto the second ferry. But as soon as they approached the shore of Devín Castle, "people shouted immediately not to bring them across" and the ferry was forced to turn back. Elizabeth's men ended up stranded on the small island "without food and drink, miserabl[e]."

Elizabeth blamed the German burghers, "the gentlemen in Bratislava," for this affront, but she was bewildered by their about-face. These men had welcomed her enthusiastically to their city a few years ago when she had promenaded the cobblestones on the arm of her late husband, the famed Black Lord. But now they had turned against her, and she was unsure why: "I do not know who had the desire to do this, they [the burghers] themselves or someone else." This "someone else" went unmentioned by name, although the only authority the free German burghers answered to was the Hapsburg emperor.

Elizabeth thought she presented no obvious threat: The men she had brought along constituted too small a force to occupy a fortress. But the burghers of Bratislava clearly thought otherwise. Even in peacetime, the sister of a Hungarian rebel, the vicious persecutor of the respectable Miss Modl, could not be allowed to install any of her men in a fortress overlooking Bratislava, within a day's ride of Vienna. Elizabeth protested that she had remained loyal to the Hapsburgs at great cost to herself: "I have never betrayed My Lord, even in times of such big destruction and misery, I have rather kept my loyalty to His Majesty, and I don't know why it was needed to do such a thing to me, that has never before occurred in my family."

Viewing this as yet another Hapsburg land seizure, and decrying "what the Germans have done to the Hungarian nationality," Elizabeth promptly lodged a grievance with the imperial court. But the Bathory family would never recover this prestigious piece of real estate.

. . .

Elizabeth's tour of the rest of her estates proceeded much less eventfully. As soldiers marched out of their forts and serfs and hajduks wound their way down from their mountain hideouts, Elizabeth recorded and mourned her losses. Although the Countess had managed to save the Nadasdy family seat of Sárvár Castle with the help of the bodyguards she had hired, most of the villages surrounding the castle had been burned down by the armies sent to protect them from the Turks. In the fall, Elizabeth sent her steward to survey the damage. One village recorded that, thanks to the mercenary soldiers under Lord Batthyany's command, they had lost "40 good milking cows . . . 26 horses . . . [and all] our crops and food, clothing and other goods." Their losses totaled close to a quarter of a million in today's dollars. Other villages detailed how troops had ransacked their homes to take small personal items like shoes, handkerchiefs, and silver buttons. The attacks weren't just restricted to their property. Some of them had been beaten so severely, they claimed, "we have yet to heal up to this day."

Outside of Sárvár, four of the five other Nadasdy estates had not fared much better. Keresztúr had been burned down at the beginning of the rebellion. Léka, where Francis had been buried with great pomp only two years earlier, was practically abandoned; there, Elizabeth wrote, "I have no serfs at all." Csepreg, once the largest market town in the region, had been grand enough to host her older daughter Anna's wedding. But now Elizabeth wrote that it was "only a devastated town." Even Čachtice in the north, where Elizabeth and Francis had liked to spend their Christmas holidays, had not escaped unscathed. The manor and castle had been spared, but the countryside and town had been ravaged, first by the Ottoman Turks and then by Bocskai's hajduks.

The question was how to encourage serfs to return and rebuild. Aristocratic landlords were now competing to attract commoners to populate their villages and towns. Elizabeth focused on restoring order and reestablishing routines. She had her stewards conduct land surveys and clearly mark property borders, and she personally organized the repair of the roads, demanding villagers show up with axes "the following Wednesday and two days following it" to help with the work. She also offered incentives. So her people might rebuild their homes, the Countess granted them free lumber from the previously forbidden manor forests. While construction was underway, they were given free lodging in other villages and allowed to fish in her manor's ponds to supplement their diets. Her people were also given an exemption from paying taxes or performing any other work or service. This concession was often granted for one to three years after devastating fires, but in some villages, Elizabeth extended the reprieve to a full five years.

It is difficult to understand how Elizabeth could have initiated, or continued, a murderous spree at this time. While the confusion of the war years might have provided some cover for such crimes, in the years following the Peace of Vienna every village was now being visited by a variety of stewards and administrators, every house and family was being cataloged, and every death was recorded. And serfs and commoners, for once, had some degree of choice. That they chose to return to the Countess's villages and towns strongly suggests that, while there may have been rumors that the great lady had heretical beliefs or treated her German servants harshly, there were not yet widespread concerns that she was a murderer.

But the Countess earned herself no new friends when she began investigating the corruption that had mired local governments since the war. That autumn, Elizabeth, now forty-six years old, complained in her letters about a new "condition" that left her "like a bruised person, sometimes better, sometimes quite sick again." The Countess may have been experiencing a slow and halting recovery from one of the many circulating epidemics, what we would term post-viral syndrome today, or these may have been symptoms of some new and more ominous ailment. Still, she did not allow her poor health to slow her down. In yet another of her crusades for *igazság*, for truth and justice, Elizabeth filed complaints against the vice chancellors of several counties, complaining they were not doing their jobs. She threatened them publicly: If their performance did not improve, she would find a way to have them removed from their posts. Soon after, finding paperwork missing on one of her estates, she accused the former provisor of embezzling funds. Elizabeth fired the man, commissioned an audit, and then, unhappy with the results of the audit, demanded he be arrested. The county decided that the man was no longer under Elizabeth's jurisdiction and she could not have him thrown in jail, although he was forced to provide a full accounting of the money spent. Although outraged, Elizabeth did not abuse her authority: She did not have the provisor imprisoned secretly, or roughed up by her bodyguard. She did what she usually did—took her grievance to the courts.

Much like her mother and brother, Elizabeth displayed a desire for order, for things to be made right, for the guilty to be held to account. Her efforts were appreciated by the downtrodden but were tiresome, even threatening, to many others. As Elizabeth sought to rebuild her estates among those who did not wish her well—German commoners, Lutheran pastors, and opportunistic nobles—she could now add to that tally a number of disgruntled former employees.

. . .

The Peace of Vienna was short-lived. Bocskai reigned in Transylvania for barely six months. On December 29, 1606, in the eastern city of Košice, the forty-nine-year-old prince took his last breaths. The general who had launched his rebellion under a strange new star—a supernova, it would turn out—ended his reign under a dark and moonless sky. His funeral procession had not yet been assembled when the battle for the succession began. The favored candidate was Bocskai's top general, thirty-year-old Valentine Drugeth of Humenne. The other aspirant was Elizabeth's nephew.

Elizabeth's brother, Stephen, had produced no biological children. He was the last male in the Ecsed line; this western branch of the Bathorys had seemed fated to extinction, like so many other ancient families. A convenient solution presented itself when one of their mother's relations from the eastern Somlyó branch left behind two young orphans. Stephen had adopted his young Catholic cousins Gabriel and Anna, raised them as Calvinists, and named them his heirs. Upon Stephen's death, young Gabriel had inherited the ancestral castle of Ecsed. Now this seventeen-year-old boy was poised to revive the Bathory family's prospects.

Lively and affable, Gabriel had a natural charisma. Men and women alike reported that he was unusually handsome, with chiseled features and the Bathorys' expressive brown eyes. Even hardened old hajduks were enamored with him. Gabriel was a gifted athlete, an accomplished rider and swordsman. He was slender but extraordinarily strong, rumored to break horseshoes in half with his bare hands. When Elizabeth's brother had declared his support for the rebellion, Gabriel, then only sixteen, had become one of Bocskai's army officers. Brave almost to the point of recklessness, Gabriel had acquitted himself on the battlefield, earning the hajduks' respect. Ever since, the boy had been carefully groomed to be Bocskai's successor.

Elizabeth was close with her nephew; while not many letters between the two survive, those that do show an easy familiarity and affection. Not only did Elizabeth seem to genuinely like Gabriel, he promised to be the male protector that she had lacked since the deaths of her husband and brother.

At news of Bocskai's death, both Gabriel Bathory and Valentine Drugeth rushed to secure backing for their respective candidacies. Gabriel Bathory, who pledged to keep Transylvania free from all Hapsburg influence, was embraced by the hajduks. Valentine Drugeth, who pressed for closer relations with the Hapsburgs, was supported by many of Bocskai's former advisers. Drugeth also received funding from many nobles across the border in Royal Hungary, including George Thurzo.

Bocskai had once publicly suggested that, should anything happen to him, Gabriel Bathory should be Transylvania's next prince. But just a few weeks before his death, Bocskai had named Drugeth as his successor in a will. There were, however, questions about that will, given the prince's poor condition. Some contemporary historians have made much of the fact that Bocskai's secretary, one of the will's signatories, wrote to a friend: "For now . . . *all will easily believe* and be reassured that His Majesty has wisely made his will."

A few days after the prince's death, the rumors of poison began. For most of the past year Bocskai had complained of symptoms like heavy, swollen feet, typical of edema from congestive heart failure. Even in the early seventeenth century, this disease was not unknown; it was called dropsy and linked to heart troubles. A letter by Bocskai's close counselors announcing the prince's death to the Transylvanian people even decisively stated that he had died of natural causes and there was no suspicion of poison. Another of his close advisers wrote that if there was anything nefarious afoot, it was simply the "curses of [the] many poor people" whose property had been looted by Bocskai's hajduks.

Still, the common people found the timing of their prince's death, on the heels of his victory and the ratification of the Peace of Vienna, to be suspicious. And in this era, every conspiracy was an opportunity.

First, a rumor was circulated that Bocskai had been poisoned by the Hapsburgs. They had, after all, tried to assassinate the rebel leader many times before. But within days, the accusations of poison were weaponized against a critical supporter of Gabriel Bathory's candidacy: Bocskai's former chancellor. Michael Katai, like Bocskai himself, had strong ties to the Bathory family. Before becoming chancellor, he had served Elizabeth's brother, and then one of her cousins. Now he championed her nephew. Katai had been imprisoned just months earlier, pending the completion of an investigation into whether he had overstepped his authority during the peace negotiations. The investigation now abandoned, he had every expectation of being released and, in fact, was reported to have begun asking, "Whose prisoner am I? Who keeps me *in arresto*? I would certainly like to know, and I will take care of them in the future." Once freed, Katai could lobby for Bathory's election and then serve as *his* chancellor.

Tying Katai to Bocskai's murder required a certain ingenuity; after all, the former chancellor had been sitting in a prison for several months. It was decided that "Katai supposedly poisoned him [Bocskai] with a drink, a few months before at a wedding in a garden." One secondhand account describes the council meeting where Katai was denounced:

> One night suddenly all the lords were called to the council house. When the lords gathered, they were all inside with burning torches and they did not know why they were summoned . . .
>
> One of the prince's intimate counselors went among them with a lit torch . . . : "What would such a man deserve who would feed his benevolent lord, his merciful prince—who by the grace of God liberated the whole country from a powerful enemy and protected the Holy Church of God and restored the country and the Hungarian nation to their old freedom like a father—a deadly poison and [slowly] kill him?"

The lords answered: "He also deserves a similar terrible punishment, because he has sinned against the whole country."

The lords asked: "Who is that man?"

[The counselor] answered: "Michael Katai is the one who did that."

Did every member of the council believe the dramatic denouncement? Did it even matter? A dangerous precedent had been set, creating a tolerance, and even appetite, for disinformation. The Hapsburg emperor's sham trials and manufactured evidence, wartime propaganda, and the histrionic language from sectarian battles had made it commonplace to accuse one's rivals of crimes without any hard evidence, based on simple hunches about their sinfulness.

In the past, Katai would have been brought to trial on an unrelated spurious charge, but the brand-new Peace of Vienna had guaranteed due process for all and fair judicial proceedings. That Katai, a career soldier and politician with no special medical knowledge, had somehow discovered a rare poison that could kill someone four months after a single dose was not a claim likely to hold up in court. Instead, it was engineered to drive hot-headed hajduks, grieving the loss of their beloved Prince Bocskai, to lose control.

Katai was told he was being released from prison and led to the town square of Košice. There, surrounded by pastel-colored burghers' houses and in the shadow of the town's grand Gothic cathedral, a small group of hajduks were waiting. One of his fellow aristocrats was waiting too. He ordered the hajduks to strike Katai down. When some demurred, they were told, "Anyone who does not cut this unfaithful traitor is a dishonorable traitor himself too!" The rest drew their swords and, a contemporary wrote, when the hajduks finished, his body was "chopped into thousands of pieces." There was so little left of him that Katai's pretty young wife had to gather up the bits "in a sheet" for burial.

This carefully orchestrated lynching was meant to send a clear message to the Bathory family: Their opponents were willing to take extreme measures to ensure that the ancient clan did not grow more powerful. Should the Bathory family persist in seeking the throne of Transylvania, more bloodshed would result.

CHAPTER 6

The Dose Makes the Poison

In the end, Chancellor Katai's gruesome death was completely unnecessary.

Neither Valentine Drugeth nor Gabriel Bathory won the crown. The newly seated Transylvanian Parliament, determined to guard the region's hard-won independence, found reasons to object to both candidates. Valentine Drugeth had been named by Bocskai as his successor in his will, and the Parliament did not want to set a precedent of princes appointing their replacements. Gabriel Bathory also made them uneasy; since there had been so many Bathory princes in the past, they wanted to avoid the appearance of a hereditary Bathory dynasty. Instead a third candidate was elected. As a more seasoned politician, already in his sixties, Sigmund Rakoczi was intended to be a stabilizing force.

Still, people were not reassured. "Visiting someone's house at this time was very scary," one contemporary pastor wrote. The rumor that the great Bocskai had been felled by some new exotic poison deeply shook many people, who became convinced that they, too, might be killed in an unexpected way. The pastor wrote, perhaps exaggerating, that "after Bocskai's death, poisoning people's food and sprinkling poison powder on saddles and chairs became customary in this country."

It was true that there were many sudden and even unexplained deaths. The plague was back again, and typhus, cholera, and smallpox were circulating widely. And then everything froze: the Thames, the Zuiderzee, the Loire, the Seine, even the Rhine up to Cologne. The birds froze, falling from their perches. Even one king's beard froze: France's Henry IV woke one morning to find his neatly trimmed *henriquatre* frosted to his face. Everyone had been muddling through the Little Ice Age, but in the winter of 1607–8, the cold suddenly intensified, resulting in the Great Frost, one of the bitterest winters in recorded history. All across Europe, death rates surged.

One of Elizabeth's fellow lord-lieutenants, Andreas Doczy, of neighboring Bars County, had a few of his friends die shortly after visiting him, including a relative of Elizabeth's. People began whispering that partaking in "Andreas Doczy's hospitality and Doczy's cup" was equivalent to taking one's life in one's hands. The next year, when Valentine Drugeth, one of the former contenders for the crown of Transylvania, also died suddenly, this was alleged to be Doczy's work too: Doczy was accused of having smeared poison upon Dugeth's saddle.

Elizabeth's peer and neighbor was arrested on multiple charges of murder. Cases of serial murder were not unheard of, and illustrated "true crime" broadsides that detailed such atrocities were bestsellers throughout Europe. Usually, though, these sorts of charges were leveled at commoners in the German lands who fell afoul of religious authorities. In this instance, the aristocracy worried that the Hapsburgs were up to their former tricks and that the murder charges were only a means to seize Doczy's title and lands. When dozens of people came forward and testified to having heard rumors about Doczy's use of exotic poisons, the Hapsburgs were accused of paying off witnesses. Fortunately, many prominent nobles also came forward to testify on Doczy's behalf, including a family member of one of his alleged victims. Without any hard evidence that the deaths were the result of poison, Doczy finally cleared his name with a solemn oath of innocence.

In an interesting twist, Doczy's accusers now found themselves in trouble. One man's slander of Doczy earned him a death sentence (the sentence was commuted, but his family was disgraced nevertheless).

This was likely the very reason that Katai's accusers had the chancellor lynched instead of brought to court. The stakes were high for those caught spreading malicious rumors.

The Doczy trial did much to restore faith in the legal system, reassuring aristocrats that even if it took some time, the Hungarian courts could be trusted to approximate something close to justice. The case also illuminated how pervasive rumors could prejudice and shape witness testimony. When dozens of people repeated the same story over and over, it didn't necessarily indicate guilt; instead, in the words of one contemporary, when "the testimonies are going in one direction, [this is] a sign that he [the accuser] has told his theory to everyone and that this very interesting story has had time to form on the lips of the public." Government and court officials were well aware that a successful (and fair) prosecution had to rely on more than just hearsay.

Doczy's trial also illuminated the ongoing breakdown in the medical system. The charges against him initially seemed credible because, with no single authority overseeing cases, recording symptoms, or providing any alternate narrative for illnesses, it was easy to blame poison, or even witchcraft, whenever someone died unexpectedly.

People were already rubbing and sprinkling all manner of odd and unknown substances upon themselves. When the doctor or barber-surgeon or "old woman" could not be found, aristocrats tried their best to treat themselves and one another. Once, in the throes of an illness, Elizabeth had begged Francis, "If Your Lordship would find some good ointment, send me some." Nobles pursued "good ointment" with the same fervor that Emperor Rudolf's alchemists sought the philosopher's stone. Some purchased theirs from the traveling healers pitching their remedies in the town squares. Others had theirs brewed up by neighbors and friends: The concoction Thurzo applied to his aching neck was sent to him by Lord Batthyany. Elizabeth's brother, Stephen, even had one ointment shipped all the way from eastern Transylvania.

Ointments were said to be able to cure almost all manner of illness, everything from the plague to tumors. In the library in Sárvár was a personally inscribed copy of the first known medical book in Hungarian, full of recipes for ointments; one incredibly complicated recipe combined herbs with "cow dung water" and claimed to cure plague, gout, and cold sores.

Many remained skeptical of these ointments' supposed abilities. Elizabeth's maid Justine, during a bout of illness—fever, chills, and swollen lymph nodes of her neck—complained about the ointment she was directed to slather on her stomach: "I didn't see any effect, so I quitted the anointing, because I always felt worse after it." Justine, like everyone else, never really knew exactly what was in her ointment. It might be cow dung water. It might be opium or willow bark or hemp. It might be just common kitchen grease, or it could be—it was rumored—baby parts. But if slathering one ointment on your stomach could save your life, it stood to reason that another ointment—or salve, or powder— could just as easily kill.

It was true both that many people were being poisoned and that many of these deaths were unintentional. Paracelsus, a Swiss alchemist and physician, had recently introduced the idea of using minerals and chemicals in medicine. In the years since, he has been credited as the founder of Western toxicology, the creator of our pharmaceutical-industrial complex, and the "godfather of modern chemotherapy." Daring to question that the four humors ruled human health, Paracelsus argued that since the human body was composed of chemicals and minerals, it could be treated by the same. He was responsible for the creation of laudanum, a tincture of opium, widely considered a blessing by anyone unfortunate enough to undergo surgery in this era. But Paracelsus also popularized chemicals known to be poisonous.

As a direct result of his work, small amounts of mercury, for example, became a leading treatment for syphilis. Another toxic heavy metal, antimony, was introduced to help with skin conditions like scabies and impetigo. But it was used most widely as a purgative, a sort of early modern cleanse to expel whatever toxin might be making one ill. Sometimes people would swallow a small pellet of antimony that worked as a laxative by irritating their digestive tracts. After the person was emptied of all supposed toxins, the antimony pill could then be fished out, cleaned off, and reused for their next illness. This remedy persisted into the nineteenth century, known as the economical "everlasting pill."

A less disgusting method of administering antimony involved letting wine sit in a cup made from antimony; the metal would react with the tartaric acid in the wine to form antimony tartrate, which induces vomiting.

Antimony was a controversial treatment. In France, for example, the medical faculty in Paris ruled against its use in 1566; it would take a hundred years, and pressure by Louis XIV, for them to reconsider. Despite this, the treatment remained popular among younger doctors and patients, as well as those who traveled in the more daring intellectual circles. Elizabeth, who counted herself among these, was reported to purchase antimony in amounts so large that the apothecary would not let the Countess's courier transport it himself. Because in that quantity the antimony could kill "a hundred people," the apothecary personally delivered it instead. It is not clear who was prescribing the antimony and in what form, but there was no doctor in residence on any of Elizabeth's estates at that time. It could have been ordered and administered by a traveling barber-surgeon or, quite possibly, by a female healer on Elizabeth's staff.

Antimony, like lead, is a cumulative poison, but ten times as toxic. It causes wheezing, nausea, vomiting, paralysis, confusion, and, in large enough amounts, death. Just as the apothecary cautioned, the purchased antimony would have led to deaths on Elizabeth's estates, although it is impossible to calculate how many this "mineral cure" caused outright and how many it simply hastened along. What did the villagers whisper among one another when one too many coffins were carted out from behind the castle walls?

. . .

In their rush to elect a new prince and protect their newly enshrined rights from outside meddling, the Transylvanian Parliament had overlooked the hajduks. These soldiers—who had agreed to fight for Bocskai in exchange for land of their own—now refused to lay down their arms until they received their due. Gabriel Bathory saw an opportunity to take advantage of their discontent. In February 1608, he signed a formal pact with the hajduks; they agreed to support his candidacy for prince of Transylvania, and in exchange, he agreed to give their captain a seat on his council and to make sure all soldiers were settled on plots of their own. One year and one month into Prince Rakoczi's reign, the hajduks threatened an armed revolt, and Transylvania had no standing army large enough to counter them. After this bloodless coup, on March 7, 1608, the now eighteen-year-old Gabriel Bathory was elected the prince of Transylvania.

When Gabriel rode into Cluj for his coronation, flanked by his hajduk troops in their feather-topped caps, the common people greeted him like a victorious general. Gabriel looked the part of the perfect prince: tall and elegant, with a neatly curled mustache. He was young and vigorous—a prince who might protect the commoners from the Hapsburgs and the Ottomans alike. This optimism was shared by the extended Bathory family. After several deaths in the family, Gabriel was not just the last male Ecsed Bathory, but the last male Somlyó Bathory too. The survival of both branches of the family depended upon the young prince; his ascension was their chance to rebuild their political influence.

Gabriel's new principality was hemmed in between two powerful empires, its wild and mountainous lands scarred from decades of near continuous invasions. It needed, more than anything, time to heal and rebuild. But the treaties with both the Hapsburgs and the Turks were new and fragile. Border skirmishes were still breaking out, and restless hajduks rampaged through the countryside. When the Transylvanian Parliament grudgingly elected Gabriel Bathory, they made their support conditional upon one thing: The new prince must ensure there was peace. He would need to keep the favor of both the Hapsburgs and the Turks and bring the hajduks to heel. Governing Transylvania at this precise moment would have been a difficult job for even the most seasoned politician, much less an untested eighteen-year-old.

Soon Royal Hungary was celebrating a new leader too. The Hapsburgs had become increasingly concerned about the mercurial Emperor Rudolf, who had come out of his isolation only to try to undo the new peace treaties and reignite both wars. Archduke Matthias again stepped in, luring some hajduks over the border with promises of land in exchange for their help overthrowing his older brother. In an episode nicknamed "the Brothers' Quarrel," Matthias forced his brother Rudolf to cede control of Hungary to him.

Plump-faced Matthias had long cast about for a suitable role to play—bishop, governor of the Netherlands, king of Poland, regent of the Tyrol—but had failed in all of them. Now, finally, he was lauded. A man of immense ambition but no particular talent, Matthias was enamored with his new title and its trappings. For his coronation, he had special coins and medals struck, banners hung, and the wooden bridge on the way to Bratislava's St. Martin's Cathedral covered with a red, white, and green carpet, the colors that would later comprise the Hungarian flag.

On November 19, 1608, the archduke was crowned Matthias II of Hungary, exactly 150 years after the coronation of the first Matthias, the Raven King, who had ushered in a new era of light and learning. Matthias II could have made much of this connection and drawn parallels between the reign of the revered king and his own. But he had little use for the legend of the shining city on a hill. He did not believe in light; he believed in lockstep. His motto? *Concordia lumine maior.* Unity is stronger than light.

Matthias I was said to have walked among his people, disguised in a homespun cloak, but Matthias II avoided getting off his horse. After the coronation mass, he rode through the northernmost city gate, St. Michael's, now the much-photographed onion-domed archway that is a Bratislava landmark. In front of the city walls, King Matthias II swore the coronation oath, in the same spot, coincidentally, where witches were burned.

These two new rulers were soon joined by one more figure: George Thurzo. In late autumn of 1609, Thurzo reached the pinnacle of his political career. As lord steward, he had helped the Hapsburgs negotiate the Peace of Vienna; in gratitude, they had made him a count. Finally, he was a peer to Elizabeth Bathory. Then, in 1609, he beat out three other candidates to be elected palatine, or royal governor, of Royal Hungary. He was now the highest-ranking Hungarian in the kingdom.

Thurzo, however, was not universally loved. He had opponents in both Royal Hungary and Transylvania. Although Thurzo claimed to be a devout Lutheran, one poem in wide circulation accused him of loving money more than his God:

> *If Baal [the devil] is your God, why do you not follow him [openly]?*
> *If you're Hungarian, why don't you pity your country?*
> *It's a shame you forgot yourself.*
> *You'd better fill your basket with gold.*

Thurzo's critics were right to be wary of his ambition. He had, along with a slew of daughters, a single son, the same age as Paul Nadasdy. The palatine was carefully grooming Emery Thurzo to be a Lutheran statesman and his successor. George Thurzo imported a professor all the way from Wittenberg to be Emery's private tutor. He also made sure Emery was highly visible at the Hapsburg court: The boy had already been chosen to serve at the table of King Matthias during the coronation banquet. Thurzo wished to clear out his son's path into politics, and he had already demonstrated he would stop at nothing to ensure his family's rise.

Eager to ingratiate himself with the Hapsburg court, Thurzo had already betrayed his fellow aristocrats more than once. The most egregious example of this had occurred back in 1600, when Thurzo had lured a young aristocrat out of hiding with promises of amnesty, right into the arms of imperial troops. Although this young man was a Hungarian war hero and the last of his family line, the Hapsburgs had him beheaded and seized his lands, to the outrage of the rest of the nobility. Thurzo had also moved viciously against his neighbors; in one instance, much as George Banffy had done to Elizabeth, Thurzo forcibly seized eleven villages belonging to another family and used his connections to delay and quash their lawsuits against him. And then, in a fit of pique, he burned down another neighbor's village and executed some of his servants. Thurzo was, in many ways, typical of the age—a man who could exchange tender missives with his wife, delight in indulging his many daughters, and then, a master of compartmentalizing, easily shift into ordering a political enemy's execution.

· · ·

Prince Gabriel Bathory was, at least at first, a popular ruler. However, his early years were marked by a series of incongruous policies and promises. Because of this, for some time historians dismissed him as impetuous, inexperienced, and "entirely unprepared to govern," although more recently his legacy has been reassessed. His contradictory positions may have been the result not of youthful indecision, but of skillful politicking.

Gabriel maintained the fragile new peace by building consensus among warring factions. For some time, he succeeded in telling each what they wanted to hear, fulfilling some promises to each while postponing others. He reassured the Calvinist Protestants of his religious bona fides, waxing on about his close relationship with his late adoptive father and guardian, the devout Stephen Bathory. But he reminded Catholics that he had been born and baptized Catholic and gave them reasons to hope he might convert back one day soon. He followed through on his promises to the hajduks, giving them twenty towns to settle, some of these villages abandoned during the war, but others from his own family's holdings, while also promising nobles that he would soon crack down on these outlaws' raucous behavior. He established friendly diplomatic relations with both the Hapsburgs and the Ottomans, convincing each that he was more partial to their counsel than the other.

Gabriel's enemies weaponized the very things that made him so appealing to the masses: his youth and good looks. They decried his inexperience and high spirits and cast the prince's every decision and appointment through this lens. Attacks on his morality followed, with critics claiming he was easily bewitched by drink and pretty women. Gabriel had grown up in the almost monastic environment of Stephen Bathory's strict Calvinist household. Perhaps the prince now indulged in all the fine wine and attractive company his position afforded him. But it is just as likely that his opponents exploited the one tactical mistake the Bathory family had made.

While Gabriel was being groomed as Bocskai's successor, he had been hurriedly married off to a Bocskai relative, Lady Anna Horvath. At the time, Gabriel was not yet eighteen. Now, his wife had become a burden—her family was no longer of political use, and the prince was unable to marry a foreign princess to strengthen Transylvania's position.

The couple was said, too, to not be particularly fond of one another; soon they were living apart.

To make matters worse, the young, handsome prince still looked like a single man. It was customary for married men to grow beards. For those eager to prove their religious devotion, the longer the beard, the better. Only unmarried men were, aside from their elaborate mustaches, clean-shaven. Gabriel kept his dashing mustache and his beard was a very close-cropped one, more like a few days' stubble. That Gabriel both bucked convention *and* was living apart from his wife unsettled many fundamentalist religious figures.

It also became grist for the gossip mill, an easy way to cast aspersions on his advisers and allies. A poem was printed up and passed around the Parliament in Bratislava:

> *I heard your news, good Gabriel Bathory,*
> *Kate Iffiu and the wine have distracted thee.*

Kate Iffiu was the wife of the prince's chief adviser, a man named John Imreffy. Imreffy had already served three generations of Bathory men; his appointment was no great surprise. But the prince's opponents insinuated that Imreffy had only been appointed because Gabriel was interested in his beautiful wife. This rumor smeared one of the prince's top advisers as unqualified and, in a society where everyone was jockeying to prove their piety, cast Gabriel Bathory as dissolute and depraved.

The rumor was also a time-tested way to rein in Kate Iffiu's own political influence. The prince valued her guidance, sometimes more than that of his male advisers. One courtier grumbled that Gabriel treated her "as if she were the sacred oracle of Apollo at Delphi." Clearly, though, anyone who sought out the noblewoman must be interested not in her intelligent counsel, only in sex. The rumor was especially sinister, though, because Kate Iffiu was not just much older, with a son Gabriel's age; she was also the prince's biological aunt.

Incest allegations against powerful women had long been a mainstay of European politics—Eleanor of Aquitaine, Isabella of Bavaria, Anne Boleyn, and Lucrezia Borgia are just some of the better-known women to be so accused. The charge that Gabriel Bathory was "distracted" by his aunt was also a preemptive strike against one of the main sources of the prince's support: the women in his family. War and disease had taken out a disproportionate number of Bathory men; Gabriel had few kinsmen to advise him. But he had a sister, several aunts, and many female cousins who offered him financial support and political counsel. The smear was intended as a warning not just to Kate Iffiu, but to all of the Bathory women.

It was imperative that Prince Gabriel not be allowed to consolidate his power. The Hapsburgs were constitutionally unable to suppress their appetites. The Spanish side of the family had overrun the Iberian peninsula, moving into the southern Netherlands, the south of Italy, North Africa, the Caribbean, and the Americas. The rest of the family occupied Germany, Bohemia, Switzerland, and Royal Hungary, and had now spread into northern Italy, eastern France, and parts of Poland and Denmark. Bocskai's rebellion had temporarily stunned and embarrassed the great dynasty, but the Hapsburgs were still determined to swallow up Transylvania too.

Gabriel Bathory might slow their march eastward. But he might also present a more existential threat. Already there were whispers that this charismatic young warrior could be the long-awaited savior who would cast out the Hapsburgs and reunite all of Hungary under one crown. Gabriel himself did nothing to disabuse anyone of this notion.

As 1609 came to a close, Elizabeth found herself under suspicion again, her fate and fortune entangled in the ambitions of three men: her nephew, her neighbor, and her king.

PART TWO

1610–1614

CHAPTER 7

Strained Relations

As 1610 dawned, noblewomen were piling their hair higher and hemming their skirts to show off their new shoes. The starving colonists across the ocean in Jamestown had no shoes; they had resorted to eating them, and next their dogs, and then one another. The theaters in London were still closed due to the plague, while one of the earliest public libraries had just opened in Milan. Galileo, peering through his newly invented telescope, first observed the glimmering moons of Jupiter.

This was supposed to be the year of Elizabeth Bathory's greatest triumphs: the year that she turned fifty and the year that all three of her children were declared to be of legal age. There should have been much to celebrate. Instead, 1610 became the year that everything fell apart.

The year began auspiciously enough, with the opulent wedding of her younger daughter, Kate, to a dashing young count. The manor house in Čachtice was the wedding venue, a midway point between the lands of the bride and groom. The festivities began on Wednesday, January 6, 1610, while snow-dusted holiday garlands still festooned the village square. At the castle above, banners and coats of arms flapped in the breeze and cannons and muskets discharged their celebratory salutes. The manor house was ablaze with candles; lutes and trumpets mingled with stamping and clapping as the dancing continued late into the night, dancing so enthusiastic that older aristocrats sought out special treatments for their gout or stiff joints beforehand so they could participate. It might have been wise for them to seek some preventative treatment for their livers too. Hungarians had a reputation for being heavy drinkers—one self-professed "sober" aristocrat drank a mere two bottles of wine per day, while a reputed drunk easily consumed six. But alcohol consumption at a wedding often overshadowed even this, with a flurry of toasts, one after the other, late into the night, with everyone required to drain their goblet each time.

This was the most crowded the village of Čachtice might ever be, teeming with inebriated strangers. A hundred different aristocratic families had been invited to the celebration, accompanied by their own servants, as well as extra cooks, coachmen, equerries, and armor-bearers borrowed from Elizabeth's other estates or hired from Vienna. Even the local commoners were invited to join in some of the festivities, which lasted for days, alternating between banquets, bonfires, more drinking, and more dancing. In such an environment, gossip flowed as freely as the wine: who had danced with whom, who had been snubbed by whom, who had been seen slipping off to a dark corner with a good-looking stranger. Jokes were made about the domineering mother of the bride and her determination to not allow anything to spoil her youngest daughter's big day.

Elizabeth had, at this point, accomplished the end goal of any aristocrat: She had defended and preserved her estates and ensured the continuation of the family line. She had done so alone, despite two wars, the pillage of her lands, and living under constant suspicion of treason. And so that year she allowed herself a little brag:

> I, as a widow, with many sacrifices, and with the gracious help of my God, have honestly cared for my three dear children—my two unmarried daughters and my little son. I took care of our goods, provided for the care and education of my children with motherly love . . .

This "care and education" is on display in her letters. Despite the violence and the high mortality rates of the times—or perhaps because of these very things—it was more common for a child to be indulged than harshly disciplined. Hungarian aristocrats, in particular, were very hands-on parents. Elizabeth brought her young children along when she traveled between her estates rather than leaving them behind with their nanny. She called upon her friends with one or more daughter in tow. Paul would have traveled with his mother too, but as he became older, he sometimes stayed behind at Sárvár to continue his studies. But even when mother and son were separated for short periods of time, Elizabeth still oversaw Paul's education. Once, when Elizabeth was away at Čachtice, she had her son write to her in Latin for practice. In a very careful hand, the ten-year-old boy coyly offers that, in exchange for his doing this homework, his mother should "remunerate these first lessons of my studies with some small gift" upon her return.

There are glimpses, too, of Elizabeth the worrier, checking in on her older daughter, Anna, after her wedding. Elizabeth's letter has not survived, but her daughter's response has, full of reassurances, including this one: "Do not worry for us, all is well with us, even his servants respect me greatly."

Her daughters' marriages were a point of personal pride for Elizabeth. She bragged:

> I was able to marry my two daughters, Anna and Kate Nadasdy, with the help of the most merciful God . . . in a manner worthy of their father's house, with a decent dowry befitting their parents' status.

Aristocrats would openly complain that grand weddings completely emptied their coffers, leaving them unable to travel or shop for months. The displays of power and wealth that Elizabeth managed on behalf of both of her daughters, while still waiting for her late husband's back pay, would have required much clever economizing and strategizing behind the scenes.

It wasn't just the grand weddings that pleased her, but the matches themselves. Her elder daughter Anna's marriage to Count Nicolas Zrinyi seems to have been a good one. Despite their age difference, the two were fond of each other. And Zrinyi had proved to be a dutiful son-in-law and a stalwart family ally, joining up with the Countess to file cases and protests in the county courts and assemblies. He and Anna visited Elizabeth often, and during the Bocskai rebellion, when the fighting had moved uncomfortably close to Sárvár, Elizabeth and her two younger children even stayed with the Zrinyis for several months. Elizabeth addressed Zrinyi as "my beloved son" and in letters treated him as such, cajoling, advising, and even scolding him. Their correspondence is replete with typical motherly admonishments. When he is slow to write to her with the latest imperial gossip, Elizabeth pouts: "I would have thought that Your Grace would write . . . to me first . . . [so] I would not have needed to ask my servant." When he makes plans to travel through a dangerous region, in a seventeenth-century version of *if all your friends jumped off a bridge*, she cautions him that "those who advise you to do this, are not Your Grace's well-wishing friends."

Elizabeth had high hopes for a similarly close relationship with her second son-in-law, Count George Drugeth of Humenne. The Drugeths were as ancient, and almost as influential, as the Bathorys. Valentine Drugeth had just competed with Gabriel Bathory for the Transylvanian throne, but the two families intermarried more than they clashed. Aunt Klara's first husband had been a Drugeth; Elizabeth's mother's second husband had been a Drugeth; and Elizabeth's brother, Stephen, had married a Drugeth woman. Not only were there long-standing ties between the two families, there were also adjacent lands. Just as Zrinyi lands adjoined those of the Nadasdys in the southwest of the kingdom, Drugeth lands bordered Bathory properties in the northeast. Elizabeth's extended family now controlled an alarmingly large swath of land arcing across all of Royal Hungary, and if the families worked together, they could consolidate and protect all their holdings.

George Drugeth of Humenne had much to recommend him—land, lineage, and even a cheerfully boyish face. Elizabeth was so enthusiastic about the match that, just outside the walls of her three-story Čachtice manor, she built another house for the newlyweds, a smaller, single-story, U-shaped affair. She even had Drugeth's coat of arms carved into the keystone above the main door. Zrinyi had estates within a day's ride of Sárvár; he and Anna visited often. Drugeth's main properties, though, were more than three hundred miles east. The Čachtice manor house could easily have accommodated the pair on any visits—it had forty-six rooms. But now Drugeth and Kate would have their own residence, a further enticement to come and visit.

Elizabeth likely assumed George Drugeth would serve as one of her protectors, since he had witnessed firsthand how his own mother, also a powerful widowed countess, had been targeted by a malicious rumor campaign. One of his mother's maids had been bribed to say that, as a toddler, the real George had suffered an accidental fall and died, and his mother had substituted a peasant child for her dead boy. Soon after, the countess was besieged by ambitious extended family and three thousand troops. She was able to repulse her attackers for some time, until they found a way to cut off her castle's water supply. Before the castle was forced to surrender, George's mother slipped away with her children, crossing into Poland. The teenage Drugeth was bewildered by the sudden shift in his fortunes. He wrote, "I was sixteen years old when our enemies accused us. I didn't know anything; I didn't take part in anything, and I never harmed anyone. And yet, the laws of the homeland condemned me to the loss of my head and property." After their flight, his family was subjected to one of the many sham trials of the era. In absentia, Drugeth was found guilty of being a pretender, stripped of his lands, and sentenced to death.

Drugeth wrote that he was furious at seeing how opportunists "robbed and plundered my mother's property over the years," and from abroad he tirelessly lobbied the Hapsburgs on her behalf. He also challenged the verdict against him. Finally, after "donating" a choice property and quite a bit of money to the imperial coffers, Drugeth had been allowed to keep his head and return to Royal Hungary. In the years since, he had ingratiated himself into King Matthias II's court, even managing to be formally exonerated.

But Elizabeth's hope that Drugeth would prove to be just as indefatigable in her defense was a miscalculation, one of many that she would make that year. Her new son-in-law was not of the same disposition as the even-tempered, dependable, and deferential Nicolas Zrinyi. Instead, he had a reputation as a charmer and a daredevil. George Drugeth was a bit of a rebel as well, having converted to Catholicism while in exile. He had also learned firsthand how truth could be manipulated. And rather than becoming a crusader against injustice, he had decided to adopt the techniques of his former persecutors for his own ends.

. . .

In January 1610, right around the same time that Elizabeth was coordinating the wedding toasts for her daughter Kate, clashes broke out along the border between Royal Hungary and Transylvania.

The next month, late at night on February 16, 1610, Elizabeth's cousin Sigmund Bathory was arrested and brought to Prague Castle "under strong guard." By the end of the week, the arrest was being discussed in diplomatic circles. The Italian envoys at the imperial court, who much admired Sigmund, wondered what he could possibly have done. One reported that Sigmund had been caught trying "to elect himself king of Hungary." Yet this was rather unlikely, given that this Bathory had made it abundantly clear he didn't want to be the king of anything. Unlike his younger cousin Gabriel—a strong, athletic, and high-spirited soldier who savored the rush of battle and political intrigue—Sigmund wanted only to be left alone to become a priest.

Prior to Bocskai's rebellion, Sigmund Bathory had occupied and then abdicated the crown of Transylvania four times. There was an established pattern of Sigmund becoming disenchanted by the constant war and political intrigue, giving up his crown, then being coaxed back with promises that the situation was more favorable, only to be horrified anew by the mess of war-torn Transylvania. He seemed unable to grasp how his own comings and goings only added to the instability he so deplored.

Sophisticated and urbane, Sigmund had a strong affinity for Italian culture, importing most of his courtiers and advisers, along with musicians, cooks, cheesemakers, and a fortune teller who helped him commune with the spirit of the Raven King. At one time, Sigmund had been the point around which the hopes of a reunified Hungary had turned: A marriage was arranged between him and a Hapsburg bride, with the expectation that their Bathory-Hapsburg offspring might then peacefully join Royal Hungary and Transylvania. But whether because he was gay or impotent, Sigmund Bathory was never able to consummate the marriage, a source of very public humiliation. His virgin bride was sent off to a convent and he ended up on a country estate in Bohemia, trying his best to stay out of politics.

The agents who arrested Sigmund subjected him to interrogations (which may or may not have included the use of torture) and seized all the former prince's documents—as well as his favorite Italian secretary. They ransacked Sigmund's letter chests, but whatever communications they were looking for, they seemed unable to find them.

Sigmund Bathory, the former Prince of Transylvania

Two weeks later, on Monday, March 5, 1610, Palatine George Thurzo opened a secret investigation into Elizabeth. In his written instructions, Thurzo claimed he was undertaking this action because he had "heard at various times credible and serious allegations" that she had "cruelly murdered one-knows-not-how-many girls and virgins and other women," at the finishing school for noble girls on her estates.

Elizabeth had inherited this finishing school—or *gynaeceum* (Greek for "women's quarters")—from her mother-in-law. Such institutions were common among the manors and castles of the kingdom's highest-leading aristocrats. One was run by Elizabeth's neighbors, the Batthyanys, and one was in Thurzo's own home, administered by his wife. Here girls from the middle or lower nobility were apprenticed to a higher-ranking lady to learn not just how to sew and sing and dance, but also how to administer the farms, breweries, and bee colonies on their future estates. These "virgins" usually ranged in age from ten to thirteen, as noble girls were married off quite young, generally as soon as they began menstruating regularly. Although many historians and artists have portrayed Elizabeth assaulting nubile young women in various states of undress, her alleged victims were prepubescent girls. Legally and socially, they were considered children.

A woodcut from 1600 featuring a noble Hungarian "virgin," a girl around ten to thirteen years old

In the lore surrounding Elizabeth, it is often said that so many families had complained to King Matthias about their disappearing daughters that he ordered Thurzo to look into the matter. But no official complaints had been recorded. There was a system in place for such complaints to be made, by both noble and commoner families, so the wronged parties could sue for compensation. The Hapsburg court kept meticulous records, the vast majority of which have survived intact. There are imperial calculations, notes, reports, and multiple drafts of letters about the Countess and her vast estates; there *were* other complaints filed about her—disputes about land borders or tax payments—but no hint of physical abuse or ill treatment or murder.

It is unclear exactly what "credible and serious allegations" Thurzo *had* heard. Was it the years-old rumors about Miss Modl's demise or the two servant girls with bandaged hands? Or a more recent rumor? The latest one was not even three months old, a tale that likely began with a drunken joke during Kate's wedding: The Countess was such a rigid taskmaster, so determined not to allow anything to disrupt her younger daughter's big day, that when two girls died, she had them buried in secret.

The week after that, while Gabriel was staying at his chancellor's home, a man crept into the prince's chambers late at night, wielding a knife.

The Bathorys were under attack.

. . .

Gabriel Bathory was an easy target, his personal bodyguard having been called away to investigate a disturbance close by. But the would-be assassin could not finish the job. Instead, he threw himself upon Gabriel's mercy and named his co-conspirators: They included some of the prince's own advisers, including his host. Only one of the traitors would be captured and executed. The others, including Chancellor Kendi, the plot's mastermind, escaped over the border to Royal Hungary.

Why had they betrayed their prince? One explanation, found in many textbooks and historical accounts even today, claims that two of the lords were angry about Gabriel Bathory's mistreatment of their wives:

> Bathory, like an unbridled wild animal, with no measure or limit to his lust, shamelessly attacked the wives [of] . . . the chancellor Stephen Kendi and the nobleman Balthazar Kornis and defiled their honor . . . Therefore, an angry conspiracy was kindled against him.

This version of events, however, was commissioned more than a decade after the attack. It built upon the circulating rumors that Gabriel was interested in pretty women, casting him as not just a playboy but also a rapist. Yet scholars have shown how it was impossible for Gabriel to have "defiled" the conspirators' wives. Chancellor Kendi had married only weeks before the assassination attempt; his wife was a foreigner who lived abroad and had never been in the same city as the prince. Captain Kornis's widow directly denied that the prince had ever had any contact with her, much less raped her.

Accounts written around the time of the attack also made no mention of vengeful husbands. The Venetian ambassador, usually prone to salacious gossip, reported only that this was one of "several" recent attempts on the prince's life, which had included a failed gunpowder explosive placed in his bedroom. The lords involved in the plot were Catholics, and so most of the prince's contemporaries assumed the attack was part of the new wave of religious violence sweeping through Europe, the work of Catholic extremists committed to the Counter-Reformation. Building upon the idea that nobles had the right to resist a tyrannical monarch, a Jesuit book proclaimed that it was moral to deprive a Protestant king of his throne. Some Catholic fanatics took this as a literal directive, and several assassination attempts ensued, including the Gunpowder Plot to blow up King James I in the English Parliament. Protestant officials were on alert throughout Europe, and one of Gabriel's supporters appealed to them with a long poem condemning the cowardly Catholic attack against "the shining star" of the Bathory family. Sympathies for the young prince were further amplified when, a mere two months later, the king of France was assassinated in broad daylight by yet another Catholic fanatic.

Gabriel's would-be assassins, after five frantic days on the run, made it over the border into Royal Hungary. Palatine Thurzo rode out to meet them. When Gabriel Bathory heard the news, he was livid and demanded the plotters be handed over. Thurzo refused; instead, he offered the men his protection. Whether Thurzo had been behind the assassination attempt from the start or was now simply taking advantage of the situation as it unfolded, his actions led many to whisper about a "secret conspiracy" against the Transylvanian prince.

That Thurzo and Gabriel Bathory had long been at odds was no secret. The two men were locked in rancorous negotiations, revisiting and renegotiating the terms of the fragile peace between their two nations. Clashes flared with increasing frequency along the border. Were these an unfortunate series of individual conflicts between undisciplined hajduks and frustrated farmers? Or were they carefully engineered to reignite long-smoldering resentments?

The Peace of Vienna had established Transylvania as an independent principality, but King Matthias seemed incapable of conceiving of it as anything other than a Hapsburg satellite. His pressure campaign on the young prince had begun almost immediately. The Hapsburg king delivered a rapid-fire series of threats and orders. Matthias demanded that Gabriel send troops to help with his empire's defense. He demanded that the prince publicly pledge his loyalty. As part of the peace agreement, Transylvania paid an annual tax to the Ottoman Turks. Now Matthias demanded, too, an annual "honorarium" of his own.

Doing any of these things, Gabriel Bathory pointed out, would risk the wrath of the Ottoman Turks. Charged with preserving the peace in his fledgling nation, Gabriel offered some concessions. He agreed that "except with the Turks, I will be . . . a friend to your friends, an enemy to your enemies." The prince, though, had some demands of his own.

King Matthias had snatched back land along the border. These lands had been promised to Bocskai in the Peace of Vienna; they also encircled the Bathory family's water castle of Ecsed. Surely a prince could not be expected to pass through Hapsburg territory—enemy territory, even—every time he wished to go home.

The challenges to Transylvanian sovereignty continued. King Matthias demanded Gabriel not mint his own money or forge his own alliances. He even refused Gabriel his rightful title. In private letters to his wife, Thurzo referred to Gabriel Bathory as the prince of Transylvania, but in public he could no longer extend him such courtesy, calling him a mere "governor."

Thurzo had also been directed to undermine Gabriel in other ways. He secretly reached out to hajduks in border towns, enticing them to swear loyalty to Royal Hungary. When, in June, Thurzo arrived to his scheduled negotiations with Gabriel, he was surprised to see that the prince had five thousand hajduks in tow. The prince had, he said, heard that Thurzo was eager to meet his hajduks, so he thought he would make the introduction himself. Gabriel made it clear that the Hapsburgs were not the only ones with eyes and ears everywhere.

That summer, talks broke down again and again. At one point, the men almost came to blows when Thurzo, yet again, refused to hand over the conspirators who had fled to Royal Hungary after their failed assassination. The entire Bathory family was impacted by the contentious negotiations. Kate Iffiu and her husband were busy scrutinizing the proffered agreements. The Bathory sons-in-law Zrinyi and Drugeth were pressed into duty too, serving as envoys between Thurzo's and Gabriel's camps in an attempt to ease tensions. Cousin Sigmund remained in his solitary cell in Prague Castle as his estates were methodically searched. And Elizabeth, with seventeen key castles and estates under her control, with claims upon a fortress within striking distance of Vienna itself, became aware she was being investigated for murder.

She was not the first Bathory woman to be called a killer. When Aunt Klara was fifty years old—the same age as Elizabeth was now—she had been similarly accused.

The allegation against Klara stemmed from events more than twenty years earlier, when she had, as a young widow, joined the anti-Hapsburg resistance. She and a group of fellow supporters were arrested and imprisoned. Her former brother-in-law volunteered to be her jailer, using this opportunity to enrich himself by commandeering her property. For two years, in Klara's own words, her brother-in-law had "held her captive."

Klara's salvation lay in the courts—and her five-hundred-year-old name. The Bathory family petitioned for her release, and the Hapsburg emperor conceded that as her family were "the most important people in the kingdom . . . we should quite rightly take the greatest account of this [Klara] Bathory." After Klara was released, her family sued, and the courts ruled her imprisonment unlawful. Klara was given the opportunity to seek formal redress; her brother-in-law having since died, she would be allowed to prosecute his widow and daughters. Klara graciously declined, testifying that her sister-in-law and her nieces were not the "initiators of her captivity at all, but these ladies were much rather compassionate and commiserating . . . and wanted nothing apart from her liberation." It did not take long for that sisterly affection to evaporate, though, and the former sisters-in-law began suing and countersuing one another for their deceased husbands' property.

After this very public tumult, Klara, with her love of red jewels and radical ideas, had further scandalized society by getting married for a third time—to a man who had no land, money, or title. She went on to have a daughter with this commoner husband. When he died a few years later, Klara wed for a fourth time, to yet another man of her own choosing, also without title or fortune. Even though such love matches were virtually unheard of at the time, the Bathory family stood by Klara; her brothers actively defended her interests in court and made sure her lower-born daughter was comfortably looked after.

By midlife, Klara had shuttered a monastery, participated in an armed rebellion, and seemingly managed to find true love. But she had also accumulated many enemies and was still embroiled in a high-profile property dispute with her former sister-in-law. For more than a decade, the two women had clogged up the local courts with their petitions and countersuits, collectively defying any men who got in their way. They were accused of everything from the "capture" of other men's serfs to preventing the Holy Roman Emperor from accessing his own lands.

They refused summonses to appear before the courts. They delayed and dodged, bouncing cases from county court to the royal court and back again, launching countersuits and appeals, and wriggling out of unfavorable judgments on clever technicalities. Aunt Klara, confident that she was entitled to the equal protection of the law, left behind an inspiring legacy for her niece.

A woman, however, might best the kingdom's judges only to find herself convicted in the court of public opinion. The year Klara turned fifty, a syphilitic Catholic bishop took the various events of her life and restitched them together into the following accusation:

> [Klara] had illicit sexual relations with one of [her second husband] Anthony's clerks. With his help she smothered Anthony as he lay in bed with a disease of the joints, and at once married this same lover. She was a woman with such a strong libido that during her imprisonment she compelled all of the lowest slaves and prison guards to have intercourse with her.

His account was a mix of truth and demonstrable lies—Klara had been imprisoned, of course, but wrongfully so, and even the most cursory inquiry would show that Klara had not remarried anyone "at once" but several years after her second husband's death. But the accusation was salacious enough to be repeated, and then included in a popular pastor's book, *On the Temptations of the Devil*, detailing the moral failings of the Hungarian people.

The old bishop was following a well-worn playbook. The usual way to get a politically powerful woman out of the way was to impugn her moral character. Gabriel's aunt Kate Iffiu's political clout had been challenged by accusations of incest. Accusations of adultery were used not just to impeach Klara's character and judgment, but to question her daughters' paternity—and their right to inherit any lands from their deceased father's estate.

Elizabeth would later be accused, here and there, of some adulterous liaisons, but these rumors never took hold in the same way those of murder did. Perhaps her virtue was considered beyond reproach.

Or perhaps Thurzo, in true Machiavellian fashion, did fulfill the request the dying Francis Nadasdy had made of him six years earlier. Francis had asked Thurzo to look after his children. Accusing Elizabeth of adultery would have called into question these children's parentage and their rights to inherit. But accusing Elizabeth of murder, even the most monstrous of murders, the murder of children, would not. In this, at least, Thurzo kept his word.

• • •

As she became aware of the investigation against her, in the tradition of her aunt Klara, Elizabeth went to court. In August 1610, at the same time Gabriel Bathory and Thurzo were renegotiating the relationship between Royal Hungary and Transylvania, Elizabeth and one of her ladies arrived at the county court just outside Sárvár. The forty-four-year-old widow Helen Hernath was from the respectable middle rungs of the nobility; both her and her late husband's families had long served at the castle. Lady Helen also helped out with Elizabeth's finishing school, where her own daughter Susanna had been one of the pupils until her untimely death.

The court documents state that Elizabeth had become aware of a rumor being circulated by "many malicious and verbose people" that she had killed Lady Helen's daughter. The rumor was that

> the Countess has inflicted wounds on the mentioned late girl Susanna before her death by flogging her most terribly and ordering her to be flogged by her servants, and she had her incarcerated, and this flogging and incarceration would have killed the mentioned Susanna within one or two or three weeks.

Lady Helen testified "of her free will and in her own voice" about the true circumstances surrounding the death of her daughter. She had been present when Susanna had been "beset and overcome by a severe illness" which took her life. Lady Helen was certain her daughter had not been beaten because, during the funeral preparations, she had been the one to wash her daughter's body and she had not seen any bruises or marks.

Lady Helen attributed her daughter's death to "predestination," a strong suggestion that she was, like Elizabeth, sympathetic to Calvinist ideas. She then "fully and publicly exonerated" Countess Elizabeth Bathory from any involvement in her daughter's death.

The court scribe copied out Helen Hernath's testimony and stamped it with a red wax seal. The Countess was given this document to take with her so that she might use it "as a warrant of her rights in the future." Elizabeth, collecting testimony to mount a legal challenge, was going on the offensive.

Her nephew was taking a similar tack. Gabriel held firm and the Hapsburgs seemingly backed down. In August, a tentative agreement was reached. The prince was given back some lands near Ecsed, which not only guaranteed the safety of his family's ancestral castle but allowed him to fulfill a campaign promise. He promptly settled more of his unruly hajduks there, giving each—finally—plots of their own. The treaty laid out not just the ownership of the contested lands, but whether Transylvania had to render aid to Royal Hungary in times of war (yes, against anyone except the Ottoman Turks) and whether Prince Gabriel was entitled to be addressed on equal footing as King Matthias II, with the honorific *serenissimus*, Most Serene: No, the prince would no longer be addressed as "governor," but he would have to settle for merely being *illustrissimus princeps*, Most Illustrious Prince.

Gabriel must have been relieved, ebullient even. But at the same time he was smiling, nodding, and signing the agreement, Thurzo was crafting a secret accord with King Matthias. An imperial envoy was dispatched with written orders to organize opposition to Prince Gabriel, to isolate the prince and prevent him from forming any foreign alliances, and to do so "in the utmost silence, lest Bathory or those on his side become suspicious." They would remove Prince Gabriel from power by any means necessary and install someone else in his place.

One of the candidates under consideration was Elizabeth's new son-in-law. In the course of carrying out his duties as envoy, George Drugeth had given the Hapsburgs some reason to believe that, mere months after marrying into the Bathory family, he might be willing to betray them.

CHAPTER 8

The Preacher of Čachtice

In September and October of 1610, Thurzo received the first set of depositions against Countess Elizabeth Bathory. He had directed two royal notaries to solicit testimonies from "people of all classes and of both sexes" throughout nine counties that bordered the Hapsburg lands. One notary was ordered to conduct interviews in four northern counties, in the vicinity of Elizabeth's estate of Čachtice, the other to work in the five western counties surrounding Sárvár Castle.

The notaries seem to have been operating with no great urgency. Despite the latitude they were given—to interview thousands of people in hundreds of towns and villages across nine counties—and the time they were given to do so—six or seven months—they gathered just fifty-four testimonies from two towns. Despite instructions to interview "both sexes," and despite the fact that only other women would have had access to Elizabeth's inner sanctum, the notaries interviewed only men.

The testimony they collected would not be sufficient to charge a noblewoman with a single murder, much less serial murder. The only credible eyewitness evidence against Elizabeth was rather underwhelming. Five years earlier, one man had seen two girls with injured hands in the Countess's retinue. Around the same time, another man saw a girl being flogged on an estate three hundred miles away. A third man had seen a girl faint. There were plenty of sensational rumors of gory torture, of black magic, but all were second- or even thirdhand. People claimed to have heard a rumor from someone who had heard it from one of the Countess's former employees. Most of the witnesses were the serfs of other landlords and had never actually seen or personally interacted with the Countess.

Those convinced of Elizabeth Bathory's guilt often cite the large number of people who testified against her. But even given the immense pressure to cooperate with an investigation ordered by the most powerful man in the kingdom, a man whose authority would have been very difficult to resist, relatively few people spoke out against the Countess. Those who did were, in the words of one legal scholar, "led to the point of absurdity" by being given a written sheet of questions beforehand, worded in such a way as to suggest the desired answers. Illiterate serfs would have had the questions read to them rapid-fire, giving the impression they themselves were being interrogated. And their responses were not written down verbatim; scribes jotted down their general summaries and impressions that were later compiled and recopied. Often, they simply wrote variations of "same as above" to indicate agreement between witnesses.

The first set of depositions to be handed in came from the north. The royal notary Andreas of Keresztúr interviewed thirty-four people, almost all from a single town that borders Čachtice, a Slovak enclave now called Nové Mesto nad Váhom. This was a free market town that elected its own judges and jurors; Elizabeth held no sway here. A conservative estimate puts the town's population at around one thousand adults, yet only thirty-three agreed to be interviewed.

Two people testified to knowing nothing at all, and another six that they had only heard the most general rumors. The remaining twenty-five repeated something they had heard from someone else. The only thing that is clear from their testimonies is that the specific rumor the royal notary was sent to investigate—the murders of large numbers of girls—originated with one man. Thurzo never stated who was making "credible and serious allegations" against the Countess, but at this point the only person documented to be telling others that Elizabeth was a serial murderer was John Ponikenus, the Lutheran pastor of Čachtice.

. . .

Čachtice, the town that had been Elizabeth's wedding gift, is nestled in a valley between two mountain ranges. Čachtice's highest promontory, a twelve-hundred-foot peak of the Little Carpathians, was occupied by an old knight's castle with two distinct *donjons*, or keeps, the mark of a great castle, this one guarding the north-to-south trade route.

An hour and a half's walk downslope was the town itself, where, on adjacent hills, the manor house and the church faced off. The church was perched on a mound in the center of town, a long rectangular nave with a five-story bell tower. Ponikenus, from the start, had been uneasy in his position, understandable given that his church had been constructed by Catholics, handed over to Calvinists, and only recently wrested away by the Lutherans. His surroundings would have only added to this impression; just like the town's castle and manor house, the church was surrounded by an ancient stone wall, as if in danger of imminent attack.

On an opposing hill stood the opulent Nadasdy manor house, with forty-six rooms and its own treasury, bakery, orchards, gardens, and vineyard. The larger of its two large halls—likely the site of Kate Nadasdy's wedding celebration—had thirteen glass windows. Only the ruins of the manor's outer wall still stand today, but if one steps inside its enclosure, it is striking how close the church is, how its bell tower looms into view. From this tower, the Lutheran pastor could see over the wall of his Calvinist mistress's manor, a mere six hundred feet away. When Elizabeth was in residence, it would have been difficult to miss her comings and goings—the carriage at the front gate, servants hanging the washing in the yard, the flicker of torches and candles in the manor's many other windows. He could watch her, but not speak with her, or at least not directly. Ponikenus was an ethnic Slovak who did not speak or understand Hungarian.

His parish had a large ethnic Slovak population, but it was close to the German lands and was administered by Hungarians. It was common for people (and pastors) in the area to have a passing knowledge of all three languages so they could converse with traveling merchants, local farmers, and their noble overlords alike. Ponikenus knew Latin, which he used for his church services and communications, but his inability to understand anything else likely contributed to his many miscommunications with townspeople and parishioners.

The first time (we know of) that John Ponikenus had encountered Elizabeth was almost six years earlier, at Francis Nadasdy's funeral. Then, he had been the brand-new pastor of Čachtice, a recent graduate of Wittenberg University. Carefully dressed in his simple dark robes, Ponikenus was likely both anxious and exhilarated, a small-town Slovak finally mingling with the Hungarian elite. He had tried to attract some notice by reciting some original Latin verse he had crafted for the solemn occasion. But the end result was wooden and clumsy, and there is no record that his new mistress acknowledged or thanked him for his efforts. It is very likely that Elizabeth barely noticed him at all. Ponikenus was, after all, exactly that sort of man—without distinctive features or talents, the sort of man you might overlook entirely, until it was too late.

In the intervening years, the pastor had been overlooked again and again, passed over for one promotion after the other. To a man who saw himself as the main character in every story, the focal point of every intrigue, these snubs did not indicate any personal shortcomings, but were evidence that he was the victim of some vast conspiracy. Now the thirty-seven-year-old Ponikenus was campaigning for another promotion. He hoped to become one of the region's bishops, and he was determined to find, and foil, the agents of the Devil before they might impede his rise yet again.

In the intervening years, the pastor had also clashed with his mistress over her improper burials of the dead. Such a charge seems much more ominous today, when "secret burials" are almost universally associated with attempts to cover up a crime. But at the time, the act of burial was a flashpoint in the sectarian battles between Lutherans and Calvinists. In the same way that uncertainty about how to commemorate the Lord's Supper had led to arrests and executions, there was great confusion over what now constituted a proper Christian burial.

At the beginning of the Reformation, Martin Luther had advocated for the abolition of "such popish abominations as vigils, masses for the dead, processions . . . and all other forms of trickery on behalf of the dead." The most radical reformers interpreted this instruction literally and began to bury one another without the usual service and hymns, without even a pastor being present. One clergyman complained that "the dead are buried without a cross or candles, in silence, like senseless beasts, like dogs."

Luther and others felt these stripped-down, simplified burials went too far. One handbook for Lutheran pastors warned that pastors "cannot allow bodies to be shamefully discarded, without any honor." Luther and his followers tried to reinstitute much of the old Catholic ceremony—a procession and prayers, sermon and hymns. John Calvin and his followers, however, decreed there was to be no praying, no preaching, no bell-ringing or singing at burials. The faithful must trust and submit to God's will, not try to ease the deceased's passage to heaven with theatrical "superstitions." In Calvinist areas, burials became quicker, quieter affairs. Even more extreme "secret burials" became fashionable in some circles: John Calvin himself was buried in secret, at night, in an unmarked grave.

A Reformation-era woodcut of a radically simplified burial—without a ceremony, a priest, or even a coffin

The Lutheran Ponikenus was sure that the Countess practiced these radical Calvinist burials. He claimed to have heard from an unnamed source that, well before he became pastor, "secretly virgins were buried in the night in the church." Ponikenus testified that upon assuming the pastorship, he had made it clear that no Calvinist burials would be allowed in *his* churchyard: He had "forbidden the Lady Widow these clandestine burials [*clandestinam sepulturam*] both in Čachtice as well as for the other areas of his parish diocese."

Ponikenus was never able to present any evidence that Elizabeth had, in fact, buried anyone in secret. He was, however, livid about a funeral she had held in Podolie, a village less than three miles away, a funeral that he felt had not followed proper procedure. Lutheran commissioners were under orders to make sure that no Calvinist townsperson "attempts to bury someone secretly in the morning or evening, without the knowledge of the pastor." Elizabeth had, seemingly, followed the rules. The burial was held during the day, and the village's Lutheran pastor was notified in advance.

Ponikenus, though, was a stickler for technicalities. Parishioners were to be buried in the closest churchyard, and his church was the closest to Čachtice manor. And then there was the matter of money. Lutheran pastors were paid for officiating burials—this was one of their more reliable sources of income. When Elizabeth had opted for the services of another, the pastor of Podolie received the gold that could have gone to Ponikenus.

Perhaps Podolie was the hometown of the deceased, or held some other significance for their family. Perhaps Elizabeth or the family desired a simpler Calvinist burial and knew Podolie's pastor to be less rigid about such things, or perhaps they only wanted to avoid dealing with Čachtice's pedantic and quarrelsome preacher. Ponikenus recounted that, when he angrily confronted Zachary Gasperides, the town's pastor, Gasperides said he had tried to warn Elizabeth that "the superiors" might not approve. The Countess had responded, "I am allowed to hold my funerals wherever I want, both in Čachtice and in Podolie, because both places are my possessions." Ponikenus would later prove to be an untrustworthy witness, but this response, in content and tone, seems exactly like something Elizabeth would have said. The woman who declared

> I won't be silent
> I will not let anyone possess what is mine
> I will have your house torn down above your head

would have no qualms telling a local pastor, whether out of insolence or indifference:

> I am allowed to hold my funerals wherever I want
> Both places are my possessions

Elizabeth's clash with Ponikenus over the funeral in Podolie, and the larger sectarian controversy over "secret burials," helps explain a rumor that comes up over and over in almost half of the testimonies collected in the northern counties: that two girls died during Elizabeth's daughter's wedding and were secretly buried. Although everyone agreed that these two girls were nobles, no one knew their names or where they came from. There was disagreement, too, on *where* they had been secretly buried, with two nearby towns both mentioned as possibilities. The pastor of one of these towns thought the girls had been buried in his churchyard, but he never offered up any evidence: He had seen no one unusual in the churchyard and had found no fresh grave or disturbed earth. Still, he was certain the girls had been brought there and "were buried without funeral ceremonies, and were laid in the grave wearing only the clothes in which they supposedly died." His issue was not secrecy, but the lack of proper ceremony. Interviewed a second time, his phrasing matches that of the Lutheran handbooks: The girls were "buried with little honor." Another witness would add that the girls had been buried "in the early dawn," at a time that was in direct defiance of the Lutheran canons.

The small number who testified—less than 3 percent of the townspeople—were clearly titillated by the gossip about two noble girls who had died during the area's most glamorous wedding. They seemed less interested in the rumor Ponikenus was trying to introduce into circulation: that Elizabeth was responsible for serial murders.

Nové Mesto nad Váhom, the market town where the first set of depositions was being collected, was just four miles north of Čachtice. Before he became a pastor, Ponikenus had served as a deacon and a school rector here, so many of the townspeople were familiar with him and his opinions about their mistress. The pastor had come of age during the first schism between the Protestants, an era of arrests and executions when it was common practice to label one's religious opponent a criminal. The factions of Bishop Beythe and the hard-liner John Reczes had printed up pamphlets calling one another murderers; so it was not without precedent for Ponikenus to publicly denounce the Countess as a murderess from his pulpit. What was unique about Ponikenus's accusation was the scale. One forty-five-year-old resident testified the pastor had told him that Elizabeth was responsible for torturing over a hundred virgins to death. The town's provost, one of Ponikenus's former colleagues, also testified to having heard these claims of prolific murder, putting the alleged death toll at around two hundred.

Ponikenus did not have nearly as much influence as he might have hoped over his former parish. While a few people repeated the pastor's claims, they don't appear to have believed them; his accusations strained credulity. The largest gynaeceums of the era only housed around thirty girls and women. A princess of Transylvania had nineteen residents in hers—two ladies-in-waiting, two maids, four "virgins," each with two attendants of the same age, and a seamstress and two laundresses to see to all of their clothing. The gynaeceum run by Thurzo's wife seems to have had a similar number of residents, with three "virgins" around ten years of age, along with a few more girls from her extended family, each of whom would have had an attendant or two. Elizabeth's finishing school was likely of a similar size. Still, even if she had the largest gynaeceum in the kingdom, with thirty girls and women in attendance at all times, to commit two hundred murders she would have had to liquidate her entire school every year, six years in a row.

Ponikenus may not have been able to convince his former parishioners of his allegations. Little matter: He now had the ear of the most powerful man in the kingdom. Ponikenus considered the pastor Elias Lany to be "like a father," and this mentor was now Palatine Thurzo's personal pastor.

When Lany told Thurzo that Countess Bathory might be murdering the girls under her care, the information must have seemed a gift. Thurzo had been in search of a justification to act against the Bathory family, and one had just been handed to him.

Did Thurzo sincerely believe that the very woman he had encouraged his wife to befriend, the woman whose engagement parties and daughters' weddings he had been honored to attend, had "cruelly murdered one-knows-not-how-many girls and virgins and other women"?

Thurzo prided himself on keeping up with current events, regularly reading all the newspapers and broadsides, which would have told him that women had indeed taken to killing large numbers of children. One contemporary pamphlet, for example, discussed how a German woman was said to have killed 80 children; another group of women were executed for having murdered over 140 children. It was, seemingly, an epidemic.

Thurzo was also aware of aristocratic women committing gruesome crimes much closer to home. A member of his own family, the wife of a younger cousin he was particularly close with, would later be convicted of beating to death nine of her female servants. Anna Rozina Listius, a countess herself, suffered from strange and violent "fits," which the Thurzo family discussed in their letters to one another; it was stipulated that "no one should use a knife in her presence, and people should care for her and be vigilant [for] when the sickness comes on her."

Countess Anna Rozina Listius would not stand trial for many years, but when she did, the majority of the testimony given against her—direct, detailed eyewitness accounts—would be admissible in courts today. For example, two witnesses described seeing one victim run out from Anna Rozina's house into the street, covered in blood. Another testified that he saw that same victim dragged back inside. A servant inside the house witnessed the murder itself, and two others said Anna Rozina confessed to them afterward that, although she did beat the victim, she did not mean to kill her.

The first of Anna Rozina's murders were said to date from this time period, and she had a manor in the same county as Elizabeth's Čachtice estate. The odds of there being *two* killer countesses operating in the same county at the same time are staggeringly small. The odds of villagers conflating rumors are much higher. Any gossip about a countess beating her charges could have just as easily referred to Anna Rozina as to Elizabeth. Was this the origin of the rumor that so frustrated Elizabeth, that Lady Helen Hernath's daughter Susanna had died from being "flogg[ed] . . . most terribly"? The villagers insisted on the story's truth, despite the protests of the girl's own mother. Were they simply blaming the wrong countess?

Thurzo may have convinced himself that it was not his cousin's new bride, but Elizabeth, who was the real threat in the region. Or he may have been trying to tie up two loose ends at once: to direct attention away from his own family while sidelining a political rival.

. . .

Weeks after he launched his investigation into Elizabeth, Palatine Thurzo, "escorted by four trumpeters, 40 pikemen, and 15 carriages," rode into the town of Zilina to convene a Lutheran church council. It should have been a very good time to be a Lutheran. Less than a century before, practicing the fledgling faith had been punishable by burning at the stake. Less than five years earlier, many Lutherans had been terrified they would be forcibly converted. Now, freedom to practice their religion was enshrined in the Peace of Vienna, and the unofficial head of the Lutheran church was the highest-ranking Hungarian in the land.

Once, the church leader Stephen Magyari had been convinced that only a strict crackdown—on swearing, meat-eating, drinking, and all other vices—could end the war with the Turks. Magyari hadn't lived long enough to see himself proved wrong. It had been an armed rebellion, and a Calvinist-led rebellion at that, that had ultimately brought peace to their lands. Like the former soldiers now aimlessly wandering the countryside, Magyari's colleagues were at a loss, in want of a new crusade.

Thurzo had invited only a small, select group of Lutheran clergy. His right-hand man was his personal pastor and Ponikenus's mentor, Elias Lany. The rest of the pastors, including Ponikenus himself, were drawn from the areas around Thurzo's estates. They held an election by secret ballot for three bishops to govern the church. Lany won one of the slots. Despite his months of campaigning, Ponikenus was passed over yet again.

The new administrators, all hard-line fundamentalists, issued orders forbidding cooperation with Calvinists and instituting strict penalties for any dissenters. They also began a crackdown on medical providers who, in trying to heal people, were subverting God's will. It was permitted, they declared, to treat illness with fresh air, herbal remedies, and special foods, but if these did not offer relief, failure of faith was the reason. More invasive medical procedures were not just unnecessary, they directly defied God.

Midwives were accused of inciting God's fury because, in the words of one Lutheran preacher, they "want to become doctors of medicine, and try to cure with superstitious instruments." Female healers of any kind became increasingly targeted. In cases of outright malpractice, when treatments led people to bleed or shit themselves to death, allegations of sorcery were somewhat understandable. But it didn't seem to matter whether the healers were successful or not. When three female healers on Thurzo's estates were burned at the stake, there were no accusations of tainted drafts or surgeries gone awry. The only allegations remotely approaching malpractice came from two people who felt they had been overcharged. One of the condemned healers in particular seemed very competent: Seven people came forward to testify to her skill. She had successfully delivered a baby, set broken bones, fixed a dislocated leg, and healed wounds and burns with her homemade ointments. The town's chief justice testified that she had healed his own child. This woman's only crime seems to have been not taking the accusations against her seriously enough; when her neighbor claimed she must be a witch because he dreamed that she came into his bedroom at night to "wrestle" with his wife, she "laughed" at him. But laughing at a man like this, a man lacking in self-awareness and petrified of his own sexual fantasies, was a huge risk indeed.

Pastor Ponikenus, a man equally lacking in self-awareness, had become fixated on the female healers in Elizabeth's circle. The most obvious target for his ire, the foreign "old woman" Anna Darvulia, had had a stroke, gone blind, and died. So he focused his attentions on the "woman scientist" from Tokorcs, the same woman who had appealed to Elizabeth for help when her property was vandalized after a dispute over her foster daughter's illegitimate child. Ponikenus denounced her as an "ungodly woman."

The other healer now under scrutiny has sometimes been called "the Farmer's Wife from Myjava," although this translation does not adequately capture the woman's true status. Myjava was a region of rolling hills to the northeast of Čachtice, home to a huge estate that provisioned Elizabeth's many other properties with grain, vegetables, eggs, milk, and hay. This woman was no ordinary farmer's wife; her husband, the *major*, oversaw the entire agricultural operation, coordinating the planting and harvesting of all crops for the Nadasdy family. As the *majorosné*, or mistress, of Myjava, she was responsible for the chickens and dairy cows. She also oversaw what would have been the largest creamery in the region, supplying Čachtice and other estates with their cheese.

The Mistress of Myjava was a powerful woman from the uppermost echelon of free commoners; she commanded her own servants, oversaw the labor of serfs, and exercised control over the local food supply. And like all *majorosnés* in charge of the breeding and raising of livestock, she possessed basic medical knowledge, much as a modern veterinarian would, as well as a thorough knowledge of local herbs. The Mistress of Myjava was also a trusted friend of Elizabeth's, with personal access to the Countess and her private quarters, tasked with concocting special herbal preparations for her lady. It is unclear if Ponikenus had ever clashed with the Mistress of Myjava directly, about provisions for his parish or household, for example, or if he just resented her power from afar.

The Lutheran church's new campaign against healers is evident in the testimony against Elizabeth. The depositions in the northern counties make it clear that villagers were being questioned about healing practices. Many of the twenty-six interview summaries mention some form of medical treatment. Six people testified to hearing rumors of girls being given cold-water baths, the usual treatment for high fevers. Two more mention that girls had needles stuck under their fingernails, a common treatment for "fingernail poison," the infected boils that seamstresses often developed. Five others mentioned girls being rolled in nettles. This would have no doubt been uncomfortable, even painful. The hairs on the leaves of the nettle plant "sting" the skin by releasing histamine, acetylcholine, and formic acid, the same acid found in bee venom. But these chemicals have long been used—by ancient Egyptians and Roman soldiers, for instance—to treat inflammatory conditions. In the early modern period, nettles were illustrated in popular European herbariums and listed in medical books, including a text in Elizabeth's large library at Sárvár. It was common for people to be whipped with nettles to alleviate the pain of rheumatism, to bring back sensation in cases of palsy, or as a treatment for typhus and cholera. Five separate witnesses would testify that Elizabeth or her old women had washed, rubbed, or whipped girls with nettles, thinking it a form of punishment instead of care.

. . .

The second set of depositions, submitted at the end of October 1610, was flawed in much the same way as the first—only a small number of people were interviewed, and in only one town. The second royal notary was working in the western counties surrounding Sárvár, which were much more densely populated. Yet even fewer people were interviewed—only twenty men, four of whom testified they knew absolutely nothing and another three of whom said they had heard only the vaguest rumors. In Sárvár, a town of thousands, only thirteen male residents testified to hearing more specific rumors of the Countess's cruelty.

There are more mentions of medical treatments—a firsthand report of sick girls being given medicine, two secondhand reports of girls being cauterized with a barber-surgeon's "hot iron." The topic of proper Christian burials comes up in this set of depositions too. Some men testified that they had heard rumors of secret (Calvinist) burials, while others contested this, insisting they saw a few girls' coffins being carried out of the castle, but this was done out in the open, "with singing"—indicating the hymns and ceremony of a typical Lutheran funeral. The current pastor of Sárvár mentioned that Elizabeth "already had a bad reputation" because of some questionable burial practices. He spoke of confronting his mistress because he heard she had put three girls in one coffin to be buried. He says that Elizabeth admitted to putting not three, but two girls into the same coffin in order to bring them out of the castle gates, but said this was only done because they died very close together and she wanted to prevent "even more gossip." This anecdote strongly suggests that more girls had recently died at Sárvár than seemed usual or typical, and that Elizabeth was increasingly worried about the optics of such a situation.

While most of these allegations against Elizabeth were about the deaths of nameless girls of unknown origin, there were accusations that she was responsible for the deaths of five girls from the kingdom's most elite families. The very first witness to testify in the north swore that he had been told by Melchior and Paul Nagyvathy that their sister had been killed by the Countess while serving as an attendant at her court. The Nagyvathy family wielded immense political power: They could count two judges, a bishop, and a royal food inspector in their recent lineage. The interviews were being conducted less than a day's ride from the Nagyvathys' properties. Six months elapsed between the time the man gave his statement and when the testimonies were submitted, plenty of time for the notary to send a messenger or call upon the family himself to confirm that a Nagyvathy girl had indeed died and learn more about the circumstances; in fact, this was exactly the sort of testimony needed to successfully prosecute the Countess in court. But there is no record of this having been done, and this Nagyvathy girl was never mentioned again in any of the later proceedings against Elizabeth.

Similarly, in the depositions collected in the west, witnesses said they heard that Elizabeth had killed the children of an old family friend, Gabriel Sittkey. The Sittkey girls would come up again in later testimony too. At least nine different people would refer to a Sittkey girl being one of Elizabeth's victims. Some said there were two Sittkey victims, some that there was just one. Some said a Sittkey girl died in Bratislava and was buried in Čachtice, others that the death and burial occurred in Sárvár. One even mentioned that the Sittkey girl might have died of the plague instead. None of the witnesses knew either Sittkey girl's first name, and they couldn't agree on the time, place, and circumstances of any supposed death.

As with the Nagyvathy family, it would have been relatively easy to contact the Sittkeys to verify whether any of their daughters had died under Elizabeth's care. Yet none of the families of any alleged noble victims were ever interviewed, or if they were, those interviews seem to have been mysteriously lost and left out of the record. While many letters and records from the Nadasdy and Bathory estates are missing, the archives of the Thurzo family and the imperial court contain multiple drafts and copies of all interviews ordered or conducted in Elizabeth's case. That these families were never interviewed is even more puzzling given that wronged nobles had the right to sue other nobles for damages. There would be no need to prove a criminal charge; as with civil cases today, the burden of proof was much lower. Yet all these powerful families chose to stay silent, even after Elizabeth had been arrested and imprisoned, and to forfeit any compensation for their loss? This is in stark contrast to how the families of Anna Rozina's alleged victims behaved; at least one large financial settlement was paid out well before she was formally investigated or charged.

By the end of the summer of 1610, despite there being no verified victims and despite the Countess's best efforts to confront the rumors head-on in a court of law, Elizabeth was growing increasingly alarmed, along with the rest of her family, that she, and her family lands, were in imminent danger.

CHAPTER 9

The Mysterious Will

As the year came to a close, Thurzo was under increasing pressure to remove Gabriel Bathory from power, and removing one of the prince's richest and most powerful potential supporters could only help him reach that goal. The Lutheran church had good reason to want to remove a powerful Calvinist aristocrat. But ultimately, it might not have been Elizabeth's religious beliefs, her advocacy for other women, or even her connection to the prince of Transylvania that sealed her fate. It may have been her son.

Elizabeth's other major accomplishment in 1610 was, on June 6, celebrating her son's twelfth birthday. She proudly declared:

> By my great care, by the grace of the great Lord God, twelve years have passed in the upbringing of my son Paul Nadasdy, who has been educated, cared for and taught, and has been sworn to the office of lord-lieutenant of the honorable county of Vas, to which I have contributed in due honor and with due expense.

In Hungarian society, a boy came of age in stages. Twelve was the age at which fatherless boys began to ease into their public roles, with the help of family and male advisers. Paul's father had been lord-lieutenant of two counties; one of the titles had been stripped from the family in retribution during the Bocskai rebellion. But Elizabeth had managed to hang on to the other title, and so now Paul Nadasdy was granted a seat in Parliament.

Young Paul resembled his father, Francis—the hairline, the hair, the nose—but while portraits of the Black Lord made him into a fierce cartoon villain, there's always a vulnerability in surviving portraits of his son, something cautious in his eyes. Although Paul had now managed to become a lord-lieutenant like his father, he would never be as feared, as celebrated, or as safe.

Paul was now, technically, one of the largest landowners in Royal Hungary, although he would not be able to directly administer his estates for some time. At sixteen he would be allowed a voice in his financial affairs, and at eighteen he would be able to buy and sell the family's "movable property"—gold, silver, and jewels. To protect the family lands and political fortunes from any impulsive testosterone-driven actions, most heirs had to wait until age twenty-four for financial control over the family's most valuable commodity—its lands.

Still, Paul's twelfth birthday technically marked the end of Elizabeth's regency, although she did not seem entirely ready to step aside. As late as May 15, 1610, two weeks before she handed over power to her son, Elizabeth was filing legal protests in the county court about a noble trying to encroach upon the forests surrounding her castle of Léka. And months after her son's inauguration, in August, she was still acting in an official capacity, instructing the county deputy to deal with bandits in the area. Elizabeth expected a more gradual transition, presumably one where she would be guiding, and chiding, her son much as she did her adult sons-in-law. The men serving as Paul's guardians—Red Megyery and Pastor Michael Zvonarics—thought otherwise.

Pastor Zvonarics was responsible for young Paul Nadasdy's religious education. He was the son of the local shoemaker, and many members of his family were employed by the Countess: His mother worked in the castle and one of his brothers was a trusted estate steward. Despite his modest background, Zvonarics had not only replaced Magyari as Sárvár's pastor, he had also inherited the leadership of the Lutheran church council. Zvonarics's elevation to such a high post was a bit of a surprise.

He had never studied at Wittenberg, Geneva, or Heidelberg like most other pastors of major estates. Because of his common origins and lack of education, he was teasingly referred to as the Shoemaker of Sárvár. Bishop Beythe once sarcastically applauded Zvonarics's "noble wisdom," a dig at his less-than-illustrious origins, and a Catholic bishop derided him as a mere "bell-ringer," unqualified to be a full-fledged minister. But the ongoing religious disputes had provided a convenient path for Zvonarics's social advancement. In contrast to the rest of his family, he likely felt more loyalty to the Lutheran church establishment than to his aristocratic landlord.

Zvonarics had been asked to give testimony against the Countess by an agent of the kingdom's highest-ranking Lutheran. He had agreed, although his testimony had been rather subdued. Yes, he had heard the rumor of the secret torture chamber, although he had never seen it himself. And he reported the anecdote about the mistress having two girls placed in a single coffin, in order, she said, to avoid gossip. Zvonarics may have said more when he was not under oath; Ponikenus told others that Sárvár's pastor was the source of some of his information.

As the sectarian disputes heated up, young Paul was caught between the faith of his mother and that of his tutor and personal pastor. We can't know what Zvonarics told Paul about his mother's religious beliefs: That they had some differences in opinion? Or that she was a damned heretic? It is clear, however, that the Shoemaker of Sárvár exercised considerable influence over Paul; the boy's Lutheran education had much greater influence than any Calvinist values his mother may have imparted to him earlier in life. Paul would remain stubbornly attached to the Lutheran faith. As an adult, his most noted accomplishment would be publishing a Lutheran prayer book.

Pastor Zvonarics's influence, however, was overshadowed by that of the family's adviser Emery "Red" Megyery. Megyery had gotten his start as a Nadasdy family retainer but had become something of a real estate mogul. Granted a bit of land for his loyal service, he had expanded his small estate through a series of savvy purchases. During the war with the Turks and Bocskai's rebellion, he lent money to cash-strapped nobles, allowing them to mortgage their estates. When many defaulted, Red Megyery snapped up their castles and vineyards as his own, further expanding his holdings. Megyery had a son the same age as Paul Nadasdy, and the boys were tutored together. Megyery hoped to use Paul Nadasdy's education and introduction at the imperial court to advance his own son's fortunes.

Elizabeth had protested the appointment of a guardian for her son from the very beginning, whether because she thought she was sufficiently capable of educating her son herself or because she was wary of the intentions and ambitions of the men at her court. Serving as an aristocratic boy's guardian was a lucrative position, with a generous salary for administering the family estates. For an estate such as the Nadasdys'—worth the equivalent of hundreds of millions of dollars—the salary would be very generous indeed. Fraud and misuse were rampant; guardians were known to help themselves to property or food stores, or to take an estate's income and invest it to make money for themselves.

Megyery had already become frustrated with Elizabeth during the Bocskai rebellion, warning her that she was in danger of falling afoul of the Hapsburgs. His fate was intertwined with hers. If Elizabeth were found to be giving any material support to her nephew Gabriel, if her lands were seized and her family lost its standing, Megyery would lose his own power and influence too. He might even lose his head. And his own son, Paul Nadasdy's companion and classmate, would lose his chance to advance at the imperial court.

Townspeople, officials, and nobles all spoke about ongoing tension between Paul's mother and guardian. Megyery had to be aware of Thurzo's investigation into Elizabeth. He was old friends with the royal notary collecting depositions around Sárvár: He and Moses Cziraky had recently worked together as royal commissioners on another project. Red Megyery never testified against his mistress, but one still feels his shadowy presence throughout the proceedings. Villagers thought Megyery was working against the Countess. Some of their testimony stated that Elizabeth was afraid of her son's guardian, that she sought out spells for protection against Megyery, or that she was even trying to kill him.

In the struggle for control over young Paul, three Sárvár officials aligned themselves with Megyery: the town's mayor and its two castellans. During the investigation, these men would parrot Ponikenus's claims of a high death toll at Elizabeth's castle. Their claims were outlandish, and directly disputed by their colleagues, but that didn't make them any less damaging.

Castellans had specific military and law enforcement duties, and in a larger town like Sárvár, it was common to have two of them. These men maintained Sárvár's outer walls, managed its weapons and gunpowder stores, and supervised any prisoners. While they were charged with guarding the castle, they did not live inside it: It was Elizabeth's private guard who saw to the family's safety. In fact, one castellan testified that he had never set foot in the residence itself except when formally summoned. Still, he insisted that he had heard a beating being administered through stone walls several feet thick, walls made to withstand direct cannon fire. He claimed not only to have heard things no one else heard, but to have seen things no one else saw. He had seen 175 coffins carried out of the castle for burial, and his colleague claimed the death toll was even higher, numbering two hundred to three hundred girls. Their accounts, however, were directly disputed by other town officials and even by their own underlings. One of their deputies insisted there had been just a single coffin, and the other testified that there had been only a few dead girls, all of whom were given proper, and public, funerals.

The castellans had been treated generously by Elizabeth, promoted and given land of their own for their loyal service. At one point they seemed to respect and even like her. What had changed? Did they believe something they had been told by a trusted pastor or church official? Or was there another reason, a more practical and banal one, intertwined with life at Sárvár?

Another theory proffered by a prominent Hungarian scholar is that the two castellans and the town mayor, and thus Megyery too, had reason to fear a countess who crusaded for *igazság*, for truth and justice, especially given her recent focus on corrupt bureaucrats and public officials who had enriched themselves during the chaos of the wars. Less than a year earlier, Elizabeth had filed complaints against the vice chancellors of several counties and had attempted to prosecute a provisor whom she had caught skimming funds. She was a woman of precision, documenting everything from the buttons and handkerchiefs stolen from her serfs during a wartime raid to the exact weight of her grain stores. She had ordered multiple censuses and audits of her properties, including an new inventory of Sárvár. Did these three officials, and Megyery, have reason to fear what a future audit might show? It is suggestive to note that, after Elizabeth's fall, under Megyery's administration of the estates, these men not only kept their jobs but advanced.

There's no way to be certain of the motives of those three men, but the archives reveal alarming conflicts of interest for other witnesses who testified during the initial investigation.

Many were financially beholden to Thurzo. For example, one witness in Sárvár, Adam Szelestey, was both in debt to Thurzo and actively trying to gain the Palatine's favor to advance his family's prospects. A letter from Thurzo to Szelestey refers to a loan of 800 florins that Szelestey has not yet repaid; in today's dollars that would be close to $250,000. Szelestey also (soon after he provided his testimony, by the way) was promoted to captain in the army and was allowed to attend Parliament. It's not unreasonable to wonder if his debt or his hopes for social advancement shaded his testimony. And whether similar ambitions and obligations might have influenced other testimonies.

. . .

Elizabeth has often been accused of being oblivious to the forces marshaling against her, but instead she cleverly used the legal system to protect herself. In addition to having Lady Helen formally exonerate her under oath, just a few weeks later, on September 3, 1610, the Countess made her will.

It is a curious will. Elizabeth often availed herself of a scribe, but this will was written in her own hand. It gives the impression of having been written in a hurry, of being a first draft even. Left margins creep right, sentences are crowded at the bottom of pages, a word is crossed out. Elizabeth signed in Hungarian, and in an unusually shaky hand, as "Batorÿ Ersebeth." This was the very informal signature she used only in more intimate letters. She was proud of her title and usually employed it, signing off to family, friends, and officials with the more formal Latin "Elizabetth de Batthory" or "Elisabeth comitissa de Bathor."

THE MYSTERIOUS WILL

(Top) A signature on a 1609 letter: "Elizabetha comitissa de Bathor mp." The "mp" stands for "manu propria," Latin for "by my own hand," indicating this is Elizabeth's own signature and not that of a scribe. (Bottom) The shakier and much more informal signature on her 1610 will: "Batorÿ Ersebeth."

In her will, Elizabeth refers to both her "advanced age"—she was only fifty—and her "weak health." Almost four years prior, Elizabeth had written to a relative about a recurring "condition" that left her "like a bruised person, sometimes better, sometimes quite sick again." That "condition," whatever it may have been, may have fully resolved itself, but in the fall and winter of 1610, Elizabeth would visit medical spas with her daughter Anna and have one of her "old women," the Mistress of Myjava, prepare special herbal baths for her to soak in. These may have been a series of unrelated illnesses, or they may have all been symptoms of some new chronic condition.

The Countess called together her court officials to witness the document, fully expecting them to leak news of the will's existence and its provisions. It was soon common knowledge that the Countess Bathory had renounced all of her earthly possessions. Elizabeth borrowed a tactic used by Aunt Klara, and a common enough strategy even today: transferring assets to prevent a court from seizing them. When Klara was entangled in the lawsuit with her former sister-in-law, she began transferring her Bathory lands over to her brothers. In exchange, they swore they would financially support her and make sure that each year she received gold, grain, wine, and a new dress. Klara seemed reluctant to give up her financial independence but agreed to the plan so she could safeguard her family's lands and her daughters' futures.

In much the same way, Elizabeth put all of her own property—"all my castles"—in her children's names, to be divided in three. At the same time, she gave her children and sons-in-law an incentive to look out for her interests: The property was placed in a sort of legal limbo, as this division of property had to wait until Paul was declared of age. A boy was usually declared of age at twenty-four, with orphaned boys sometimes allowed to do so earlier, at eighteen or so. With this clever provision, Elizabeth bought herself some time—probably another six years, maybe as many as twelve, plenty of time for the political tides to turn.

The will also served as an announcement that the Countess would be stepping away from public life and no longer contesting Megyery's guardianship over her son. This must have been hard, to leave her cherished son in the care of a man she didn't entirely trust, although it was not an entirely unexpected outcome. This information comes from a passage in the will that has often been mistranslated: "As for my bridal gown, I shall wear it until my death." The phrase conjures up a seventeenth-century Miss Havisham, wandering the castle ramparts in a moldering white gown. But the Hungarian word used here, *jegyruha*, is not a single piece of clothing. It means the same as *morgengabe*, or morning gift, in German. This refers to property a wife is given after consummating the marriage, property that belongs entirely to her. Elizabeth's morning gift had, most generously, been Čachtice Castle and its estates. This phrase has, quite understandably, been mistranslated and misunderstood because women were often buried in their wedding gowns, the most ornate item of clothing they possessed. But Elizabeth was stating that she intended to reside in her bridal *property*, her morning gift of Čachtice, until her death. It was common, when an aristocratic mother ceded control of the family's main estate to her son, that she then moved to another manor. In this tradition, Elizabeth was formally announcing her retirement, declaring her intention to allow Paul to take over the family seat of Sárvár.

Had the Countess decided to retire to another property, a Bathory estate in the east, for example, closer to the Transylvanian border, we might have never heard mention of her case today. There, she would have been closer to the estates of her nephew and other extended family members and have had access to political support and avenues of escape.

But she gave up Sárvár's moat and gleaming white walls for the more compact manor house of Čachtice, traded the plains of the southwest for the northern peaks of the Little Carpathians. Čachtice was a place of great sentimental importance to her, where she had spent many happy Christmas holidays with her husband. Here, too, she would not be too far from Anna and Paul, and of course her daughter Kate had a newly built home to stay in whenever she visited.

However, Elizabeth was also moving closer to the very man who was investigating her and across the street from a pastor who was openly hostile to her. She would be leaving behind in Sárvár the private security force she had assembled at great cost to herself, who owed their loyalty only to her. Rather ominously, Red Megyery was reported to have told others that as soon as the Countess moved to her new home, she would be arrested.

Even if she anticipated trouble, Elizabeth also had many reasons to be optimistic. King Matthias II, despite his machinations against Gabriel, was eager to keep the Hungarian nobility happy, to keep up at least the appearance of judicial reform. The recent case against Elizabeth's neighbor and peer Andreas Doczy, based on widespread rumors of poison, would have been encouraging. Doczy had been acquitted after he asked other nobles to testify on his behalf. Elizabeth appeared to be following a similar tactic, having her attendant Lady Helen Hernath record her testimony to exonerate Elizabeth in the county courts. If the Countess could find out the names of other alleged victims, she might be able to have their parents do the same. She was a woman with friends from every denomination and walk of life, from Catholic bishops to Lutheran commoners, whom she could certainly call upon to do the same.

. . .

When Elizabeth settled into her new home in the autumn of 1610, Čachtice was dark with religious discord. When Thurzo held his Lutheran church council with only a handful of clergy, sixteen new church laws were adopted; Thurzo had these immediately printed up and distributed throughout Royal Hungary. Other Lutherans, outraged at being excluded from the decision-making process, refused to accept the new church administration and its laws. The nobility demanded that the three new bishops, including Elias Lany, be removed from office and another round of elections be held. Seven towns rebelled outright, refusing to attend services. Other congregations threatened to defect to the Calvinists. Pastors were physically run off from their churches; others barred their church doors, refusing to allow church administrators to enter.

Ponikenus, already sore from losing his election, was now being challenged by his own parishioners. He complained of a close encounter with "the living instrument of Satan" when one villager dared to "openly contradict" him during his sermon and then stamped out in protest. Another day, a member of a wedding party threatened him, shouting, "You whoreson priest, I will drag you out of this church by your hair, like a dog!" Ponikenus, thoroughly shaken, fled. He later wrote to his superiors, begging for protection.

The region was becoming a powder keg. The unrest sparked by the Lutheran church's new administration spilled over into clashes between aristocrats' households. In late October, a fair was held in a nearby market town. One of Thurzo's attendants, Caspar Tatay, drank too much and got into a shouting match with an unnamed servant of Elizabeth's. Tatay wanted to fight. He attacked Elizabeth's servant with his fists, then drew his sword. Luckily, bystanders intervened, took Tatay's sword, and separated the men. But Tatay was not willing to drop the matter. Rather than sleeping off the alcohol, he snuck into the town's stable and cut the tendons of the man's horse, rendering the poor animal permanently disabled. In a society where horses were incredibly expensive, and where people often formed close bonds with them, this was an assault not just against the servant, but against the Bathory family. Tatay later rode down to the Čachtice manor house, sword drawn, cursing and challenging Elizabeth's servant to a duel. Tatay was defeated, having his sword broken, and fled. But he returned yet a third time, trying to duel again.

When Elizabeth wrote to Thurzo she was furious and insisted her servant had done nothing to provoke the attack: "The beginning and the end of all things was Caspar Tatay, which I cannot suffer without the law." She let the palatine know the events had been witnessed by the servants of her daughter Anna and son-in-law Zrinyi, who had been visiting at the time, and rather cuttingly reminded Thurzo of his duties to all Hungarians: "I rather expect protection from you and your servants."

There is a report of another similar incident right around the same time. A former local judge from Sárvár recounted how his servant had also gotten into an altercation with one of Elizabeth's servants. Here the Countess's servant is named: the teenage footman John Ujvary, who went by the nickname "Ficzko," for "lad." He was a war orphan whom Elizabeth had raised on her estates since he was a baby.

Ficzko won this fight, pummeling the judge's servant. The servant went back to his lord and insisted he had done nothing to provoke the beating, and so the judge set out to physically discipline Ficzko as punishment. Elizabeth intervened, though, protecting her servant and coming to his defense, to the great annoyance of the judge.

That autumn, a land dispute Elizabeth had brought before the courts was also reaching its conclusion. The case had been winding its way through the court system for the past four years, ever since George Banffy had seized the property of Lendava in 1606 and Elizabeth had spiritedly threatened to retaliate: "I will have your house torn down above your head." Significantly, it was the notaries who had been collecting testimony against her who were asked to weigh in on the case. Not surprisingly, they ruled against Elizabeth. This was a crushing blow not just for Elizabeth, but for the woman she had promised to help regain her property, the widow of Caspar Banffy.

It was the time of year when a bitter chill began to creep under blankets and furs and the sunlight retreated. The dark was creeping in, in more ways than one. It is often asked why Elizabeth, fully cognizant of the dangers she was facing, didn't try to run. Many aristocrats facing criminal charges simply slipped over the border into another kingdom. Elizabeth's new son-in-law George Drugeth had done this very thing as a teenager, and in the future, her neighbor and fellow accused serial killer Anna Rozina Listius would abscond too.

The most logical place for Elizabeth to go would be Transylvania. Some of the lands she had newly inherited from her brother were right along the border; under the pretense of visiting one of these properties to attend to some administrative matter she could have slipped into the principality and lived at her nephew's court in great comfort. Poland was another possibility; her uncle had been king of Poland, and she still had relatives and contacts there. A last resort could entail heading south, through the lands of her son-in-law Nicolas Zrinyi, to the seaside, where the Republic of Venice controlled numerous nearby ports. Cardinals and bishops from the Bathory family had lived and worked in this fair city, and she could have found shelter there.

But flight was a last resort, and Elizabeth expected to have plenty more time. The first liberty of any noble, as carefully set out in the law, was: "They can never be arrested . . . without being first cited or summoned and condemned by judicial process." Any noble charged with a crime would receive a summons to appear before Parliament when it was in session. It was inconceivable that she would receive a summons over the holidays, when Parliament was not in session, judges were home with their families, and heavy snow made travel difficult.

And if, in the spring, she was ordered to appear before Parliament, she would still have time to decide what to do; many aristocrats viewed a summons as optional. Oftentimes they would not immediately show up, which would delay the case until the next time Parliament was in session; being tried in absentia would later give them grounds for appeal. Even if Elizabeth did appear, she would expect to spend weeks or months waiting in Bratislava for an audience, or be given lengthy extensions so her lawyers might gather documents and prepare the case. She was the type to stay and fight, but if her calculations changed, there was always time to flee.

But once again, Elizabeth miscalculated. She fully expected to be called to court; she never expected a raid.

CHAPTER 10

The Raid

They came for her on a Wednesday night when the moon was high in the sky and nearly full, and the pines slumped under heavy snow. On December 29, 1610, around seven in the evening, a small group of men assembled outside Čachtice village. Led by Thurzo, in a fur-trimmed cloak and a feathered hat, and trailed by a small detachment of soldiers, they rode the short distance to the gates of the manor house.

When Thurzo dismounted and gave the order, the soldiers forced their way into the manor house and spilled down its corridors. Thurzo limped along behind them—his gout had been troubling him since summer. At first, the thick Turkish carpets would have muffled the sounds of their boots, and except for a guard or two, they would have encountered little resistance, as Elizabeth's carefully assembled and fiercely loyal bodyguard had remained behind in Sárvár.

Thurzo would later claim that he surprised Elizabeth in the middle of a torture session, but that was a lie. Even the letter Thurzo wrote home to his wife immediately after the arrest makes no mention of Elizabeth being caught red-handed, and another, less biased source records that Elizabeth was surprised only in the act of eating dinner, seated in one of the manor's two dining halls, at the head of a long table, dining and drinking from her solid silver plates and goblets, conversing with a small group of her companions.

The manor was thoroughly searched: the two wings, the forty-six rooms, the treasury, the kitchen, the bakery, the storerooms, even the five cellars. Relatively quickly, Thurzo would have realized he had a problem. The bodies. The dozens, the hundreds of bodies. Where were they all? And the torture chamber he had been assured he would find—where, exactly? He found, instead, exactly what one would expect to find in the infirmary of any aristocrat providing health care not just for girls in her finishing school, but for female servants and serfs across the twenty-one villages that were a part of her estate. He found what one would expect during a winter outbreak—one dead girl, one girl who was clearly still very sick, and others still in quarantine.

On Christmas Eve, just five days earlier, a group of Lutheran pastors had called upon Elizabeth. One of these, Nicolas Baroseus, the pastor of Vrbové, wrote that they wanted to caution the Countess about all of the tales that "were circulating about her." He testified that during this visit he saw "a virgin still alive, but worn down and very frail, who at the time of the Lady Widow's incarceration was found dead. He also saw other virgins in similar condition." The girl is described with the Latin *maceratam* and *debilem*, both of which mean "weak"; the other girls are *similiter affectas*, similarly affected. This is a clear reference to illness, not injury. Most significantly, Pastor Baroseus did not describe any bruises or burns or other injuries.

Having been informed by the pastors of a group of sick girls, and then hearing word of a death at the manor, Thurzo may have been hoping for more than one body. That certainly would have made his task much easier. For his evidence of serial murder, Thurzo now only had the body of a girl who had been very ill just days earlier. But he had to plow ahead. Elizabeth's fate had already been decided. The show must go on.

Thurzo's claim that he surprised Elizabeth in the middle of a torture session, a claim repeated even today, was a critical part of that performance. By failing to issue Elizabeth a summons to appear before the court, and then forcing his way into her manor with his private army, Thurzo had himself committed a crime: The "invasion of houses; the

PICTURING ELIZABETH BATHORY

On the evening of September 22, 1991, thieves broke into the Čachtice Museum and made off with a single oil painting—a portrait of Elizabeth Bathory. This painting was a copy of a 1585 original of the young Countess.

Another copy of the 1585 portrait of Elizabeth, featuring a different color scheme. Notice, too, the difference in her collar and pearls.

This is the only other representation of the Countess, painted after her death. It was likely commissioned in the 1630s by her daughter-in-law as part of a set of matching portraits for the family gallery.

The only surviving contemporary portrait of Elizabeth's nephew, Prince Gabriel Bathory.

A portrait of King Matthias II, as a young Hapsburg archduke.

IN THE COUNTESS'S FOOTSTEPS
SÁRVÁR, THEN AND NOW

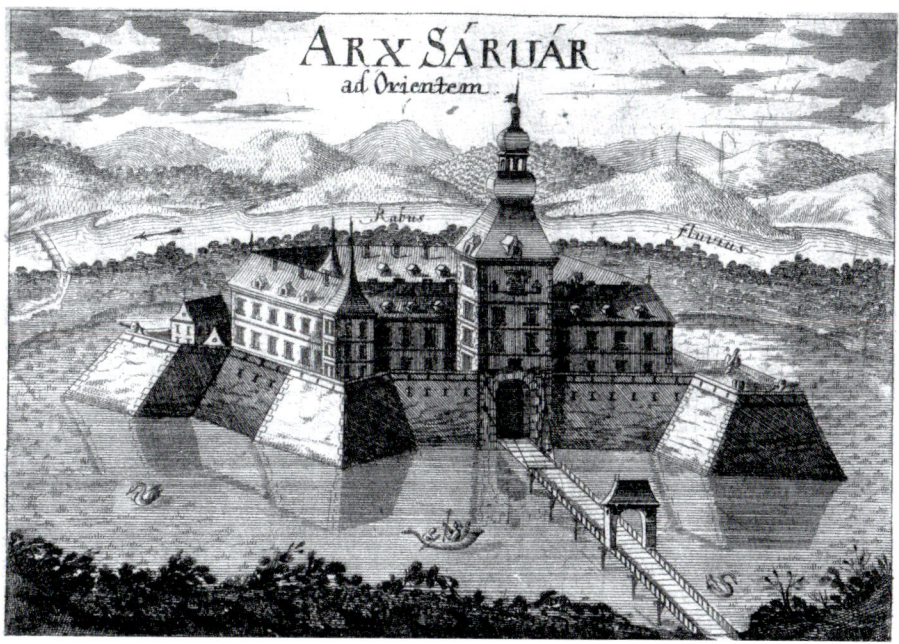

A seventeenth-century copperplate of Sárvár Castle, where Elizabeth spent most of her life.

Sárvár Castle today; the former moat is now a grassy lawn.

ČACHTICE, THEN AND NOW

An artist's sketch of Čachtice Castle, as it would have appeared in Elizabeth's lifetime.

A postcard from 1919. The Bathory legend and the ruins of Čachtice were already a popular tourist attraction.

The ruins of Čachtice Castle as they appear today.

The parish church in Čachtice. Here, Pastor John Ponikenus denounced the Countess from his pulpit.

The cellars and tunnels under the old Čachtice manor house are a tourist attraction today.

killing, beating, wounding of a noble or detaining him without just cause" were all capital offenses, and as Doczy's poisoning case had shown, a sloppy frame-up could backfire.

The only legal exception that might justify Thurzo's raid? A noble could be arrested without proper judicial process if they were caught in the act of committing a capital offense.

A noble *man*, that was. There were different rules for the weaker and gentler sex. A noblewoman caught in the act of killing one of her servants could be hauled before a court and forced to work out compensation for the victim's family. However, the law stated that they could not be charged with the capital crime of murder unless she killed an immediate family member. The only exception was if the homicide was especially egregious—if, for example, the murder involved mutilation of the body.

To justify his raid, Thurzo needed to somehow catch Elizabeth in the act of murder, and in order to imprison her, he had to show she had mutilated her victim.

The next morning, Thursday, December 30, George Thurzo gathered a crowd of villagers and servants together—at least fifteen men. He proclaimed that he had surprised the Countess in the very act of murdering one of her maids. The townspeople were then shown a special exhibit—the naked corpse of the sick girl carried out in a cart. Her name was Doricza, and hers is the only known body in the whole sordid affair. We don't know her last name. It was later said that she came from a faraway Croatian village and had only been in Elizabeth's employ for a month. Her family was never interviewed. It seems most likely that she was a commoner and a servant, for had Thurzo been able to cast Elizabeth as the murderer of a noble girl, a girl with an ancient name and important family, he surely would have capitalized upon this in the copious documents that followed.

Lady Helen's testimony months earlier—that she had "not seen or found any sign on" her own daughter's corpse—shows that part of the rumors against Elizabeth were about marks or signs on corpses that were taken to be evidence of beatings and rough treatment. Now, the villagers examining the body on display saw the marks they were intently looking for, dark purplish spots they were told by Thurzo were evidence of torture. This was likely livor mortis, the discoloration of the skin that can begin as early as around a half hour after death, but is usually most pronounced twelve hours after death. Others were convinced the redness around her neck was evidence Doricza had been shackled or strangled, but this could also have been a common postmortem hemorrhage that occurs when a dead body is left in a prone position.

Thurzo, already certain of Elizabeth's guilt, may have been similarly confused, seeing what he wished to see. Still, he had spent a great deal of time on battlefields and seen an enormous number of corpses firsthand. Thurzo had a world-class library in the tradition of the Raven King, with more than eight hundred books, including the era's preeminent books on medicine. While an ordinary villager might be confused by a purpling body, it is curious that he would be. More sinisterly, it is entirely possible that a prosecutor, in need of a mutilated dead body, had his own men create one. It would not have taken much effort to rough the body up a bit—postmortem bruises have misled even present-day coroners about cause of death.

A doctor was brought in to examine the surviving girls, the ones who had been suffering with a "similar condition." The doctor's observations about their symptoms and condition may have shed additional light upon the cause of Doricza's death, although he would never be called to testify. So without any alternate explanation offered, the villagers seem to have accepted Thurzo's assertion that the blue and purple marks were indeed welts, burn marks, or bruises.

The villagers were next presented with a living servant girl, her dress pulled down to display deep, pus-filled wounds on her back, as well as a mangled hand. She was an eighteen-year-old peasant named Anna, the daughter of a widow named Barbara from a small village near Trenčín, and her right hand became an object of much fascination and speculation. The girl would be brought to the barber-surgeon in Nové Mesto nad Váhom for treatment, and many villagers would later visit her there to gawk at or ask after her hand. One villager testified that Anna told her that Elizabeth had done something painful to "bruise" it, and also that another woman "cut the dark and purulent flesh with a pair of shears."

It is significant that the girl speaks of first having "dark and purulent flesh," and next having that skin cut off with shears, and not vice versa;

this is, even today, the medical treatment for gangrene, to prevent its spread. Elizabeth may have manipulated the girl's injured hand in such a way as to cause pain, but a bruise would not have caused necrotic skin tissue. One historian thinks that Anna's injuries most closely match up with those from an attack by a wild animal—an accidental encounter with a starving wolf or even a hibernating mother bear would not be uncommon at that time of year. The creature had raked Anna's back with its claws and bitten her hand as she held it up to shield her face; Anna had been taken to the closest thing to a woman's hospital in the area and was being treated by Elizabeth's staff.

The public presentation of the dead and injured girls was important. News of Thurzo's raid would have already begun circulating, and he had to make sure his version of events, of catching Elizabeth red-handed, was also circulating. When dozens of people repeated the same story about Andreas Doczy being a serial killer, this was described as being "a sign that [the accuser] has told his theory to everyone and that this very interesting story has had time to form on the lips of the public." Thurzo, the accuser, likewise needed to make sure that his "very interesting story" had plenty of time to circulate, from village washerwoman to country squire's wife, from mistress to her friends, from one of those friends to her brother or husband in Parliament.

After his presentation, Thurzo wrote to his wife on December 30, sounding more annoyed than horrified that he had been delayed returning home on account of "that damned woman." This phrasing was usually reserved for his religious opponents—those damned Catholics, that damned Turk. He reported to his wife, "I have arrested Madame Nadasdy and she is being detained in the castle." In the best of weather, the steep, winding walk from the manor up to the castle would take a good horse three quarters of an hour. But given the deep snow, the trudge uphill took much longer. There's no record of how the Countess spent the time, whether she showered threats upon her "heavy guard" or glowered in silence.

Thurzo had also apprehended Elizabeth's closest and most trusted servants. After the death of the "old woman" Anna Darvulia, Elizabeth had hired another midwife and healer, the widow Dorothy Szentes.

Dorothy was often assisted by Helena Jo, the nanny who had raised Elizabeth's children and would have served as the pediatrician at court. The washerwoman Katherine Benczky also assisted in some capacity: The injured peasant Anna named her as the one who had snipped away her necrotic flesh. Alongside the court healer, the nanny, and the washerwoman, the teenage footman John Ujvary, or Ficzko, was also arrested. Ficzko was still, legally, a child, but he, along with the old widows Dorothy, Helena, and Katherine, were all tortured immediately after their arrest.

. . .

The next day, a Friday and New Year's Eve, Ponikenus visited the Countess in her new prison. Ponikenus was trailed by two pastors from neighboring parishes, both of more peaceable sensibilities. Zachary Gasperides, of nearby Podolie, had already been berated for allowing Elizabeth to hold a funeral in his churchyard. The other, Nicolas Baroseus of Vrbové, had been among those to call upon Elizabeth before Christmas to warn her of the gathering storm. He had seen the maid Doricza, whose corpse had been the previous day's main attraction, while she was still alive, and observed the other sick girls quarantined with her.

Although Gasperides and Baroseus were technically beholden to Ponikenus—he was the pastor of the largest parish in their diocese—they knew he needed them, especially today, to interpret and translate. Unlike them, he spoke only Slovak and clumsy Latin, and could not converse with the great Hungarian lady in her own tongue.

Two written accounts of this visit have survived. Both claim that the Countess was not at all pleased to see the clergymen. Ponikenus's version of Elizabeth's greeting: "You priests are the cause of my captivity!"

Either Ponikenus's interpreters tactfully omitted a few words, or Ponikenus was unwilling to repeat them; Baroseus reported she challenged their morality and motives: "You ungodly and malicious priests are the cause of my captivity!"

Gasperides defended himself. And Elizabeth softened, at least toward him: "If you are not the cause, the pastor of Čachtice surely is. He has fulminated against me in quite a number of his speeches."

"Your Ladyship should not believe this," Gasperides reassured her.

"I can prove with witnesses that he has done so."

Ponikenus objected, "I have preached God's words. If this sometimes burdened Your Ladyship's conscience, I am not the cause; I have never named you."

Ponikenus was lying. Or perhaps he was splitting hairs; he might have never mentioned the Countess by her given name, since he and Lany had another name by which they referred to her: "our Jezebel," after the biblical pagan queen who defied the prophet Elijah.

As if she really were a pagan queen, the three pastors then began quizzing Elizabeth on basic Christian beliefs: "Do you believe that Christ was born and has died for you, and he was resurrected so you might aim for forgiveness for your sins?"

She answered: "Even Peter the Carpenter [i.e., the average Joe] knows these [facts]."

She was handed a Bible and told to read it during her imprisonment.

"I don't need to," she said.

When they next asked her to confess her sins to them, Elizabeth was incredulous: "How could I do this when all of you are my enemies?"

Elizabeth was not the first woman, or the last, to call these men her enemies. While she remained imprisoned in her own castle, another woman would accuse George Thurzo and his cadre of Lutheran preachers of framing her too.

She was also given a biblical nickname: Pythonissa, after a pagan soothsayer in the first Book of Samuel. Pythonissa was accused of witchcraft, but even under torture, she would not name any accomplices or confess. Despite this, she was still tied to the stake and the kindling was lit. As dark smoke and the thick scent of burning flesh filled the square, Bishop Lany complained, "She did not even want to acknowledge her sins in the middle of the flames, calling out from time to time: *I leave this world innocent!*" That Pythonissa insisted upon her innocence, throughout painful torture and even throughout the horror of being burned alive, did not make these men doubt her guilt, or their own powers of deduction, for even a moment.

This Pythonissa must have had an exceptional tolerance for pain. Few were able to resist the torture they were subjected to. Elizabeth's own servants had already been made to say that they and their mistress had committed "many and terrible" offenses.

Elizabeth challenged this so-called evidence, asking the pastors, "To what would even you not admit if you were tortured by fire or otherwise?"

Elizabeth spoke of the futility of coerced confessions, of the witnesses that she would summon, and of her right to keep her own counsel about her defense. She even invoked her right to silence. When Ponikenus demanded information, she responded: "I am not obliged to tell you." She refused to repent and told the pastors that she placed "her trust in her [legal] case" instead.

Pastor Baroseus found her declarations of innocence convincing; he did not seem to think that Elizabeth had hurt anyone herself. He said she had become "entangled in horrible crimes" but did not accuse her of directly committing them. He posited that her healers were incompetent but that she had allowed the old women to continue practicing because "even she herself was also afraid of them."

Perhaps Baroseus, worried about directly defying Ponikenus, was trying to construct a face-saving alternative, one in which no one had deliberately committed murder. The idea of the Countess being afraid of anyone, though, was completely at odds with her demeanor.

She directly challenged the pastors, "What do you think? Will there be no commotion because of this?" Both Ponikenus and Baroseus reported her next threat in near-identical words: She had written to her nephew, and "the prince of Transylvania will avenge this injustice against me." Both pastors seemed genuinely concerned that Elizabeth might summon her nephew's fearsome hajduks to rescue her. Ponikenus reassured himself that Elizabeth was secure in her prison, "enclosed by a wall," and that any rescue attempts would be fruitless.

Rescue, though, could come in more than one way. The case against Elizabeth was in danger of unraveling. If Ponikenus had hoped that the Countess would be so scared that she would confess outright, sparing everyone the trouble of prosecuting her case, he had sorely underestimated her. The Countess, too, had many powerful friends and allies with whom she still seemed to be communicating. Ponikenus complained to his superiors that she had been receiving messages and furiously writing letters. The pastor could not count on public support: His parishioners were already on the verge of revolt, and other Lutheran pastors did not seem to share his enthusiasm for the case.

In the diocese of Čachtice, there were thirteen Lutheran parishes, yet only Ponikenus and three other pastors would become involved in the proceedings. The pastor of Beckov would protest that he "knew nothing," and the other eight pastors would not testify, although doing so would have curried favor with Thurzo. In the western counties, too, clergy seemed reluctant to get involved. There were dozens of Lutheran parishes in the area, but only Sárvár's pastor Michael Zvonarics testified. (No Calvinist pastors, obviously, were consulted.) Even Thurzo, after publicly accusing the Countess of murder and mutilation, seemed to be softening his stance. When he wrote to his wife, he shifted the blame for the "torturing and killing" elsewhere—to a group of "wicked females" and their "trusted assistant." The counternarrative that Pastor Baroseus had proposed—that there were no murders, only inept and unskilled healers—might easily gain traction.

Ponikenus was adamant that this not happen. Writing to Bishop Lany on New Year's Day of 1611, the day after his visit to the Countess, he leveled even more charges against the Countess. He detailed what her servants should be made to confess: "I write this with the aim that those three old women who were led away, and the lad Ficzko, will be well interrogated. So they will tell what pleasure these wicked women took in so many and such horrible murders, and what a monster they supported." He was determined to have a witch trial. He accused Elizabeth, in specific, gory detail, of something that Jews, Turks, werewolves, and witches all allegedly indulged in: cannibalism.

> Here we hear from virgins who still live that some of them were coerced to eat their own roasted flesh; others, young men, were served the flesh of virgins instead of mushrooms, cut into bits and cooked, but they didn't know what they ate. Oh, Thyestes-like feasts! No torturers under the sky have been crueler than this, according to my judgment.

This detail from his letter, despite not being corroborated by a single other witness, would make its way into the final report that Thurzo later sent to the king, who would express his shock at hearing so many girls at the Countess's court had "their flesh ripped out, roasted on the fire, and this roasted flesh then allowed to be served." Ponikenus had not overestimated his influence in this case.

This makes his next accusations all the more heartbreaking. Ponikenus formally accused two healers the Countess had supported, the "woman scientist" of Tokorcs and the Mistress of Myjava, of witchcraft. This was no offhand complaint. He knew what wheels he was setting in motion by denouncing these two women in writing.

The Tokorcs healer, he claimed, had advised the Countess to "take a black cat, kill it with a white rod, keep its blood . . . [and] smear your enemies with that blood." The Mistress of Myjava had created a spell that called upon "the mighty Lord of Cats"—the Devil himself—to send ninety-nine cats to "bite into and eat the heart of King Matthias and of the Lord Palatine and of the Lord Red Megyery and also of Moses Cziraky [one of the notaries], so Elizabeth Bathory shall not be harmed!"

Ponikenus had convoluted explanations for why, even though these healers posed credible threats to public officials, all of their intended victims were still alive and well. Although the Mistress of Myjava had composed her murderous invocation, it had not yet been uttered: The Countess had sent a servant to Myjava to retrieve the spell the night of her arrest, but he returned too late, after the Countess was already in custody. The pastor also knew of another attempt she had made on the lives of Elizabeth's enemies: "On Christmas Eve the Mistress of Myjava made a bath with different herbs for Her Ladyship, and as I heard, they wanted to bake bread with this bathwater so her enemies ate it, but they were betrayed." Ponikenus relished the near miss, the adrenaline surge of having cheated death over and over again. The murderous spell delivered an hour too late! The plot to bake enchanted bread interrupted!

The pastor rambled on, but the last sentence of his letter returned to the Mistress of Myjava again. Aware that he had painted her as incredibly powerful, so powerful that the local bailiffs might be reluctant to arrest such a witch, he closed with this assurance: "As I hear, the said Mistress has greatly shrunken by now." The woman's powers had somehow diminished just days after her attempts on the lives of the king and palatine; the men sent to arrest her would find not a fearsome demon, but just an ordinary old woman.

In a hasty postscript, Ponikenus relayed the following anecdote that happened to him after supper:

> I go again to my room to say my ardent prayers to God. My wife follows me shortly after and we are speaking about this miraculous and dire thing [i.e., the Countess's arrest] that happened. After this, I don't know why, a cat is meowing in the top floor . . . I recognize that this is not the natural voice of a cat. I go looking and find nothing. I say to my servant, "John, if you see cats running in the yard, kill them, don't be afraid."
>
> We don't find anything.
>
> My servant says, "Master, many mice are peeping in this chamber."
>
> I run there and find nothing.
>
> And I say, "There is nothing here," and I go back down the stairs. When I have only two or three stairs to go, immediately six cats and, I have to add, dogs, start to bite my right leg.
>
> Then I say, "Go to hell, you devils," and I hit beside my leg with a piece of wood.
>
> At this, they all clear off into the courtyard; my servant runs after them, but doesn't see or find anything. Your Lordship sees [this is] the Devil's work.

Other men may have been troubled that the Countess's secret torture chamber could not be found and that no one yet knew where her many victims were buried. But Pastor Ponikenus was more certain than ever. That the Countess had called upon Satan to send phantom animals to torment him could only mean one thing: He was, at last, getting very close to the truth indeed.

CHAPTER 11

The Servants' Trial

Ponikenus's letter to his mentor made it clear that, even before she had been interrogated or tried, Elizabeth Bathory's punishment had been decided upon: She was to be imprisoned for life. The pastor was not the only one with advance notice of her supposedly "deserved punishment." Red Megyery had been apprised of the proceedings against Elizabeth and knew she would be arrested once she moved to Čachtice. He had not warned his mistress, but he had alerted other court officials about the upcoming action. Elizabeth's sons-in-law had also been consulted. Zrinyi, the more loyal of the two, had held out for some time. He defended his mother-in-law until he found himself dragged before the Privy Council and accused of treason, of having "surrendered to the Transylvanian prince, sworn allegiance to him, and moreover promised him that he would bring the neighboring countries and provinces . . . under his rule by force of arms." He was, under threat to life and limb, made to renounce Prince Gabriel Bathory and swear allegiance to King Matthias II. Only then did Zrinyi tersely agree to allow his mother-in-law to "peacefully stay" in Čachtice, so that the rest of the family lands "shall not be diminished" and the rest of the family could avoid the "grave mark" of treason.

There was no need to threaten Drugeth with any ultimatum: Thurzo had already struck a deal with him. Well before Elizabeth's arrest, Thurzo met with Drugeth and Red Megyery to decide how to best divvy up her property. Drugeth desired Elizabeth's northeastern properties that abutted his own family lands, and Megyery wanted to solidify his control of the area around Sárvár. Zrinyi was furious to have been left out of these negotiations and threatened to raise a clamor: "I will contradict this [process] . . . publicly." In exchange for his silence, Zrinyi demanded, "I want for myself an equal part of everything, from the property on this side of the Danube as well as from that on the other side."

The interests of all three of Elizabeth's children—Anna, Kate, and Paul—were now represented by their guardians and spouses. In this, Thurzo had managed to thread the needle between the conflicting interests of his king and the nobility: He had sidelined one of Prince Gabriel Bathory's key allies while also keeping his promise to Francis Nadasdy to be his children's "guardian and protector," making sure the family kept their lands.

Nicolas Zrinyi, however, may not have entirely betrayed his mother-in-law. Finding himself also under suspicion of treason, he may have thought it best to first clear his and his wife's names, secure the family lands, and then work to see his mother-in-law released or pardoned. A pardon was not out of the question, even given such serious charges. Elizabeth's son-in-law Drugeth had been fully exonerated many years after his supposedly treasonous offenses, and when Thurzo's own in-law Countess Anna Rozina Listius was later sentenced to death for the murder of nine women, she would be granted a full pardon one year later. Perhaps all Elizabeth had to do was stay in the castle, keep quiet, and let her family petition, again and again, for her release.

The servants arrested alongside her had no such prospect of pardon. Days after their arrest, the four servants were hustled out of Čachtice to Thurzo's family seat of Bytča for their trial. This was a fifty-mile trip that would have taken at least three days given the heavy snow and bitter cold, on some of the shortest days of the year. It was no simple feat to transport four chained prisoners in carts through a narrow pass in the Carpathian Mountains alongside a frozen river. Given the considerable time, risk, and expense involved, this was, to say the least, an unusual action, one that showcased the control Thurzo exercised over every aspect of Elizabeth's case. It was his private army that broke into and searched Elizabeth's home, it was his men who tortured her servants, and it would be his court that ruled on their guilt.

Commoners were usually tried in the locality where they had been arrested or where their crime was alleged to have been committed, to ensure witnesses would be available to testify. If Thurzo was genuinely worried about the Čachtice justice system favoring the Countess, he could have easily moved the trial a few miles north to the free market town of Nové Mesto nad Váhom, which had its own independent judges and jurors. Trying the servants closer to Sárvár, where most of the crimes were alleged to have occurred, would have been another option. But his earlier investigation had shown that most people in both towns, while certainly eager to share and spread gossip about the Countess, did not hold any specific animosity toward her. In these regions, Thurzo might not be able to dictate the outcome of the case. If her servants were acquitted, or convicted of much lesser crimes, Thurzo's imprisonment of Elizabeth and the division of her property would not stand.

The servants' trial began shortly after their arrival in Bytča, on January 2, when they were formally questioned. Ponikenus's letter would have just arrived to Bishop Lany, detailing his hope that the servants would be "well interrogated." They had been roughed up already, threatened and tortured, but that was in makeshift quarters in Čachtice shortly after their arrest. Now the torture sessions would be conducted much more deliberately by Thurzo's own employees, two local magistrates and the castellan of Bytča. Thurzo told these three men that he was certain the servants had committed hundreds of murders, but he wasn't sure exactly how or when or where. Their task was to confirm the most damning testimony, and quickly, or his case would collapse.

The four servants did confess to some rather shocking things. Much more shocking, however, is how modern audiences have repeated, believed, and even delighted in these confessions, especially given what we know about how interrogations were conducted during this period. Consider the account of Johannes Junius, the mayor of Bamberg, who confessed to having sex with a succubus, attending demonic gatherings with other townspeople, and desecrating the communion host. In a heartrending letter to his daughter, smuggled out of prison just before he was burned at the stake, Junius declared his innocence and described how his confession was coerced, through thumbscrews (which crushed his digits and made him unable to use his hands for a month), painful leg screws, and the repeated use of strappado, or what he called "the hanging torture." People's hands were tied behind their backs and they were suspended from a rope attached to their wrists. First a person's shoulders would become dislocated, then, if left hanging for too long, kidney damage and even death would ensue. Junius told his daughter, "They never stop with the torturing until one confesses something. No matter how pious a man might be, he will confess . . . No one escapes, not even a lord." He said even the executioner begged him, "For God's sake, confess to something, whether it's true or not! Invent something—for you won't be able to survive the torturing they plan for you. Even if you do survive, you'll never go free . . . That's how all these trials go, each one just like the other." Even those who somehow survived the torture and were miraculously allowed to go free never fully recovered. In one case, in a town close to Sárvár, an exonerated farmer filed a legal appeal because the thirty-three weeks of torture he had endured left him unable to work: His captors "let me stretch and tear to pieces, so now I have to be a poor man all my life."

The statements of one teenage boy and three old widows under such circumstances can hardly be called "testimony," and any agreement between their statements is more likely to be the result of a dogged interrogator than proof of any conspiracy. But even with the incentive of the strap and the iron, the servants could not be made to agree on who, exactly, had been murdered. The boy Ficzko thought there might be thirty-seven victims, and the healer Dorothy thought thirty-six, but both the nanny Helena Jo and the washerwoman Katherine claimed there were fifty. They all had trouble naming or describing specific victims. Ficzko and Dorothy at first couldn't name a single one, and Helena Jo described nine supposed victims but only in very vague terms: "a large, tall girl, the daughter of a nobleman" or "a girl from the south of Poland."

THE SERVANTS' TRIAL

They could agree that the Sittkey girls, who were at this point the subject of widely circulating rumors, had somehow been killed, but even in this the servants' testimonies were at odds: Ficzko said a single Sittkey girl was killed for stealing a pear (an odd end for a noble girl, with her own attendants who could have secured her as many pears as she wished), while Helena Jo and Katherine insisted there had been two Sittkey girls, although they could provide no further details about how they had died.

A scribe was present at these sessions, but his enthusiasm for recording the proceedings seems to have flagged the longer they went on. The man resorted often to brief summaries and phrases like "everything like the other witnesses" or "she said the same as the others." It's unclear whether, as the screams and pleas increased in tempo and volume, he found it harder and harder to keep up, furiously jabbing his quill in the inkpot and scribbling across the parchment, or if each subsequent defendant, already traumatized by the cries of those tortured before them, just agreed outright with anything the interrogators suggested.

The servants' confessions don't clarify who the Countess's alleged victims were, but they do give an idea of what the interrogators wanted to know, the sort of questions they shouted over and over while they crushed, stretched, burned, and flayed the terrified servants. The men were desperate to figure out the location of Elizabeth's torture chamber.

If Thurzo had truly stumbled across the Countess in the act of torturing her maid in Čachtice, as he claimed, he would already have known the answer to this question. Though he and his men thoroughly searched the premises, they never reported finding any space that was obviously designated as such. There was also supposed to be a secret torture chamber at Sárvár; the Lutheran pastor Michael Zvonarics and the castellan of Sárvár had both testified that one existed. Surely such esteemed men could not be lying. Megyery was now administering Sárvár for young Paul Nadasdy and had full access to the castle, including the former women's quarters. Yet he, too, had been unable to find this secret chamber.

The women couldn't come up with any likely torture chambers either, stating that the torture was performed everywhere. Helena Jo, the nanny, did mention, oddly, that a "bloodstained stone wall [was] washed."

This makes sense only in light of the testimony given earlier by one of the castellans of Sárvár, who insisted he once saw a bloodstained wall. When no such wall was discovered, the terrified nanny was made to agree that the blood must have been washed away.

If there was no torture chamber, then where had the crimes taken place? The scribe summarized Ficzko's response to this question: "In Beckov she had them tortured in the chamber in the kitchen building. In Sárvár they were tortured in the inner castle, where not everyone could enter. In Keresztúr in the privy. In Čachtice within the kitchen building. When we were traveling, she herself tortured, beat, pinched and poked them with a needle, in the carriage." These very informal settings make more sense if one substitutes "treated" for "tortured"—drafts being prepared and cautery administered in a kitchen near the fire, for example, or menstrual care conducted in a privy. Privies, kitchens, women's bedrooms, and carriages were also places men would not ordinarily be, which neatly accounted for the lack of eyewitnesses.

There is also mention of torture being conducted in Vienna, at the town house Elizabeth shared with her neighbor Lord Batthyany, torture so obvious that "the monks threw pots at the window as they heard the wailing [of the girls]." This town house was less than two hundred feet away from the Augustinerkirche, the looming Gothic court church of the Hapsburgs, the likely residence of any neighborhood monks. Both are right next to the massive Hofburg palace. This scenario has Elizabeth torturing people right under the Hapsburgs' nose, close enough that monks are throwing pots at the windows in complaint, in the middle of a crowded, cosmopolitan city, with not a single one of these monks, or Elizabeth's neighbors, or the many Hapsburg courtiers passing by ever filing a complaint.

This is one of the many questions and inconsistencies that crop up throughout the coerced testimony. There are numerous others. For example, the washerwoman Katherine testified that the nanny Helena Jo had always been a favorite of her mistress, so much so that Elizabeth paid for the weddings of the nanny's two daughters and gave them fourteen "beautiful skirts." While this detail was no doubt meant to prove the close relationship between Helena Jo and the Countess, it is evidence of the guiding hand of a male interrogator who knew little of women's fashion and its cost. Elizabeth's own aristocratic trousseau, the trousseau of arguably the wealthiest heiress in the kingdom, listed only six skirts. That the daughters of her nanny would receive fourteen skirts, even if they were all hand-me-downs, would be virtually inconceivable.

Unable to uncover the names of victims or the location of a torture chamber, the interrogators were desperate to find bodies, of which they were certain there must be dozens, if not hundreds. "Who were the ones who hid these bodies, where were they buried, and how were they hidden?" the scribe recorded.

In the servants' responses, the sectarian debate over burials shows up again and again: The scribe makes a distinction between "hidden" Calvinist burials and those aligned with Lutheran tradition, such as girls "buried publicly by the priest." The nanny Helena Jo in particular seems to have been interrogated about her mistress's adherence to Lutheran doctrine. Her torturer's specific question was not recorded but Helena Jo's defense of her mistress was. All girls were buried according to the church canons: during the day, with singing and a proper ceremony. In Keresztúr, she said, burials were even done "with students," a reference to the custom of hiring students from the local Lutheran schools to sing at funerals. Such public events should have left a paper trail of some kind—letters and receipts—that could be confirmed or disputed in court.

The interrogators were keen to know about one specific incident: They seemed to think a few girls had died fairly recently at Čachtice, all around the same time, and wanted to know where they might be buried. The scribe summarized the servants' answers this way:

> FICZKO: These old women have hidden and buried those girls here in Čachtice.
> HELENA: She doesn't know where the corpses were buried now, but she knows that Mrs. Dorko [Dorothy] and Mrs. Kata [Katherine] carried five corpses into a wheat storage pit.
> DOROTHY: Within one week and a half five girls died in Čachtice and she had them piled on each other in the chamber, and then she went to Sárvár [with the Lady], and this Mrs. Kata [Katherine] carried them into a wheat storage pit with other servants.

The last interviewed, the washerwoman Katherine, proved to be the most loquacious. Her response seems especially disjointed; it is not clear if this is a reflection of the terrified washerwoman's own speech patterns or of the scribe's flagging skills.

> KATHERINE: The five girls, about whom Mrs. Dorko [Dorothy] knows where they died, because she was with them and she piled them under a bed and had alcohol poured upon them, and after that they brought food for them every day, as if they were still living in there, although they died long before. After that, the woman [Dorothy] went to Sárvár and ordered this witness to dig up the floor of the house and bury them, but she didn't, because was not enough to do that [sic], but those poor corpses were rotting so much and the whole castle stank so badly that all of this [evil] could be felt outside. But then the witness—not knowing what to do—buried them at night in a wheat storage pit, for God's sake, together with Bulia and one maid, Barbara, and Katus, who was together with Mrs. Dorko day and night as long as they both lived.

This testimony doesn't bolster the case against Elizabeth at all; if anything, it casts doubt upon it. This is evidence not of murder but, at worst, medical malpractice and illegal burials. It clearly describes girls dying of natural causes during an epidemic, not being tortured and killed. Dorothy stated that "within one week and a half five girls died," and Katherine also used the verb "died." They both described an elaborate ruse constructed to hide these deaths from their mistress, bringing food to the already dead girls to pretend they were still alive, and waiting until after Elizabeth had traveled back to Sárvár to move the bodies out of the house without her knowledge.

The story was, on the face of it, plausible. The Countess was not the only one whose nerves were fraying that autumn. Her entire household had been under immense strain. Servants witnessed villagers coming to blows and locals haranguing the pastor; one of Thurzo's men had shown up on their doorstep, drunkenly brandishing his sword. In the midst of such tumult, if five girls *had* died under Dorothy's care, the healer may have panicked and tried to hide the fact from her mistress.

The wheat storage pits (*verem*) mentioned by all three women were similar to root cellars; lined with bricks and plaster, they were cool, dark places to store either grain or seeds. It was customary for bodies to be kept in cool, dark places, sometimes on ice, until a funeral could be arranged. Bodies were usually laid out in cellars, but if a cellar was full, it would not be odd to use a wheat storage pit for this purpose.

It is curious that there should be exactly five corpses in this anecdote. Five corpses were exactly what Thurzo had hoped to find when he stormed into Elizabeth's manor. Certainly, five girls could have died in October and another five could have *almost* died in December. But Thurzo's retainers garbled and conflated many other facts in an attempt to help their master; it would not be surprising if, believing there had to be five corpses, the interrogators had tortured their charges into admitting such.

None of these bodies, however, were ever recovered. The grain storage pits would have been easy to locate and in three months' time, any remains would not have disintegrated. The servants did not admit to having moved the bodies elsewhere, and there were no recent graves in the local churchyards. How had five bodies completely disappeared? Finding them would have bolstered Thurzo's case. Yet the other Čachtice servants said to be involved—Bulia, Barbara, and Katus—were never questioned. There seem to have been no further efforts to discover these deceased girls' names or final resting places.

The only thing the interrogators managed to do was get the servants to turn on one another. The washerwoman did her best to save herself. She had not willingly participated in any secret burials. It was all the healer Dorothy's fault: Dorothy had given the orders and even after she left town, her best friend Katus remained, supervising and watching. Katherine even accused Dorothy of one other dreadful deed: "And Mrs. Dorko buried one [body] herself under the sewer, who was then pulled out by the dogs from there, and also Mr. Zrinyi's servants saw this."

If this incident actually happened, it would have had to occur in October, when Elizabeth's daughter Anna was visiting with her husband.

The washerwoman was tortured last, so the other servants could not be made to confirm her story. Zrinyi's servants, though, were said to be eyewitnesses, and surely they would remember seeing or hearing about the manor dogs dragging around a girl's decomposing body. The dozens of Čachtice locals employed in the manor house should have heard mention of such a dramatic event too. This was exactly the sort of story that should have set tongues wagging; it was every bit as dramatic as the various tales of Miss Modl's supposed mistreatment. Yet this account never made its way into the local gossip, never wound its way into Ponikenus's fiery sermons, and was never mentioned again in any official account.

Bewildered and in pain, Katherine might have grasped for, or had suggested to her, a common enough trope. True-crime broadsheets and pamphlets loved to illustrate the moment a murderer was unmasked; many of these woodcuts portrayed dogs uncovering hastily buried bodies. Much of what the servants confessed to echoed recent news stories and well-known folklore. Throughout the proceedings, the interrogators were less concerned with gathering names of potential witnesses or victims and more interested in hearing tales of detective dogs and child-beating bogeymen.

The three men seem to have enjoyed, above all else, witchcraft narratives. The Sárvár administrator Stephen Vaghy had accused the Countess of practicing witchcraft, stating that she possessed a pretzel-like cake, into the center of which she placed a communion host, which she then used as a sort of enchanted mirror to spy on her enemies—the king, Thurzo, and a local judge—and pray for hours that they would not cause her harm. Rumors and even charges of witchcraft had previously been leveled against many foreign women of high rank, including duchesses, a princess, and even three English queens. In Royal Hungary, one of Elizabeth's aunts and her mother-in-law had also been accused in their lifetimes. Other aristocrats had specifically been suspected of communing with the dead or spying on their rivals through supernatural means. One of Thurzo's own relatives had been publicly accused of talking to angels via a crystal. So Vaghy's tale of a supernatural spying device was not without precedent. At the end of his torture session, the teenage boy

THE SERVANTS' TRIAL

Ficzko was made to confirm it: Yes, his mistress would pray for hours before a pretzel with a mirror in the middle.

Immediately after that, Ficzko also corroborated one of Ponikenus's stories about the Mistress of Myjava attempting to murder the king, Thurzo, and Megyery with two enchanted cakes made from Elizabeth's bathwater. The assassination attempt was foiled when the men all got a stomachache from eating the first cake; they were so suspicious that the Mistress decided not to bake the second cake that would have finished them off. This account, though, is easy enough to disprove: While Thurzo may have dined at Elizabeth's, and Megyery most certainly did in the course of conducting estate business, the king never did; in fact, Matthias II had never set foot on any of Elizabeth's estates.

But Ficzko had been forced to accuse the Mistress of Myjava nonetheless. As Mayor Johannes Junius explained to his daughter: "One has to denounce other people, even if one knows nothing at all about them, as I have had to do." There is evidence of the servants resisting doing so, instead blaming the dead or absent. Ficzko, for example, at first blamed the dead "old woman" Anna Darvulia and a mysterious figure called "Ironhead Steve" who had since left and gone "beyond the Danube" and so would be unable to be found. Two of the women also blamed the dead Darvulia for the murders.

Other times, those being tortured blamed their fellow defendants: They knew they were all past saving. And sometimes, in a show of justified rage, spite, or defiance, they cleverly turned on their accusers. Ficzko seems to have said only the bare minimum against the Mistress of Myjava. In contrast, he was much more loquacious when speaking out against a fellow servant who had given evidence against him and the others. Helen, the widow of "the bald coachman," had backed Ponikenus's tales of supernatural assassination attempts, claiming:

> When she served there, more than thirty girls were killed by multiple tortures owing to the Lady Nadasdy and her helpers . . . The Lady Nadasdy was very skilled in magic and sorcerer's crafts . . . With certain incantations and charms she made a treacherous attack on the life of His Royal Majesty, our merciful Lord, and the Lord Palatine,

as well as Emery Megyery and others, by murmuring certain cursing formulas.

Perhaps Ficzko, then, felt less compunction blaming this Helen as one of the prime abusers and murderers at the finishing school. He said Helen pricked girls with needles, burned them with irons, and beat them up to ten times a day. But Ficzko's testimony about Helen's cruelty would be completely disregarded, and the widow was not subjected to additional interrogation or charged.

If the coachman's widow managed to escape further scrutiny, others were not so lucky. The legends and lore surrounding Elizabeth always spotlight her as the mastermind and prime agent of the murders, assisted by a few loyal servants. What is so often overlooked is how many other women—especially noblewomen—ended up entangled in the case.

Thurzo may have intended to prosecute only Elizabeth and her closest confidantes, but the interrogators assumed a murderous satanic kidnapping ring was a group effort and conducted their interrogations accordingly. The servants named thirteen other people who helped Elizabeth "recruit and lure" girls to court. One was a man, Elizabeth's stablemaster, but the other twelve were women. One accomplice is easily identifiable: Lady Drugeth of Humenne was Elizabeth's younger daughter, Kate. Others are nearly impossible to track—"the Slovak woman in Sárvár," for example, or three different Mrs. Szabos, all of whom share a married name as common as Smith or Brown might be in the United States today. The alleged accomplices who are more easily identifiable were Sárvár noblewomen whose families had long histories of service to the Nadasdy family. They were accused of recruiting victims, accused even of sacrificing their own daughters. They, too, were not interrogated or called to testify.

The servants were judged by a tribunal of twenty men (although only sixteen of them signed the final ruling; it's unclear if the others were merely absent when the verdict was read or if they did not attend at all). Alongside the servants' confessions, the tribunal reviewed testimony from thirteen people, all from Čachtice. The first nine witnesses, all low-ranking men, had witnessed Thurzo's display of Doricza's corpse.

They all testified to having seen the body taken out of Elizabeth's manor house in a cart and to there being marks upon her flesh. Some of the men also testified to having seen the peasant Anna's injured back and mangled hand.

For the first time, the testimony of women was included as well—three of Elizabeth's female servants were deposed. The young servant girl Susanna was the first to testify, sharing what she knew "from hearsay"—a tale of one of the Countess's administrators discovering a signed list of 650 victims. This detail seems to have been borrowed straight from a popular true-crime story; the press was full of sensational accounts of a German serial killer who kept a diary listing the names of each of his 964 victims. Susanna was followed by a widowed servant named Sara, who testified to knowing of eighty deaths, having heard that number from the warden of Sárvár. Next came Helen, widow of the bald coachman, with her accusations of black magic at the court. The last to testify was a local noblewoman named Anna, widow of Stephen Gonczy, who claimed that her ten-year-old daughter died while at Elizabeth's court: "When she wanted to see her daughter, they didn't let her in, causing her the utmost pain." Although she never saw her daughter in her final days, the Widow Gonczy was certain the girl had not died of natural causes. This is the first instance of a family member directly accusing the Countess of murder and one of only three verified deaths, along with that of the servant Doricza and Helen Hernath's daughter. The other two deaths were the result of illness, and this one may have been as well: The mother's mention of being turned away is highly suggestive of a quarantine.

On January 7, 1611, a mere five days after the proceedings began, the tribunal pronounced their judgment. Their written declaration begins with praise of Thurzo, and then rewrites his raid of Elizabeth's manor home, placing Megyery and both of the Countess's sons-in-law on site. (The men had not been near Čachtice at the time, although they had sent representatives in their stead to make sure Thurzo did not overreach and seize the family property.) The tribunal stated that Thurzo found the dead body of the maid Doricza at the very entrance of the manor, and seeing the body right there gave the palatine cause to enter the Countess's manor to arrest her. And there is the mention of two badly injured girls, although all of the witnesses testified to there being just one—Anna of the mangled hand. The tribunal also seems to have reviewed the summaries of the torture sessions rather quickly or hardly at all, mixing up Ficzko's testimony with those of Helena Jo and Dorothy.

Nevertheless, the nanny Helena Jo and healer Dorothy were determined to be the most guilty, and the severity of their sentence reflected this: "All the fingers of their hands which they steeped in Christian blood and which were the instruments of murder shall be torn out by the executioner with iron tongs, after which they shall be placed alive on the fire." Ficzko, on account of his young age, was sentenced to be beheaded first, and then have his dead body burned.

It was only the washerwoman Katherine who was shown mercy, at least temporarily: "She shall be kept in close confinement until her guilt may be determined." She had been the one most willing to elaborate for her torturers, giving them a very detailed story about dead girls made to seem alive and dogs dragging around a corpse. Her connection to the town's pastor may have also been what saved her: The Shoemaker of Sárvár, Michael Zvonarics, still led the ruling council of Lutheran clergy. Katherine was friends with Zvonarics's mother, another castle employee; Zvonarics's mother had helped Katherine secure her position as washerwoman. A tribunal of devout Lutherans may have been reluctant to publicly execute a woman with ties to an esteemed pastor's family. Katherine is not heard from again in the records; it's unclear if she died in jail or was later discreetly released.

Eyewitnesses in ongoing criminal cases were not supposed to be executed. A few decades earlier, when an eighty-one-year-old former artillery commander had been accused of witchcraft, he had petitioned to keep all witnesses alive in prison at his own expense so they could be cross-examined in court. They were burned instead. But the man took his complaint all the way to the imperial court in Vienna, which issued a ruling criticizing the use of torture and the execution of potential witnesses. This admonition, however, did not deter Thurzo.

The kindling was piled high in the cobblestone town square next to a hurriedly assembled scaffold. There's no mention of how Ficzko, Helena Jo, and Dorothy Szentes met their fates—pleading and shrieking or silent and stoic. Or maybe barely conscious: Some defendants were so broken that they had to be laid on the block or tied upright to the pyre. Even in these cases, defendants were sometimes forced awake. The tribunal said they wanted the executions to be a deterrent to others, a show of the palatine's power, and so the gorier and more horrific the better.

Two weeks later, the villagers of Bytča were forced to witness yet another execution. The Mistress of Myjava, under torture, had confessed only to the most tangential connection to the case, to having sent girls to deliver cheese to Čachtice who later ended up dead. What doomed her was Pastor Ponikenus's accusations of murderous spells and magical cakes, confirmed in part by Ficzko's coerced confession. There seems, however, not to even have been the pretense of a trial. At least no records of such have survived. What has survived is a brief record of her end: "On January 24, the Mistress of Myjava was burned to death in the village square of Bytča as a witch."

CHAPTER 12

Her Day in Court

Twelve-year-old Paul Nadasdy was told the nanny who had slept outside his door every night, who had cuddled him when he was scared and smoothed his hot head when he was feverish, the woman who had helped raise him, was a demonic killer. He had to have been shaken, even as Pastor Zvonarics celebrated the boy's narrow escape from the Devil's clutches.

At night, when the boy closed his eyes after his prayers, did he ever envision his former nanny having each of her fingers ripped out and then screaming as the flames crackled higher? Or did he replay the many scenes of eternal damnation that surely awaited him if he dared mourn her? Paul could not call for his mother, as a boy might want to do in such distressing circumstances, nor even go to visit her in her prison in Čachtice without the permission of Red Megyery. He was also told that his mother had participated in the gruesome torture and murder of hundreds, that she had cannibalized corpses, and that his sister Kate had helped procure one of the victims. Young Count Paul Nadasdy had to be terrified, traumatized, and now even further isolated from any familial support.

His guardian Megyery had him write a letter to his mother's prosecutor, thanking the palatine for his handling of the case. In the even and neat handwriting his mother had helped him practice, Paul expressed his gratitude to Thurzo for the "Lordship's goodwill toward me and my sisters." Paul was allowed to take issue with the manner of his mother's unusual and unlawful arrest: "The writ of summons should have been made earlier." He agreed, however, that a trial "is not necessary, as my poor mother's present punishment is even more bitter than death, let alone that in the future her life could be taken by execution" if a court found her guilty. He (or his guardian Megyery) preferred to have her remain imprisoned, with the family lands divided among the three children. The boy agreed to help Thurzo and make sure that "I do not harm Your Lordship somehow in His Majesty's eyes with my petition, as we understood this intention from Your Lordship's letter (which we keep secret)." The palatine was desperate to make sure Paul Nadasdy did not petition the king on his mother's behalf. He may have convinced the boy that he was acting in his best interests, but he was really most worried about his own—Thurzo had drawn the ire of King Matthias II with his handling of the case.

Thurzo had waited to notify King Matthias II of both the investigation into and arrest of Elizabeth until after her servants had been tried and executed. Thurzo had claimed at the start of his investigation that he was acting "by the will of said Royal Majesty," a claim parroted by his tribunal in Bytča. But the Austrian Archives, bursting with painfully long reports on the most inconsequential of matters, have no records of any such orders, and King Matthias seemed to be hearing of the matter for the first time.

In a letter written one week after the servants' executions, January 14, 1611, the king writes to Thurzo, responding to a missive that has since been lost. But based on his response, it is clear that Thurzo has been highly selective in his reporting of events. For example, the king is led to believe that Elizabeth was found to have killed "more than 300 innocent virgins and women." It is unclear how Thurzo settled on that number, when fifty victims, the highest number claimed by one of her servants, was sufficiently horrific. Thurzo presumably did not mention that only one body had been found and that so far there was only a single direct allegation made by a family member, the mother of the ten-year-old Gonczy girl.

As for the manner of these three hundred women and girls' deaths, the king had been told that "their bodies [were] mutilated, burned with hot irons, their flesh ripped out, roasted on the fire, and this roasted flesh then allowed to be served." The detail about cannibal feasts came from Ponikenus's letter. Other testimony, no matter how dubiously it had been coerced, was still a matter of public record; in contrast, this information was only found in private correspondence.

The king was sufficiently horrified, but he also seemed unwilling to accept Thurzo's claims at face value. He was encouraged in this by Elizabeth herself, who was playing a very active role in her own defense. The canonical legend has the Countess locked away, walled up, even, in a tower. This was a fate some of her female contemporaries suffered, but Elizabeth remained under a sort of glorified house arrest. Čachtice was a working castle, and her days would not have been entirely quiet ones: whinnies from the large stables, shouts of drilling soldiers, constant chatter of the maids and squires in the many kitchens and warehouses. She remained free to entertain visitors, write and receive letters, and interact with the dozens of servants and soldiers in residence. She met and strategized with friends and family members, asking her newest, charming son-in-law to manage one of her properties in the northeast of Royal Hungary for her; Drugeth promised to use the income to help pay for her upkeep and defense. Unbowed and undeterred, even after learning the horror of what her associates and friends had endured, Elizabeth undertook a letter-writing campaign and used her network to try to force her case to go to trial. She wanted her day in court. And she very nearly got it.

. . .

King Matthias, as he learned more details about Elizabeth's arrest, chastised Thurzo: All proceedings against the Countess should have been carefully conducted "in accordance with the law." With news of the Countess's crimes "becom[ing] so widely known," the king wanted her to be properly tried and punished. He commanded that, within fifteen days, Elizabeth be issued a summons for her or one of her representatives to appear before the court. He wanted a copy of the testimony collected so far sent to the kingdom's court chamber, and he demanded the "names and circumstances of the deaths" of the alleged victims. He also, undercutting Thurzo, wanted additional testimonies to be collected, and so ordered the two royal notaries involved in the case to go back out and collect another round of depositions.

Thurzo, of course, could not allow this to happen. He would not be able to provide the "names and circumstances of the deaths" of three hundred girls. And should Elizabeth appear in court, with witnesses of her own, it might come out that when Thurzo forced his way into her home, she had not been actively killing her servant Doricza, but eating dinner. He might be the one to end up on trial. And so, in all of the correspondence that followed, Thurzo hedged, prevaricated, delayed, and even outright defied his sovereign to keep Elizabeth from appearing in court.

Many Bathory scholars and enthusiasts have long defended Thurzo, positing that he must have been, however clumsily, just trying to help. The greedy King Matthias II wished to avoid paying back the $1.5 million he still owed the Countess and hoped to seize some of the Countess's lands for himself; Thurzo's delays were his way to keep his deathbed promise to Francis Nadasdy to protect his children. Thurzo wished to spare the children from public shame and from the loss of their lands, so he had Elizabeth quietly imprisoned. For her own good.

Yet King Matthias remarked that, in the month since her arrest, news of the Countess's alleged crimes had "become so widely known." The case was already quite public. Thurzo's investigation, dragged out over the past year, had done much to seed the rumors. And the longer Thurzo delayed Elizabeth's trial, the more petitions before Parliament there would be, the more witness interviews—in short, the more public attention. In the absence of a court case and a clear verdict, conspiracy theories flourished.

Further, the king learned very quickly that Elizabeth had given away her lands in her will and there was very little property he might seize. He was still hopeful that there might be some way to profit from the situation, some property unaccounted for in her will. Thurzo wrote to Megyery and Elizabeth's sons-in-law, informing them that their deal was in danger of collapsing. Paul and his sisters were further terrorized with threats that their mother, if she were publicly tried, might not be fully exonerated like Doczy but instead brutally executed. While this was a possibility, in most cases involving high-ranking aristocrats, especially women, death sentences were commuted or a pardon was issued. It was the land that everyone was most worried about, land that might end up seized by the imperial crown, no matter how careful Elizabeth thought she had been in preparing her will.

The king's demand that Elizabeth be granted a trial became a steady drumbeat throughout 1611. In February, King Matthias sternly chastised his palatine again: "Nothing precludes or should prevent said woman from appearing in court . . . We ask firmly that you handle this Nadasdy complaint no differently [than others] and that you proceed according to the law . . . We expect your loyal and immediate response." When, in March, the king had not yet received a response, he wrote to Thurzo that he was instructing the Hungarian Court Chamber to begin reviewing the case.

Thurzo finally replied, full of apologies—he had been busy, he had somehow only received the king's orders after the court had already been sent home. But Thurzo still would not follow orders to turn over documents so the trial might begin. Instead, he assured the king of Elizabeth's guilt: "There is no risk that complaints about her innocence will reach the ears of Your Benevolent Majesty." The palatine had consulted with lawyers and the Council of Lords, and all were in agreement that Elizabeth could remain imprisoned.

In April, the king again requested that proper procedure be followed. Thurzo apologized, promised to pick up the pace, but somehow, it managed to be one thing after the other. The royal notaries took an exceedingly long time to collect additional testimonies, and by the time Thurzo had them in hand (the fourth set of depositions was submitted at the end of July, the fifth not until the middle of December), Elizabeth had been imprisoned for nearly a year.

While Elizabeth's right to due process was being debated, there was an imperial effort in progress to isolate her young nephew Gabriel. Even after the signing of the latest treaty between the two nations, the prince had, rather sensibly, been wary of the Hapsburgs. He had sent his envoys to the Turks—the damned Turks—asking whether, should Transylvania be invaded by the Hapsburgs, they would send military support. The fledgling principality had to do whatever it could to protect its very existence.

At this precipitous moment, a mysterious letter was intercepted in Constantinople. The Hapsburgs released its contents: It was a declaration by Gabriel Bathory that he planned to hand all of Transylvania over to the Turks. The prince's representatives, though, pushed back forcefully. They insisted this was a "fake letter," a skillful forgery "written in such a way as to pretend Gabriel had written it himself." The Hapsburgs declared the letter was genuine, proof that the prince had betrayed his own people. Transylvanians, however, had been warned before that their leader was a secret Muslim—the Hapsburgs had leveled this same charge against their beloved Bocskai. Gabriel's subjects remained loyal. When subterfuge failed, the Hapsburgs tried force.

Just as Gabriel had long feared, an army from Royal Hungary invaded Transylvania, seeking to overthrow and execute him. The Hapsburgs justified their incursion to the rest of Europe with creative, and circular, logic. That the prince had asked for help in case of an invasion meant he deserved to be invaded: "He, before our party had any intention of wanting to enter Transylvania, had already completely submitted himself to the Turks, and therefore he could not or should not be favored by any Christian."

Elizabeth's nephew was now under siege, and in a painful and public betrayal, her newest son-in-law had ridden out with the invading army. The ever-restless George Drugeth was now a commander in Transylvania, with hopes of being appointed Gabriel's replacement. Drugeth seemed insatiable. He not only pushed for the crown of Transylvania, he pushed Elizabeth for more of her land, seeking to control valuable trade routes that ran through the eastern part of the country. At one point Elizabeth became alarmed that Drugeth had designs on her gold and jewels. When her older daughter Anna visited, Elizabeth had her head down to the manor house afterward. There, seemingly on her mother's instructions, Anna had the door of the treasury forced open and spirited away most of its valuables. Drugeth was infuriated; he, along with his newest ally Red

Megyery, threatened criminal prosecution. But Elizabeth's jewels—her diamonds, sapphires, rubies, emeralds, turquoise and pearls; her many pendants, cuffs, and rings—remained, for the time being, beyond their grasp.

. . .

The handling of Elizabeth Bathory's case was not the only thing Thurzo and King Matthias disagreed about. Thurzo thought the invasion of Transylvania a mistake. Even though he and King Matthias had long been united in their aim to remove Prince Gabriel Bathory from power, they were at odds over how to best accomplish this. Thurzo loathed the idea of Hungarians fighting against one another. Worse, most of the army's commanders, including Drugeth, were Catholic. The Lutheran palatine could easily see how, should the invasion succeed, a Catholic ruler in Transylvania working with the Catholic Hapsburgs in Royal Hungary would doom his hopes for a unified Protestant Hungary. They might even doom Thurzo's own political career.

One of the king's top German advisers wrote that Matthias was "not a little annoyed" at his palatine's reactions and questioned Thurzo's loyalty to the fatherland. In August, when Thurzo again protested to King Matthias, the king snapped back: "Bathory's wicked and destructive intent and practices, [his] tyrannical mind and clearly hostile Turkish spirit . . . should not be protected and fostered under the cloak and pretext of religion." In an unpublished part of the letter, the king ordered Thurzo not to dare try to recall the army from Transylvania.

On September 8, 1611, a declaration by the king was read aloud to the assembled county council of Vas County, where either Paul Nadasdy and his guardian Red Megyery or their representative sat in attendance. Prince Gabriel Bathory was formally declared an enemy of Royal Hungary. The subtext was clear: Any open support for Elizabeth, the county's former lord-lieutenant, would now be construed as treason.

In a head-spinning about-face, just weeks later, though, the king announced that Gabriel Bathory was the kingdom's friend. All hostilities had ceased and Royal Hungary and Transylvania were entering into peace negotiations instead. What the king did not announce: The invasion of Transylvania had been a resounding failure. Prince Gabriel had managed to rout the Royal Hungarian army. Their path home obstructed by unfamiliar mountains, the army wandered lost for ten long days, forced to eat their horses to stay alive. The army finally made it back to Royal Hungary with less than half its men, its leaders the subject of widespread ridicule. For the second time in five years, the Hapsburgs were forced to admit defeat in the face of a smaller, less-equipped foe.

At the beginning of 1612, mad, isolated Emperor Rudolf met his Maker. King Matthias, newly married to his Hapsburg first cousin, inherited his older brother's throne, becoming Holy Roman Emperor. Gabriel Bathory had managed to repulse Matthias once, but could not be assured of managing to do so again, especially now that the new emperor had even more resources at his disposal. And the prince had endured a series of misfortunes, some self-inflicted, some secretly engineered. He began fighting with his allies in Wallachia and Moldavia. The Turks, his bulwark against Hapsburg interference, seemed increasingly annoyed with Gabriel after a series of late tax payments and diplomatic snafus. Increasingly isolated, nervous about Transylvania's ability to defend itself against the entire Holy Roman Empire, Gabriel finally agreed to the very thing the Hapsburgs had long been pressuring him for: a secret alliance against the Turks.

. . .

By the summer of 1612, Elizabeth learned that a deal was in the works to grant her long-desired day in court, or even an outright release. With Transylvania and Royal Hungary now allies, Elizabeth was no longer a potential traitor. Cousin Sigmund had already been released from his Prague Castle jail, and Elizabeth hoped her nephew could help petition for her freedom too.

In December 1612, the Hungarian Court Chamber reached out to Emperor Matthias, wanting to know "whether this widow should be prosecuted . . . or if her case should be silently neglected." There were still potential charges of serial murder hanging over the Countess, but her alleged body count was no longer six hundred, or even one hundred: The chamber referred instead to the alleged murders of "*several* decent women and innocent girls." The chamber began planning to hold a trial when Parliament convened early that next year, and they requested they be given all related case documents fifteen days beforehand. In January 1613, King Matthias and Thurzo began making preparation for Elizabeth's trial.

After her arrest, Elizabeth had stubbornly refused to confess; she told the pastors that she placed "her trust in her [legal] case" instead. Now it seemed as if her faith in the legal system had finally paid off. The king even contemplated having the Countess released in advance of the trial, musing in writing "whether she should be kept imprisoned or if this is rather unsuitable, whether she should be summoned, freed from the prison with a sufficient bail?" He reminded Thurzo—twice—that the circumstances of her case were highly unusual, as the Countess had been "incarcerated after not being legally summoned, nor even convicted."

Emperor Matthias called in his legal experts. He no longer seemed to entertain any hope of seizing any of the Nadasdy properties, so Megyery and Elizabeth's sons-in-law had little to fear. But he was eyeing "her own ancient possessions," the many Bathory family castles Elizabeth had inherited from her own parents and brother. A likely outcome would be the imperial court pressuring Elizabeth to trade one or more of these properties for her freedom. The emperor also succeeded in getting Thurzo to turn over all of the documents related to the case—the depositions from his initial investigation, the summaries of the servants' interrogations, the third round of testimony featuring the thirteen witnesses from Čachtice. The compiled copies made to fulfill the king's request are the ones now available to researchers in the Hungarian National Archives.

Among these files were the last two rounds of depositions collected at Emperor Matthias's insistence. The fourth round of depositions seem especially overwhelming upon first glance, with 225 people offering testimony. This time the royal notary traveled outside of Čachtice to many of the nearby villages: Kostol'any, Vrbové, and Beckov. He even interviewed some women. However, upon closer examination, these depositions are just as problematic as the earlier ones. Some witnesses were interviewed in groups, all of their testimony lumped together. One group of 10 men is recorded as all saying they know nothing, then another 10, and another, and yet another. Out of 225 witnesses, well over 80 percent did not testify against the Countess. Most seemed to have no specific knowledge of or information about the case.

Pastor Ponikenus testified, but while under oath his accusations were considerably more subdued. There was no mention of cannibalism and supernatural assassination attempts, or of phantom cats and dogs. He recounted having seen Thurzo's display of the dead girl after Elizabeth's arrest. He told how the Countess had once buried someone in Podolie without his permission. The pastor also reported that a servant told him that he had spied on girls being treated and saw that they were lying down naked surrounded by candles, possible evidence of a satanic ritual. His testimony begs the question of why an adult male servant was peeping at a naked prepubescent girl to begin with, but also offers evidence of another healing practice—cupping, used since the time of Hippocrates to balance the humors. Glass cups were suctioned to the body to draw out excess humors, the suction created by exhausting the air inside the glass with burning candles.

The fifth set of depositions, collected in the western counties around Sárvár, took Moses Cziraky almost a full year to complete, but he was only able to secure twelve additional testimonies. Another family member testified that her daughter died at Elizabeth's finishing school, although she was unsure of the cause. That brought the number of confirmed deceased girls to 6, but in all of these cases it was not clear what had caused their deaths. Two of Elizabeth's court officials, Jacob Szilvasy and Benedict Deseo, gave some of the most incriminating testimony, but at this point they themselves were under suspicion, having been mentioned in the servants' interrogations as among those complicit in covering up the Countess's atrocities. Szilvasy, the supposed holder of the list of 650 victims, recounted 11 deaths that had taken place throughout the years. Deseo repeated nearly every rumor that had been mentioned so far, and also delivered an additional, sensationally gruesome charge, one that combined the legend of Miss Modl with Ponikenus's charges of cannibalism: "The Lady cut with a knife a lot of flesh from the backside of a young married woman named Modl, and she had that poor woman eat it raw, and she finally died in Sárvár after a lot of torture."

HER DAY IN COURT

The notaries still did not collect testimony from any of the reported survivors: Anna of the mangled hand; the sick girls at Čachtice manor and the doctor who examined them; a peasant woman called Chiglei; or even the servant from Elizabeth's inner circle who had been spared, the washerwoman Katherine. There were still no interviews of the noble families of supposed victims—the Nagyvathys, the Sittkeys, the Zichys, the Szells—to confirm whether any of their daughters had indeed died.

But there was, for the first time, some attempt made to track down the Countess's accomplices, the noblewomen who recruited and trafficked her supposed victims. Arguably the most fascinating of these alleged accomplices is Lady Helen Hernath, the twice-widowed noblewoman who gave a deposition in Elizabeth's defense at the Vas County court, stating that she had been present when her daughter Susanna had died at Sárvár, had personally prepared her daughter's body for burial, and had seen no signs of foul play. As such, Helen Hernath was an important witness who could speak on Elizabeth's behalf. Was her name suggested to the servants during their torture? The nanny Helena Jo and the healer Dorothy both referred to her, claiming that she had enticed several women and girls to Elizabeth's court "although she knew that they would be killed."

Lady Helen Hernath was the third person interviewed in the very last round of testimony. No mention was made of her earlier deposition exonerating Elizabeth from harming her daughter, although that was a matter of public record. Lady Helen testified to having seen Elizabeth punish girls with beatings, but also to witnessing acts that corresponded with medical treatments: washing girls with nettles, for example, or sticking their shoulders with pins. She mentioned the death of one girl, Kate Fekete, on the estate of Keresztúr; she also was clear that Miss Modl had not been killed, just flogged and chained.

This round of depositions also included the testimony of forty-five-year-old Lady Anna Velikey, another noblewoman who was employed at the finishing school. She had been named by the washerwoman Katherine as someone who brought two victims to her mistress. Lady Anna would not admit that there was any torture at Elizabeth's court, saying she had only ever seen girls whipped or with bruised faces. She did relay an anecdote that seemed to be designed as a quiet show of defiance. Lady Anna recounted a time when she questioned her mistress about the "many bad and horrible things [that] are said about you far and wide." In response to this, the Countess said of her accusers, "Those whores were lying." This was one way for Elizabeth, unable to testify herself, to have her denial entered into the record. Lady Anna, though, soon found herself accused by subsequent witnesses of having lured girls to Elizabeth's court for nefarious purposes, even of helping to kill the niece of another employee.

This points to the intimate nature of the accusations. In legend, Elizabeth killed legions of anonymous, interchangeable peasant girls; in reality, she was said to be dispatching the daughters of old family friends and loyal retainers, recruiting her victims from among her confidantes and neighbors. Her trial would have to untangle a complex web of loyalties and resentments and feature family members testifying against one another. It promised to be a salacious event.

When Parliament finally did convene, expecting they would be trying Countess Elizabeth Bathory in open court, Ponikenus had prepared a poem in clumsy Latin for the event. He praised both Thurzo and Emperor Matthias as the "parents" of Hungary and, anticipating a guilty verdict, thanked them in advance for their help in uncovering Satan's minions among them: "Now that God himself scatters the conspirators . . . the golden nation reigns."

But despite the time and expense put into gathering more testimonies, the land surveys and consultations and careful preparations, even the attempts to sway the jury, no trial commenced.

CHAPTER 13

The Last Bathory

In the end, it would not be Thurzo, the king, or even her scheming family who would wreck Elizabeth's hopes for a public trial. It was an unlikely and (seemingly) unobtrusive character, one of Prince Gabriel's advisers. Gabriel Bethlen was the prince's senior by eight years, although he appeared much older, with his stiff gait, heavy beard, and "untidy mop of hair." Official contemporary portraits manage to make Bethlen presentable, but certainly never attractive. In council meetings, next to Prince Gabriel, whom allies and enemies alike found distractingly handsome, or even alongside the many elegantly attired courtiers and charismatic military commanders, Bethlen would have been easy to overlook. He had one gift, though, that would ultimately help lift him out of obscurity—his piercing dark eyes. No detail escaped them.

The tendency of others to overlook him played perfectly into his hands. It was Bethlen who had left behind a letter that compromised Bocskai and forced him into open rebellion against the Hapsburg emperor. It was Bethlen who failed to show up at a few key battles in time to help Prince Gabriel, and it was Bethlen who strained Gabriel's relationship with the Ottoman Turks by making sure the annual tax payment was sent late. Bethlen was at the center of all manner of curious coincidences. When he decided something was the proper course of action, he pursued

Gabriel Bethlen in a 1620 engraving

it doggedly, no matter the cost. He had served under three Bathory princes, but now he decided that the proper course of action was for him to become prince himself.

Sometime in 1611, Bethlen turned traitor, becoming an informant and spy for the Turks. When Prince Gabriel and the Hapsburgs formalized their secret alliance, Bethlen wrote to the Ottomans with the news, begging them to overthrow Prince Gabriel and install him on the throne instead. In early September 1612, after some of his correspondence with the Turks was intercepted, Bethlen fled to Ottoman territory.

Gabriel wrote to Thurzo: "[Bethlen] has long been plotting against us." The prince and the palatine found themselves, for once, united against a shared adversary. In his postscript, Gabriel reported that he had just received a missive from his disgraced advisor "begging for mercy." He closed on an optimistic note, "We believe that God will grant us good fortune in all our affairs." To the young prince, so much seemed within his grasp—the ascendence of his family, the reunification of Royal Hungary and Transylvania, the restoration of the Hungary as "the star of Europe."

This should have been the end of Bethlen, a life spent in exile, looking over his shoulder for potential assassins. But for Bethlen the truth was warm wax in his hands, to be prodded and molded. Even given the damning chain of correspondence between him and the Turks, Bethlen recast, reinvented, rewrote; he offered implausible reasons for his flight to Turkish territory, so many that it is a wonder he could keep his stories straight. He seemed, even, to sincerely believe each of the conflicting versions he told.

Each version was tailor-made to appeal to the prejudices of its audience. To George Thurzo, Bethlen denied any dealings with the

Ottomans. "I have not come here [to Turkish territory] to improve my condition in any way," he protested to the palatine. The reason for his flight? A Bathory woman.

Bethlen laid all his troubles at the feet of Kate Torok, a first cousin and key supporter of the prince. She had inherited so much property from her family and her late husbands that she was now the largest landowner in all of Transylvania—she was Elizabeth Bathory's counterpart in the east. Kate Torok's current husband, her third, was a prominent general and war hero who, although he had been actively courted by Thurzo, had stayed loyal to Prince Gabriel.

Bethlen told Thurzo that he had discovered that Kate Torok and Gabriel Bathory were lovers. Kate Torok had demanded that Bethlen be silenced before he told anyone about their affair, and so he had been forced to flee. This tale of an incestuous affair seems crafted to arouse the sympathies of the puritanical Thurzo, who already believed the young prince to be depraved. It would also have delighted Thurzo—perhaps the palatine could now convince Kate Torok's cuckolded husband to join forces against the prince.

In an alternate version of events, Bethlen casts the same Kate Torok not as an adulteress, but as the agent of his salvation. Gabriel Bathory was preparing to eliminate any potential political rivals, but Kate Torok, having a soft spot for Bethlen, warned him of his imminent arrest. And in yet another version of events, Bethlen stated it was not a woman at all, but his own principles that made him flee: He simply disagreed with Gabriel Bathory's policies and could not bear to see the country ruined.

Many years later, Bethlen would concoct a fourth version of events: He had fled Transylvania because Gabriel had raped his wife and Bethlen could not bear the dishonor. This version of events was constructed only after his wife had died. The very detailed account of the supposed assault, as told to a Spanish adventurer, seemed designed to titillate: Bethlen detailed the flimsy nightgown his wife was wearing at the time and how handsome and strong Gabriel was (one snippet: His wife, "a delicate, fragile lady," encounters "a tall, robust young man, with an exceedingly handsome face," in possession "of tremendous strength, [able to] control a horse with just his two knees, and stop a two-horse chariot with a single hand"). Bethlen then claimed that, after he relayed this story to the Ottomans, they were so outraged that they offered to invade Transylvania to avenge his dishonored wife.

Invade they did.

Bethlen wrote most of these letters protesting his innocence at the same time he was traveling from one regional pasha to another, then meeting with the grand vizier, and finally the sultan, to plead his case. At the beginning of October, Bethlen invaded with eighty thousand Turkish troops, the largest Ottoman army to set foot in Transylvania. The Ottoman Turks ordered the Transylvanian nobles to hurriedly assemble for a parliament and, on October 23, 1613, under their watchful eyes, Bethlen was declared prince. One commoner quipped: "Out of fear, they [the nobles] freely elected him."

The Transylvanian Parliament composed a farewell letter to Bathory, firing him from his role. The deposed prince retreated to Castle Várad, a border fortress he knew well, having spent his childhood there, to await reinforcements from Royal Hungary. This Turkish invasion was the first test of the new Hapsburg-Transylvanian pact. Surely Emperor Matthias, after hounding Gabriel for years to join together to fight the Turks, would come to his aid.

Thurzo did send troops, but only a small army of two thousand—enough soldiers to make it clear Gabriel had indeed double-crossed the Ottoman Turks and formed an alliance with Royal Hungary, but not nearly enough to actually be of use. These troops camped close to Várad. After learning of the massive size of the approaching Turkish army, morale was understandably low. Four days after Bethlen's "election" as the new prince, Gabriel was encouraged by two advisers to ride out from the castle to personally inspect the Hungarian troops at the nearby camps to help rally them for the battles ahead. One of these advisers, Andrew Giczy, had been a former contender for the Transylvanian throne himself, and had even recently rebelled against Gabriel. He had begged for, and been generously granted, a pardon. The other was one of Thurzo's men, Nicolas Abaffy, the captain of the reinforcements sent by Royal Hungary.

Gabriel trusted their advice, and so he set out on the afternoon of October 27, 1613, in his light, glass-windowed carriage. He was usually accompanied by at least some of his personal bodyguards, soldiers nicknamed the "blues" due to their distinctive uniforms, but this time he was accompanied only by the repentant Andrew Giczy, two young pages, and his beloved dachshund.

The prince reviewed the troops without incident, and upon his return, sometime between three and four in the afternoon, as the prince's distinctive carriage rattled over the cobblestones toward the gates of the castle, Gabriel became aware of a commotion outside. Horsemen forced the carriage to the side of the road and shots rang out.

Giczy fled from the carriage, presumably to get help. Gabriel was hit by one bullet in his side, but he still managed to jump out of the carriage, followed by his two pages, and run to a nearby willow tree. With his back against the enormous tree, he unsheathed his sword and waited for his attackers. Chronicles record how the prince fought bravely and furiously, but he was set upon by fifty men, led by four hajduk captains he knew well, men he had personally promoted and richly rewarded. Eventually, mortally wounded, he collapsed at the feet of his former friends. Gabriel's body was stripped and then tossed into the shallow waters of the Pece stream. Some chroniclers also related how Gabriel's dachshund survived the fracas and stayed by his master's body, furiously barking and chasing away onlookers. One wrote: "The dog was more faithful than all his friends and supporters."

This version was recorded by contemporaries, but not by eyewitnesses. Another account has surfaced, found among the letters of Thomas Nadasdy, a cousin of Elizabeth's late husband. This was written by an actual eyewitness, albeit a biased one—Abaffy, the leader of the Hungarian reinforcements who helped plot the assassination. According to him, there were no gunshots. The young prince, with his carriage waylaid, managed to draw his sword. But Gabriel didn't exactly die fighting: He was quickly knocked down with calvary lances, trampled by horses, and then, lying on the ground helpless, stabbed with a sword. Gabriel's body was not thrown in a stream, nor guarded by his loyal dog, but simply left overnight in the street, naked.

· · ·

Gabriel's stunned "blue" guards came the next day with an oxcart and took his corpse to a nearby town where it was temporarily buried, before it was dug up by his infantry captain and transported to the Bathory family stronghold of Ecsed.

Although it was the treacherous hajduk captains who struck the fatal blows, they were not the ultimate masterminds of the plot. Many interests converged with the death of the young prince, some of them the same as those entangled with his aunt's case. The main suspect was, of course, Bethlen, who began disseminating counternarratives as soon as Gabriel's death was confirmed, some as creative as those he had told about his flight to Turkish lands. While disavowing any knowledge of the plot and claiming to be horrified by it, he also made sure there were no witnesses left. Giczy, the adviser who had been in the carriage with Gabriel, likely anticipated being rewarded with a position in Bethlen's court. But Giczy had already betrayed a prince twice, and Bethlen did not wait to see if he would try a third time—rather than being promoted, Giczy was executed.

The only known plotter to survive was Abaffy, captain of the reinforcements sent from Royal Hungary. As soon as he was certain Gabriel was dead, Abaffy set out for Vienna via the fastest means possible—the mail coach—to deliver the "good news" to the Hapsburg court. His choice of words is striking: The Hapsburg court saw the death of their new ally as "good" news? Even though one of Emperor Matthias's closest advisers later bragged that he had organized the assassination, Thurzo was suspected of being the plot's mastermind. Abaffy had served under and been given land by Thurzo. And when Abaffy wrote to his patron, he warned Thurzo that the rumor mill thought him responsible.

Abaffy did not escape entirely unscathed; weeks later he wrote that not only had former friends turned against him, he was now facing frequent death threats. A full seven years after Prince Gabriel's death, Abaffy had trouble staying employed, and even Bethlen would not allow the former captain to stay at his court, thinking it was too dangerous: There were simply too many plots against him.

Although Bethlen had assured the Ottoman Turks that Gabriel was wildly unpopular, the reaction to the prince's death shows this was not the case. While there were some who certainly celebrated Gabriel's demise, others compared the fallen prince to a famous Trojan warrior ("Hector of Transylvania") or Alexander the Great, or mourned him as the "guardian and protector of Transylvania." Anonymous eulogies were circulated, listing the prince's accomplishments: his support of the hajduks, his defense of Protestant ministers, his expansion of Transylvanian territory. "Poor Gabriel Bathory," wrote the people of one town, "is mourned by all orders [social classes], even by the women and children . . . Bathory has done countless good deeds for us." Even years after the assassination, one of Bethlen's court historians was forced to admit that rather than being forgotten, Gabriel's "fame has soared higher than Olympus."

Some refused to believe the young prince was truly dead, while others cast him as a holy martyr. At the Bathory family seat of Ecsed, where Elizabeth had spent her childhood, when Prince Gabriel's body was laid out, it was observed to be sweating for several days. A Calvinist minister recounted, "Everyone who was around him witnessed this with their own eyes, and they even wiped the sweat off him many times with a handkerchief." Even Catholic clergy were unsettled by this supposed miracle. One bishop wrote to another that the prince's assassination "is a cause for regret, since his body, a few days after his death, was still sweating profusely, as if he were still alive, and his body was still flexible, as if life had just left it. This sweat is proof of his innocence, crying out for vengeance, for the punishment of the vile murderers who had killed him."

Even the assassins themselves underestimated public opinion. The hajduk captains who had ambushed and killed Gabriel showed up at the Transylvanian Parliament, expecting a reward, but instead they were handed over to the military and executed.

The news would have reached Elizabeth quickly in her quarters in the tower of Čachtice Castle, where she lived in diminished circumstances, certainly, but not entirely cut off from the world, with her chest of deeds and documents, her inkpot and parchment, visited by family and messengers. Prince Gabriel's assassination was a devastating blow. As long as her nephew lived and exercised power, she was a valuable hostage, one whose fate could be negotiated just like that of a castle or vineyard. But now? And it was not just her own circumstances Elizabeth was apprehensive about. The prince's death was devastating for the entire Bathory family. Gabriel was the last direct male heir of both the eastern Somlyó and western Ecsed branches. While Elizabeth's brother had left significant holdings to his sister in his will, the bulk of his estates went to his male heir, Gabriel. Now, given the prince's death, it was Bathory women who would inherit, and need to protect, this considerable property.

In Transylvania, Bethlen was eyed with suspicion, having just spent over a year in foreign exile and then marched in at the head of an infidel army. The Ottomans, not having the appetite for a new lengthy occupation, withdrew shortly after Bethlen was installed on the throne and had sworn to pay their yearly tribute and serve their interests. But the Ottoman army itself, just by virtue of its size, had devastated the principality and "enslaved countless virgins and slaughtered many Hungarian warriors." There was active opposition to the new prince, and he was very short on money. Bethlen identified several estates of strategic importance that would bring in much-needed income. But these estates lay in the hands of three Bathory women: the slain prince's sister, aunt, and cousin.

Gabriel's younger sister, Anna, was his heir; she had her own extensive properties and a sizable fortune, and now she controlled most Bathory estates in the east. Gabriel's aunt Kate Iffiu had been the wife of his top adviser; his cousin Kate Torok was Transylvania's largest landowner. When Bethlen sent three hundred soldiers to capture one of her castles, her much smaller garrison fought back and won. She, and her relatives, were prepared to resist.

Both of the Kates were extraordinarily wealthy new widows, with many potential suitors. Should they remarry men with political ambitions, they could position their new husbands as challengers to Bethlen. Anna Bathory had a young son who might grow up to one day depose Bethlen in revenge. Bethlen's position was tenuous, and the three presented a genuine threat. But as in Royal Hungary, women could not be charged with treason because women were assumed not to be political opponents. As 1613 came to a close, echoing earlier rumor campaigns,

Bethlen charged all three Bathory women with both "incestuous fornication" and "charming witchcraft."

At the beginning of 1614, a head-spinning reversal of fortune occurred at the Transylvanian Parliament. The men who had been hiding out in Royal Hungary under George Thurzo's protection, the men who had attempted to assassinate Prince Gabriel Bathory back in March 1610, were welcomed back with great ceremony. They had all of their titles and lands restored. At the same session, the three Bathory women went on trial. The Parliament usually only heard treason cases. But they deigned to try the women in quick succession for offenses that had, until now, always been left to the lower courts.

The first to be tried was Kate Torok. Despite the same shortcomings found in the case of her cousin Elizabeth, she was found guilty of both incest and witchcraft and sentenced to death and the loss of all of her lands. The death sentence was not carried out, as Kate Torok went on to marry again, but her lands were seized. Gabriel's aunt Kate Iffiu was tried immediately after, for the same crimes, and received a lighter sentence, only having her lands confiscated.

Anna Bathory's trial followed. She was only twenty, married with one young son, and she had not seen her older brother for long stretches of time while he was off on foreign campaigns or away at his court. During the course of her trial, in order to make the allegations of incest match up with Prince Gabriel's known whereabouts, she was accused of seducing her brother when she was just ten years old. The parentage of Anna's one son and heir was also questioned; the same witness declared the baby had been fathered by another man who had since mysteriously disappeared. Anna Bathory's trial was abruptly stopped and no sentence was declared. Why?

In May 1614, at the time Anna Bathory's trial was finishing up, Bethlen was facing a backlash. There was much public sympathy for Anna's deceased brother. Bethlen was criticized for leaving his predecessor unburied, as a pagan might, and his opponents interred Gabriel Bathory with full military honors in his family crypt in Nyírbátor, just outside Ecsed. Accusing the grieving sister of a young murdered prince of incest had seemingly offended the sensibilities of many in Transylvania.

But this groundswell of support for the Bathory family came too late for Elizabeth.

. . .

Elizabeth, now fifty-four, seemed to know she did not have much time left to get her affairs in order. Unable to go to a local court to record a declaration, she had the court come to her. On Saturday, July 31, 1614, two priests trudged up the steep limestone hill in the summer heat and were admitted by the guards to the Countess's private chambers.

The local priests, acting in their capacity as notaries, witnessed the Countess's final decree, her last attempt to protect her family's land. Her son-in-law George Drugeth of Humenne had overstepped yet again, even after his failed attempt to take the crown of Transylvania away from the Bathory family. Now he pushed to take more than his wife Kate's allotted inheritance. One property he had been given to manage during his mother-in-law's imprisonment—to help pay for her defense—he now tried to claim as his own. But Elizabeth was firm in her declaration: "She bequeathed nothing more to Lord George of Humenne." The three-way division of property between the heirs still stood.

Three weeks later, on the evening of Wednesday, August 18, 1614, Elizabeth approached her guard, who reported that she said, "Look how cold my hands are!"

"It's nothing, my lady," he reassured her. "Will you not retire for the night?"

The moon was full that night, its light spilling across the limestone walls, down the precipitous slopes, down into the hollow far below, with its terraced vineyards, thatched roofs, thin wisps of curling smoke. The Countess went to bed under its unblinking eye, praying and singing hymns, placing her pillow under her feet instead of her head.

The next morning she was found dead.

Epilogue

Three prominent Bathorys had been targeted at the same time; now, in the span of less than eighteen months, all three were dead.

Cousin Sigmund, after being released from prison, had died under mysterious circumstances, alone on his Bohemian estates, just six months before Gabriel's spectacular assassination. And now Thurzo's secretary added Elizabeth to that tally, recording the date of her demise in his diary and adding a snide marginal comment. It was a couplet in Latin which, translated, reads:

> Few kings descend to the underworld without slaughter and blood,
> and few tyrants die a dry death.

The secretary's characterization of the Countess as a "tyrant" may have been a criticism of a woman who had usurped political power that was supposed to be wielded by men. The term was also his era's shorthand for a religious opponent; the insult was first leveled at Elizabeth Bathory in 1602, during her clash with the Lutheran pastors, and last deployed by Thurzo's court in Bytča, who condemned her *satanica tyrannide*.

A "dry death" is a bloodless, tranquil one; the same phrasing is used by Shakespeare in *The Tempest*, written during this time: "but I would fain die a dry death." Elizabeth Bathory was not only spared a gory execution, she received a proper funeral. The Countess was not buried immediately, as a common criminal would be, but three months later, as was customary for aristocrats. Her body remained on ice in an underground cellar while her family made the arrangements and their travel plans. On November 25, 1614, her coffin was draped with an expensive black silk cover and brought into the church where she was once denounced. The Countess, accused of conducting quiet Calvinist burials, was given a Lutheran funeral, one that presumably included all of the singing, bell-tolling, and ceremony she eschewed in her lifetime. Afterward, she was "buried in the Čachtice church," most likely in the crypt underneath its floor, the space most commensurate with her rank. If so, Pastor Ponikenus, who never advanced beyond his position as pastor, conducted his subsequent services with the Countess interred directly underneath his feet.

Outside of Thurzo's small circle, there was no mention of Countess Elizabeth Bathory's passing in any surviving letters. Her reputation had been savaged by sermons and whisper campaigns, but now a very curious silence surrounded the entire case. Pastors had decried her secret Calvinist burials, and a witness had even testified that she had desecrated the communion host. Pastors perseverated on other long-ago sins, but published no new sermons denouncing the Countess's heresies.

The Countess had been accused of torturing the girls in her charge—whether 5 or 650. And, just like her mother-in-law, just like other Bathory women—including her niece, an aunt, and a few cousins—the Countess had been accused of witchcraft. She hosted cannibal feasts; she commanded an army of invisible cats and dogs. She was "very skilled in magic and sorcerer's crafts" and tried to use "certain incantations and charms" to kill her king and palatine.

The seventeenth-century public adored sensational "true crime": Accounts of the demonic crimes of witches and the cruelties of accused serial killers sold well and circulated widely. Even Aunt Klara's supposed adulterous crimes had been included in a popular book. Surely a story about an aristocratic, treasonous, child-killing witch would have been a bestseller. Yet there were no poems narrating Elizabeth Bathory's crimes, no broadsides illustrating her cruelties.

EPILOGUE

Perhaps some had the good sense to be embarrassed. The death of their Jezebel did nothing to ease God's wrath: the cold did not relent, their harvests did not improve. There were plenty, too, who remained skeptical of the entire case. A small, strident minority had denounced the Countess, but thousands had refused to join in. Alongside every pastor writing a brimstone sermon and every servant girl passing along a gruesome rumor, someone else had been calling for calm, for cooperation, and for compromise.

Perhaps people had too many other things to worry and write about. Four years after the Countess's death, another anti-Hapsburg revolt began, this one in Bohemia. Fearing, just as Bocskai and his rebels once had, that the Hapsburgs were moving to outlaw the Protestant faith, a group of defiant aristocrats tossed three Catholic officials out the window of Prague Castle. This, the second Defenestration of Prague, plunged most of Europe into the Thirty Years' War, one of the longest and most destructive conflicts in Western history.

Or perhaps their attention had just shifted to another Bathory woman. At the start of the Thirty Years' War, Bethlen was desperate to consolidate his power in Transylvania, but still faced bitter opposition from Gabriel Bathory's former supporters. The slain prince's sister, Anna, was hauled back into court. Bethlen accused her of witchcraft yet again, adding on a charge of murder. When Anna Bathory steadfastly refused to confess, Bethlen had one of her court officials arrested and accused him of being Anna's lover. Anna was interrogated again and again; some claim she was even subjected to torture. Still, she managed to hold out and to negotiate for her freedom, giving up her main estate and most of her jewels.

Just a few years later, in 1621, Bethlen had Anna, that "devil" and "murderous whore," arrested for a third time. This time, he had already decided the outcome of her trial for witchcraft and murder, ordering his underlings to "bring Anna Bathory to trial and, when the verdict is delivered, to kill her . . . the guilty shall be burned." But then, in a bizarre turn of events, Anna's execution was postponed when Bethlen's wife took ill. The sick woman was convinced that Anna (younger, prettier) had somehow bewitched her and possibly her husband. Bethlen's wife insisted that Anna cure her. Anna refused. Bethlen's wife eventually died, and he got busy battling the Hapsburgs, so he agreed to spare Anna Bathory's life. But in exchange, Anna had to give up the crown jewel of the Bathory estates—the family stronghold of Ecsed, the water fortress where Elizabeth had spent her childhood.

Having deprived the Bathory family of its ancestral seat, its gold and valuables, and its good name, Bethlen now had Gabriel Bathory's corpse dug up again. He had called Gabriel an incestuous fornicator, a rapist, and even a vampiric "blood-sucking prince." Now, determined to appease any remaining Bathory resistance, Bethlen funded an elaborate state funeral where the fallen prince was publicly praised as "elegant" and "brave" and always "ready to serve his country and people." One noble wrote in his memoirs that when the coffin was reopened, Bathory's corpse appeared incorrupt: It "did not rot, but was beautiful, as if it had only recently been put there: There was no smell either." In yet another head-spinning reversal, the young prince was rehabilitated, transformed from a drunken lecher to a sober statesman and then, a saint.

Whether her slain brother was seen as a reprobate or a martyr, Anna was, like so many other widows of her era and station, broken and penniless. The new palatine of Royal Hungary took pity on her misfortune, declaring, "The order of this world is a wonder. Her grandfather was one with [i.e., closely related to] King Stephen of Poland, and she in turn with the prince of Transylvania, and now she is almost a beggar, and a wretch too." He gave her a modest manor house and a small country estate so she might live out the rest of her days in some degree of peace and comfort.

Even out in the countryside, Anna Bathory would have heard word of the other accusations of witchcraft, the mass trials, intensifying throughout Europe. In Bamberg, 278 people were executed; in Würzburg, over 600, the youngest victim just seven years old.

Hopefully, far out on a small and not particularly desirable estate, Anna felt, for even a short time, safe. Here there was no one to smell the accusation that still clung to her hair and skirts, an accusation passed down for three generations. *Witch.*

· · ·

EPILOGUE

A witch burning illustrated in a mid-sixteenth-century news pamphlet

Palatine George Thurzo died just two years after Elizabeth, on Christmas Eve of 1616, right after three female healers on his estates were burned at the stake as witches. His widow, the sickly Elizabeth Czobor, assumed his position as lord-lieutenant for some time. But she found herself the target of the same tricks her husband had once employed against other women; she would die an impoverished and broken woman.

The son Thurzo had intrigued and connived to advance would never see his twenty-fifth birthday. Thurzo's many daughters survived, but their father had not done much to make their lives easier. He had seen firsthand what a struggle it was for his wife to learn to read and write as a teenager. His only son was given a world-class education. But for his daughters, while Thurzo spared no expense building an elaborate wedding palace in which to host their nuptials, he would not pay for a tutor. As adults, his daughters all struggled with reading and writing, and they would become only as educated as their own husbands wished them to be.

Elizabeth's older daughter, Anna, died less than a year after her mother, childless. Her younger daughter, Kate, proved hardier. Kate had one son, John Drugeth X, with her daredevil double-crossing husband,

and later a daughter, named Elizabeth in honor of her grandmother. Once widowed, Kate fought for herself and her children fiercely, to try to recapture some of the Bathory family estates. She sent in her own troops, who were not successful, and launched a court battle, which ultimately *was* successful. Her son, John, would even take up residence in Čachtice, the site of his grandmother's imprisonment, for some time.

While Kate was defiant, the youngest Bathory child, Paul, proved pliant, completely under the thumb of Megyery and his circle. And even more unfortunately, in 1616, he suffered a serious head injury after a fall from a horse, a fall so bad that for a time it was even reported that he had died. Afterward, he would suffer from epilepsy.

The following year, when he was just nineteen, the wealthy heir to one of the largest estates in Royal Hungary would marry the daughter of Moses Cziraky, the notary who had collected testimony against his mother. This match, with a family that was much lower-ranking than his, seems inexplicable unless one takes into account Megyery's influence and the friendship between Megyery and his old friend Cziraky.

When his first wife died, rather unexpectedly, a year later, Paul got married again, to a woman who was not only from another much lower-ranking family, but was also close with Megyery. Judith Revay was not an aristocrat herself; she had been a lady-in-waiting in the Batthyanys' neighboring court. Perhaps both marriages were love matches, as his great-aunt Klara's had been, or perhaps Paul simply had no ambition to make a great marriage, as his sisters had done, and docilely accepted whichever candidate Megyery placed in front of him. Paul dutifully ensured his family's survival, producing a male heir, but under him the Nadasdy family lost much of its stature and political influence. He would fail to distinguish himself in any way, except by his staunch Lutheranism.

It was Paul's son, the judge and general Francis Nadasdy III, who would display some of his grandmother's defiant spark. He joined his Zrinyi relations in a plot to overthrow the Hapsburg emperor. If her grandson's rebellion had been successful, it's likely we would still know the name of Elizabeth Bathory, but in a completely different context. She would be—along with her aunt, brother, nephew, and

EPILOGUE

daughter—part of a long line of anti-Hapsburg rebels. Her story would be that of a middle-aged mother, an aristocratic widow, snatched from her home in the night and denied due process. But Elizabeth's grandson Francis was captured and convicted of treason, losing both his head and the family's land.

· · ·

Speaking before the Hungarian Parliament in 1609, Thurzo himself had declared, "Even a criminal caught in the act cannot be condemned without an interrogation." This was the law of the land.

Was the Countess ever interrogated? There are suggestions she was. When the pastors visited Elizabeth after her arrest, they brought with them "the points of the interrogation," although these could have been the questions already put to the servants during their first, more informal round of torture. Later, though, one pastor asked her "whether she remembered these and stood by these," the clear implication being that "these" referred to statements or testimonies that Elizabeth had given in the forty-eight hours since her arrest.

If Elizabeth was not interrogated, Thurzo violated not just his own counsel, but the law of the land. If she was, the record of this interrogation did not survive. Any documents that would have comprised the Countess's defense—not just this possible interrogation, but the many letters, petitions, and complaints she wrote—have disappeared. The ancient family had no one left to preserve its archive. It's important to note, however, that every testimony against her was recopied several times and carefully preserved, ensuring that Thurzo's campaign would outlast its creator.

In November 1705, a low-ranking nobleman carried some of these testimonies into his local church chapter, the organization responsible for authenticating and storing official documents. It is not clear how this noble had come across these old documents, but now he requested that his finds be recopied and entered into the public record. His actions meant that these tales of an illustrious countess torturing and killing prepubescent girls and practicing witchcraft were in the chapter's records, where, twenty-four years later, a Catholic priest stumbled across them.

It was Father Laszlo Turoczi who revived, and popularized, Elizabeth Bathory's story. The Jesuit had already spent considerable time in the vicinity of Čachtice, teaching at a nearby seminary, before he decided to try his hand at a travel guide of Hungary. The lurid accusations against Countess Bathory made for an interesting anecdote, the sort of "local lore and legends" common in guidebooks. The accusations also made for a useful cautionary tale.

By the eighteenth century, the Ottoman Turks had finally been expelled from the Hungarian lands and Transylvania had lost its independence. The Raven King's former kingdom had been reconstituted, but under Hapsburg rule. The Hapsburgs' territorial conquests had been matched by religious ones: Their Counter-Reformation had prevailed. The children and grandchildren of the Calvinists and Lutherans who had bitterly argued and plotted and brawled found themselves rounded up and imprisoned together. Now, Jesuits like Father Turoczi were tasked with uncovering and converting any remaining Protestant holdouts.

Turoczi decided that Elizabeth Bathory had been born a Catholic, an easy enough assumption given his sloppy scholarship and the Bathorys' overgrown family tree—entire branches of the family were Catholic. Turoczi also decided to embellish the trial records to make the story even more compelling. In the 179th chapter of his travel guide, he confides that he had wrestled with whether to include the story, out of respect for the great Bathory family. He then launches into the tale, and has the supposedly Catholic Countess converting to Lutheranism to please her husband. Having turned her back on the Catholic faith, Elizabeth Bathory became unnaturally vain and obsessed with her appearance. Father Turoczi details her grooming routine in great detail, having her adorn her hair with complicated curls and jewels with the help of numerous attendants. When one of the attendants pulled her hair, the Countess slapped her. The girl's blood splattered across one side of her face. After she wiped her face, the Countess became convinced that this blood—virgin blood—had made her face look younger. So the Countess had her trusted servants supply her with a steady stream of virgins so she might bathe in their blood to appear eternally young.

The priest's grisly tale would easily be at home in contemporary QAnon chat rooms about adrenochrome theory, which claims that global elites kidnap children to harvest their blood for a particular chemical they need for their youth elixirs. This idea of a secret cabal harming children has deep roots: Romans once charged Christians with ritually slaughtering, and then devouring, children. Christians then deployed these accusations against Jews, accusing them of the ritual murder of Christian children to obtain blood for their ceremonies. When some European towns drove out their Jewish populations in the hysterical overreaction to these tales, other groups ended up accused of the same crimes—social outcasts, failed healers, and religious opponents.

Father Turoczi's introduction of the blood bath also mirrored a shift in the larger culture, exhausted by witch trials and in thrall to a new boogeyman: vampires. Father Turoczi was writing at the height of an alleged epidemic of vampirism in the Hapsburg lands. Rumors that aristocrats were doing strange things with the blood of children were spreading throughout Europe. Paris was gripped by a conspiracy theory that King Louis XV was "a leprous prince whose cure required a bath in human blood, and there being no blood purer than that of children, these were seized so as to be bled from all their limbs." Throughout Paris, commoners brandishing bricks and torches frantically searched for these abducted children. Variations of this conspiracy theory persist even today, such as Pizzagate and Frazzledrip, leading to the 2016 incident where a man, brandishing an AR-15, showed up at a Washington, D.C., pizza shop, determined to rescue imaginary children.

Father Turoczi's tale of a blood-bathing countess would be used as a case study in the emerging field of psychopathology and then wind its way into a Brothers Grimm folktale. It would be amplified by other travel guides, incorporated into local histories, poetry, and magazine stories, and then adopted by metal bands, video games, and horror films. The canonical legend of Elizabeth Bathory confirms what many remain desperate to believe: tired old myths about menopause, female vanity, and the dangers of leaving women, unsupervised, in charge.

Today, Elizabeth Bathory is a staple of the Central European tourism industry. One can take any number of tours, from Bratislava to

Budapest, that purport to tell her story. It is not Palatine Thurzo's but Father Turoczi's version of her life that prevails. On my most recent visit to Bratislava, during a "spooky" city tour, I was told of a countess who missed her husband terribly while he was off fighting the Turks. The stress of the separation and the bad genes of her ancient family took their toll. Determined to still be young and beautiful when her husband returned from the front, the Countess began bathing in blood. Elizabeth Bathory has unfortunately become both a jump scare and a joke.

Sárvár, where Elizabeth Bathory spent more than three decades of her life, where she ruled as the county's lord-lieutenant, has been, in turn, the site of an artificial silk factory, a refugee camp for Poles fleeing the Nazi invasion, and an internment camp for Yugoslav POWs, and is now a spa town known for its thermal springs and kids' water park. The pentagonal Renaissance castle still stands, its former moat now a green lawn. The castle is largely overlooked by foreign tourists but a seeming favorite for local schools' field trips. Although Sárvár was said to be the site of the Countess's gory torture chamber, Elizabeth Bathory is not the focal point of the museum there. There is one display, however, that contains reproductions of Nadasdy family portraits, including one of Elizabeth herself, along with the actual Sárvár printing press that sparked so much discord in her lifetime.

Čachtice, where Elizabeth was arrested, imprisoned, and spent her final years, has fully embraced the Blood Countess legend. On the way into the village, one passes the Bathory Oil gas station; in the town itself, one can eat at Pizzeria Bathory or the Countess's Court inn. One can pick up a bottle of Bathory Blood wine, fermented in the tunnels underneath Elizabeth's manor house, and then ride a bright red tourist train uphill to the castle ruins. In one of the castle's remaining interior rooms, I visited a half-hearted display featuring a wooden iron maiden and a female mannequin strapped down on a table. The mannequin's cotton nightdress had been hiked up and her panties pulled down by a previous visitor as a prank. In the courtyard, a local historical group was, uncannily enough, performing a reenactment of the European witch trials.

Countess Bathory's contemporaries routinely confessed to fantastical and gruesome acts. Who still believes the two young boys who testified that their father and older sister were werewolves; or the couple who swore that, at night, they shape-shifted into bears; or the man who confessed to feasting on the hearts of unborn babies? Who thinks of the hundreds of thousands who were imprisoned and tortured, or the tens of thousands who were beheaded, hanged, or burned at the stake, as anything other than innocent victims? Three old women and one teenage boy testified under torture that they helped their mistress commit unspeakable acts: How is that any different?

In the past decade, the last Salem witch has been cleared, memorials to the falsely accused have been installed throughout Europe, and groups in Spain, Switzerland, Scotland, Belgium, and Norway have formally rehabilitated those accused of witchcraft and sorcery. Alleged murderers who once occupied slots alongside Elizabeth Bathory in *The Guinness Book of World Records* have since been acknowledged to be fictional and stricken from the record.

Just as this book was going to press, Elizabeth Bathory was not quite exonerated, but her gruesome title was quietly revoked. *The Guinness Book of World Records*, which for over fifty years has maintained that the Countess was one of the world's most prolific serial killers, decreed:

> Though the Hungarian "Blood Countess" Erzsébet (or Elizabeth) Bàthory (1560–1614) is alleged to have tortured and murdered as many as 650 victims, her life history is so shrouded in legend that it is impossible to separate fact from fiction.

Instead of being given a public apology or a plaque, Elizabeth Bathory has, once again, been dismissed.

. . .

Elizabeth Bathory's legend has long been profitable because it is such fun: in her former castles one can find innumerable iron maidens, plenty of fake blood, and dark underground passageways decked out with plastic witches. The legend is also much less terrifying than the truth.

Elizabeth Bathory and her contemporaries had been promised all sorts of things: A reformed, impartial judicial system. The right to worship however they chose. Groundbreaking new medicines to relieve their suffering. They had been assured that a new technology would better connect them to one another; instead, the printing press taught them to fear that their neighbors were heretics, cannibals, and witches.

We prefer our monsters to be maniacally insane individuals, broken from birth, rotten to the core. This is preferable to wondering what it might take for all of the good, decent people in our lives—the co-workers we joke with, the neighbors who sit next to us in church—to denounce us, too.

We can throw up our hands and declare the past inscrutable, claim that no one can ever really sort it all out. Or we can acknowledge that our legends are all too often platforms for another era's extremists. We can keep negotiating what we might still owe the past.

In her own time, Elizabeth Bathory demanded justice. In our time, may she receive it.

ACKNOWLEDGMENTS

I'm certainly not the first to cast a skeptical eye at the accusations against Countess Elizabeth Bathory. I'm indebted to the researchers and scholars in central and eastern Europe who, beginning in the 1980s, challenged the canonical Bathory legend. Chief among these were the historian László Nagy and the lawyer Irma Szádeczky-Kardoss. More recently, this reclamation project has been led by the scholars Gábor Várkonyi and Tünde Lengyelová. I am especially grateful to Dr. Lengyelová for taking the time to share her research with me. I also want to acknowledge the work of Tony Thorne, whose 1997 book, *Countess Dracula*, was one of the first to make the troves of European sources accessible for English-speaking audiences. Mr. Thorne was kind enough to entertain my questions as I began this project.

I've had the great fortune that, in the past decades, archives have continued to find and catalog primary sources relevant to Bathory's life. I owe a great debt to the National Archives of Hungary, as well as the Austrian State Archives, the National Archives of Romania, and the Slovak National Archives. I am also grateful for the generous librarians and archivists at many other institutions—in Hungary, the National Széchényi Library, the Central Archives of the Lutheran Church, and the Archives of the Primate of the Catholic Church in Esztergom; and in Slovakia, the Archives of the Bishopric of Spiš. The collections of the New York Public Library and the Metropolitan Museum of Art also proved to be invaluable resources.

Without accurate transcriptions and translations of these primary sources, this book would not be possible. I must sing the praises of two talented (and patient!) experts. Dorottya Szabó, a former chief archivist, gave advice on navigating the Hungarian archives and provided crucial context, corrections, and analysis. Judit Babcsányi, of Historia Translation, demonstrated an extraordinary ability to decipher old handwriting—no matter how blotted, blurred, or fussy the script—and to work out archaic turns of phrase.

I would also like to acknowledge the generosity of several scholars, archivists, and librarians who went above and beyond: Dr. Vladimír Olejník at the Bishopric of Spiš; Dr. Mihály Balázs at the University of Szeged; Gábor Szibler at the Ferenc Nádasdy Museum in Sárvár; and Christoph Pálffy.

I'm so grateful for my indefatigable agent, Mackenzie Brady Watson, and all of the Bloomsbury editors who championed this project. Thanks to Ben Hyman for acquiring, to Morgan Jones for her keen edits, and to Colleen Lawrie for shepherding the manuscript across the finish line. I'd also like to acknowledge the rest of the Bloomsbury team, especially Ava Grandfield, Barbara Darko, and Rosie Mahorter.

More than two decades ago, my cousin Andrea Petriková first introduced me to the legend of Elizabeth Bathory during a twilight visit to one of the Countess's castles. Much more recently, Slavomír Dzvonik guided me to another of the Countess's castles—the infamous Čachtice—and the many small village churches involved in her tale. Miroslav Bitarovský of the Čachtice Underground showed me the manor house's last crumbling wall and gave me a private tour of its cellar and underground passages. Throughout this adventure, Nate Miles proved an invaluable companion, contributing his good humor, flawless sense of direction, and photography skills.

Lastly, I want to acknowledge all of the other women I encountered over the course of researching this book, women who were similarly denounced and accused of horrific crimes. Their stories, fragmentary as they may be, chilled, infuriated, and deeply moved me. This book is for the scapegoats, each and every last one.

BIBLIOGRAPHY

ARCHIVAL MATERIALS

AUSTRIA

ÖStA   Österreichisches Staatsarchiv (Austrian State Archives, Vienna)
- HHStA   Haus-, Hof, und Staatsarchiv
- FHKA   Finanz-und Hofkammerarchiv

HUNGARY

EPL   Esztergomi Prímási Levéltár (Archives of the Primate of the Catholic Church, Esztergom)

EOL   Evangélikus Országos Levéltár (Central Archives of the Lutheran Church, Budapest)

NSZL   Országos Széchényi Könyvtárban (National Széchényi Library, Budapest)

MNL   Magyar Nemzeti Levéltár Országos Levéltára (National Archives of Hungary, Budapest)

E 142	Acta Publica
E 148	Neo-regestrata acta
E 156	Urbaria et Conscriptiones
E 185	Archivum familiae Nádasdi
E 196	Archivum familiae Thurzó
E 204	Missiles
Jzk	Jegyzőkönyvei
P 47	Benyovszky család
P 1314	Batthyány-missilisek
VVL	Vas Vármegyei Levéltára

ROMANIA

ANR   Arhivele Naționale ale României (National Archives of Romania)

SLOVAKIA

ARBSP Archív Rímskokatolíckej cirkvi Biskupstva Spišské Podhradie (Archives of the Bishopric of Spiš)

SOBA Štátny oblastný archív v Žiline so sídlom v Bytči (State regional archive in Žilina, Bytča)

    OK-TK   Oravský komposesorát—Thurzovská korešpondencia

OTHER PRIMARY SOURCES

"1572 dezember 21. Báthory Erzsébet (Nádasdy Ferencz mátkája) arany-ezüst míveinek, készpénzének és egyéb ingóságainak összeírása" (Inventory of the gold and silver items, coins, and other personal property of Elizabeth Bathory [Francis Nadasdy's fiancée]). Edited by András Komáromy. In *Magyar Történelmi Tár 4*. Vol. 9. Budapest: Historical Committee of the Hungarian Academy of Sciences, 1908, 59–60.

"Acta et Conclusiones Conventus seu Synodi . . . Solnae congregatorum" (Proceedings and Conclusions of the Synod . . . assembled at Zsolna [Zilina]) March 28–30, 1610). In *Urkundenbuch zum oesterreichisch-evangelischen Kirchenrecht*. Edited by Karl Kuzmany. Vienna: Wilhelm Braumüller, 1855, 189–93.

"Adatok Csejthe Történetéhez" (Chronicle of Castle Čachtice). Reprinted in *Magyar Történelmi Tár 3*. Vol. 22. Budapest: Historical Committee of the Hungarian Academy of Sciences, 1899, 722–24.

Batthyany, Francis. "Levelei" (Letters). Edited by Gyula Nagy. *Magyar Történelmi Tár 3*. Vol. 2. Budapest: Historical Committee of the Hungarian Academy of Sciences, 1879, 96–123.

Bornemissza, Peter. *Ördögi Kisértetekről* (On the Temptations of the Devil). Sempte, 1578.

Bullein, William. *Bulwarke of defence against all sicknesse, soarenesse, and vvoundes that doe dayly assaulte mankind*. London: Thomas Marshe, 1562.

Forgách, Francis. *Rerum Hungaricarum sui temporis commentarii* (Commentary on the Hungarian Affairs of His Time). Edited by Elek Horányi. Bratislava: J. M. Landerer, 1788.

Frankovith, Gergely. *Hasznos És Fölötte Szükséges Könyv* (A Useful and Very Necessary Book). Monyorókerék: János Manlius, 1588.

Fumee, Martin. *The historie of the troubles of Hungarie*. Book 5. London: Felix Kyngston, 1600.

Herber, Caspar. *Erschröckliche newe Zeytung Von eine Mörder Christman genannt, welcher ist Gericht worden zu Bergkessel den 17. Juny* (Horrible new Zeitung: Of a Murderer named Christman, who was tried in Bergkessel the 17th of June). Mentz, 1581.

Junius, Johannes. "Letter to His Daughter and Trial Transcript, 1628." In Clifford Backman, *Cultures of the West, Volume One: To 1750*. 3rd ed. Oxford University Press, 2023, 26–266.

"Listius Anna Rozina Bünprehez" (The trial of Anna Rozina Listius). Edited by Andras Komaromy. *Magyar Történelmi Tár 3*. Vol. 20. Budapest: Historical Committee of the Hungarian Academy of Sciences, 1897, 626–52.

Magyar országgyűlési emlékek (Records of the Hungarian Parliament). Vol. 10: 1602–1604. Edited by Vilmos Fraknói and Árpád Károlyi. Budapest: Athenaeum, 1890.

Magyari, Istvan. "Az országokban való sok romlások okairól" (On the causes of decay in our country). Sárvár, 1602. Reprinted in *Régi magyar könyvtár*. Vol. 27. Budapest: Hungarian Academy of Sciences, 1911.

Urbáriumok xvi-xvii. Század (Urbariums of the 16th and 17th century). Edited by Francis Maksay. Budapest: Akadémiai Kiadó, 1959.

Melius, Péter Juhász. *Herbarium*. Kolosvár, 1578.

Nádasdy Tamás nádor családi levelezése (Thomas Nadasdy's family correspondence). Edited by Árpád Károlyi and József Szalay. Budapest: Akadémia Könyvkiadó-Hivatala, 1882.

Oláh, Miklós. *Hungaria*. 1536.

Pápai, Páriz Ferenc. *Pax corporis*. Kolosvár, 1690. Reprinted 1764.

Pázmány, Péter. "Mint kell a keresztyén leányt nevelni" (On the education of Christian girls). In *Pázmány Péter művei*. Edited by Márton Tamóc. Budapest, 1983, 1021–42.

"The Peace of Vienna with the Prince of Transylvania." June 23, 1606. In *Rebels and Ottomans—The Habsburg Monarchy Makes Peace*, German History in Documents and Images. germanhistorydocs.org/en/from-the-reformations-to-the-thirty-years-war-1500-1648/ghdi:document-4513.

Rexa, Dezsö. *Báthory Erzsébet, Nádasdy Ferencné (1560–1614)*. Budapest: G. Benkö, 1908.

Szepsi, Laczkó Máté. *Krónikája és emlékezetre méltó hazai dolgoknak rövid megjegyzései. 1521–1624* (Chronicle and brief notes on memorable domestic events. 1521–1624). Edited by Imre Mikó. Cluj, 1858.

"*Szerelmes Orsikám . . .*" *A Nádasdyak és Szegedi Kőrös Gáspár levelezése* ("My Beloved Orsika . . ." The correspondence between the Nádasdys and Gáspár Kőrös of Szeged). Edited by Tivadar Vida. Budapest: Szépirodalmi Könyvkiadó, 1988.

Thurzo, George. *Bethlenfalvi Grof Thurzo Gyorgy Levelei Nejehez Czobor-Szent-Mihalyi Czobor Erzsébethez* (Letters of Count George Thurzo Bethlenfalvi to his wife Elizabeth Szent-Mihalyi Czobor). 2 vols. Edited by Edmund Zichy. Budapest: Athenaeum, 1876.

A Thurzó-Levéltár Protestáns Egyháztörténeti Iratai (Historical Documents of the Protestant Church in the Thurzó Library). Edited by Balint Ila. Budapest: Hungarian Protestant Literature Society, 1934.

Turóczi, László. *Ungaria suis cum regibus compendio data* (An overview of Hungary and its kings). Trnava: Academicis Societatis Jesu per Fridericum Gall, 1729.

Von Elsburg, R. A. *Die Blutgräfin: Ein sitten-und charakterbild* (The Blood Countess: A portrait of morals and character). Breslau, 1904.

Wagner, Michael. *Beytrag zur Philosophischen anthropologie und den Damit Verwandtn Wissenschaft* (Contribution to Philosophical Anthropology and Related Sciences). Vienna: Stahl, 1796.

Warhafftige und erschreckliche Beschreibung, von einem Zauberer (Stupe Peter genannt) der sich zu einem Wehrwolff hat können machen, welcher zu Bedbur . . . ist gerichtet worden, den 31. October, dieses 1589. Jahrs, was böser Thaten er begangen hat . . . (A true and terrifying description of a sorcerer [named Peter Stupe] who was able to transform himself into a werewolf . . .). Pamphlet. Gedruckt zu Cölln, Niclas Schreiber, 1589.

SECONDARY SOURCES

Acsády, Ignác. *A pozsonyi és szepesi kamarák, 1565–1604* (The Chambers of Bratislava and Szepi, 1565–1604). Budapest: Magyar Tudományos Akadémia, 1894.

Agoston, Gabor. "Where Environmental and Frontier Studies Meet: Rivers, Forests, Marshes and Forts along the Ottoman-Hapsburg Frontier in Hungary." In *The Frontiers of the Ottoman World*. Edited By A. C. S. Peacock. Oxford University Press, 2009, 57–79.

Angyal, Dávid. "Báthory Gábor uralkodása" (The reign of Gabriel Báthory). *Magyarország Története II. Mátyástól III. Ferdinánd Haláláig*. Budapest: Athenaeum, 1898.

Atwal, Sanji. "Was Elizabeth Bathory Truly the Most Prolific Female Serial Killer Ever?" Guinness World Records, June 6, 2023. guinnessworldrecords.com/news/2023/6/was-elizabeth-bathory-truly-the-most-prolific-female-serial-killer-ever-751852.

Bak, János M. "Online Decreta Regni Mediaevalis Hungariae: The Laws of the Medieval Kingdom of Hungary" (2019). *All Complete Monographs*. 4. digitalcommons.usu.edu/lib_mono/4.

"The Balance Sheet of War." In *History of Transylvania*, vol. 1. Edited by László Makkai and Zoltán Szász. New York: Columbia University Press, 2002. mek.oszk.hu/03400/03407/html/120.html.

Balázs, Mihály. "Ecsedi Báthori István levelei Bocskaihoz 1605 március 8–július 12" (Letters of Stephen Bathory of Ecsed to Bocskai, March 8–July 12, 1605). *Acta Historiae Litterarum Hungaricarum Tom. X–XI* (1971): 43–51.

Bariska, István. "Nádasdy II. Tamás és a Bocskai-felkelés" (Thomas Nadasdy II and the Bocskai uprising). *Századok* 144.4 (2010): 823-848.

Barkley, John M. "The Worship of the Reformed Church in Hungary." *The Church Service Society Liturgical Review* (May 1970): 1–20.

Békefi, Antal. "A vasi várak zenei élete a török megszállás idején 1526-1686" (The musical life of the castles of Vas county during the Turkish occupation 1526-1686). *Vasi Szemle* 17, no. 4 (1965): 516–55.

Benda, Borbála. "Egy uradalmi központ egy korabeli étrend tükrében (Csejte, 1623. november 1–1625. augusztus 31.)" (A manor house as reflected in a contemporary menu [Čachtice, November 1, 1623–August 31, 1625]). *AETAS* 23, no. 4 (2008): 24–48.

Benda, Kálmán. "A kálvini tanok hatása a magyar rendi ellenállás ideológiájára" (The influence of Calvin's doctrines on the Hungarian ideology of class resistance). *Helikon* (1971): 322–30.

———. "Válasz Hetyéssy Szilviának" (Response to Szilvia Hetyéssy). *Élet és Irodalom* 24, no. 3. (January 19, 1980): 2.

Bitskey, István. "'Erdély Hektora' avagy 'tirannusa'? (Báthory Gábor alakja a kora újkor irodalmában)" ("Hector of Transylvania" or "tyrant"? [The figure of Gabriel Bathory in early modern literature]). *Báthory Gábor És Kora*. University of Debrecen, 2009: 29–36.

Bobory, Dora. *The Sword and the Crucible: Count Boldizsár Batthyány and Natural Philosophy in Sixteenth-Century Hungary*. Newcastle upon Tyne: Cambridge Scholars, 2009.

Bódi, József, et al. "Csepreg történeti településföldrajza a Kiegyezésig" (The historical geography of Csepreg until the Austro-Hungarian Compromise). *Településföldrajzi Tanulmányok* 5, no. 1 (2016): 38–59.

Boner, Patrick, editor. *Kepler's New Star (1604): Context and Controversy*. Leiden, Boston: Brill, 2011.

Borbély, Zoltán. *A Homonnai Drugethek Felső Magyarországon a 17. század első évtizedeiben* (The Drugeths of Humenne in Upper Hungary in the first decades of the 17th century). PhD dissertation. Esterhazy Karoly College, Eger, 2015.

———. *A kisvárdai várday család* (The Várday family from Kisvárda). ACTA Universitatis, Sectio Historiae, Tom. XLVI: 65–74.

———. "A végvárrendszer kiépítésének társadalmi hatásai Felső-Magyarországon" (The social impact of the construction of the border castle system in Upper Hungary). *Mozgó frontvonalak. Háború és diplomácia a várháborúk időszakában, 1552–1568*. Studia Agriensia 35. Eger, Hungary, 2017: 169–95.

Borzelleca, Joseph F. "Paracelsus: Herald of Modern Toxicology." *Toxicological Sciences* 53, no. 1 (January 2000): 2–4. doi.org/10.1093/toxsci/53.1.2.

Botik, Jan. *An Ethnic History of Slovakia: Multi-ethnicity, Minorities, and Migration*. Translated by John Peter Butler Barrer. Bratislava: Stimul, 2021.

Branecky, Jozef. *Trenčín, Trnava: historicke povsti a clanky* (Trenčín, Trnava: historical accounts and legends). Trenčín: Spolok Svätého Vojtech, 1939.

Burr, George L, editor. "The Witch Persecutions: The Witch Persecution at Wurzburg." In *Translations and Reprints from the Original Sources of European History*. Vol. 3. Book 4. Philadelphia: University of Pennsylvania History Department, 1896, 28–29.

Buzás, Gergely. "The Royal Palace in Visegrád and the Beginnings of Renaissance Architecture in Hungary." In *Italy & Hungary, Humanism and Art in the Early Renaissance*. Edited by Péter Farbaky and Louis A. Waldmann. Florence: Villa i Tatti, the Harvard University Center for Italian Renaissance Studies, 2011, 368–407.

Codrescu, Andrei. "Looking for the Blood Countess in the Bowels of the Empire." In *The Muse Is Always Half-Dressed in New Orleans and Other Essays*. New York: St. Martin's Press, 1993, 179–90.

Craft, Kimberly L. *Infamous Lady: The True Story of Countess Erzsebet Báthory*. 2nd ed. CreateSpace Independent Publishing Platform, 2014.

———. *The Private Letters of Countess Erzsebet Báthory*. CreateSpace Independent Publishing Platform, 2011.

Csepregi, Zoltán. *ELEM, Proszopográfiai rész. I. A reformáció kezdetétől a zsolnai zsinatig (1610)* (Evangelical ministers in Hungary [ELEM] Prósopography I, from the beginning of the Reformation to the Synod of Zsolna [1610]). 3 volumes. Budapest: Magyar Evangélikus Digitális Tár, 2015.

Cziraki, Zsuzsanna. "Erdély Szerepe Melchior Klesl Fennmaradt Írásos Véleményeiben 1611–1616 Között" (The role of Transylvania in Melchior Klesl's surviving written opinions from 1611–1616). In *Bethlen Gábor és*

Európa. Edited by Gábor Kármán and Teszelszky Kees. Budapest: Komáromi Printing and Publishing, 2013.

———. "Szemelvények Melchior Khlesl És A Bécsi Titkostanács 1611 És 1613 Között Keletkezett, Erdélyivonatkozású Írásos Véleményeiből" (Excerpts from the written opinions of Melchior Khlesl and the Vienna Privy Council regarding Transylvania, written between 1611 and 1613). *Levéltári Közlemények* 83 (2012): 319–69.

Daboczi, Denes. "Haban Ceramics in the Collections of the Savaria Museum." *Acta Ethnographica Hungarica: An International Journal of Ethnography* 60, no. 2 (December 2015): 323–26.

Daniel, David P. "Hungary." *The Early Reformation in Europe*. Edited by Andrew Pettegree. Cambridge University Press, 1992, 49–69.

———. "Piety, Politics, and Perversion." In *Women in Reformation and Counter-Reformation Europe: Public and Private Worlds*. Edited by Sherrin D. Marshall. Bloomington: Indiana University Press, 1989.

Deák, Éva. "The Wedding Festivities of Gabriel Bethlen and Catherine of Brandenburg." *Hungarian Studies* 26, no. 2 (2012): 251–71.

Dienes, Dénes. "Az imádkozó nagyságos úr. Ecsedi Báthory Istvánról" (The praying nobleman: István Báthory of Ecsed). *Széphalom* 15 (2005): 187–89.

Dillon, Virginia. "News of Transylvania in the German Printed Periodicals of the Seventeenth Century, from István Bocskai to György II Rákóczi." PhD dissertation, University of Oxford, 2013.

Dominkovits, Péter and Géza Pálffy. "Küzdelem az országos és regionális hatalomért. A Nádasdy család, a magyar arisztokrácia és a Nyugat-Dunántúl nemesi társadalma a 16-17. században" (The struggle for national and regional power: The Nadasdy family, the Hungarian aristocracy, and the noble society of Western Transdanubia in the 16th and 17th centuries). Part 1. *Századok* 144, no. 4: (2010): 769–92.

Duchoňová, Diana. "'We Are Pleased to Expect You on This Joyful Day . . .': Weddings as an Important Part of Family Festivities of the Esterházys in the First Half of the 17th Century." *Historický časopis* 60. Supplement (2012): 19–42.

Eamon, William. "Kepler and the Star of Bethlehem." *The Professor of Secrets* (author web page). December 24, 2011. williameamon.com/kepler-and-the-star-of-bethlehem/.

"Ecsedi Báthori Ersebet erkölcsének bővebb megesmertetése" (A more detailed description of the immorality of Elizabeth Bathory of Ecsed). *Tudományos Gyűjtemény* 23, no. 8 (1839): 42–60.

Elton, G. R., editor. *The New Cambridge Modern History: The Reformation 1520–1559*. 2nd ed. Vol. 2. Cambridge University Press, 2008.

Erdélyi, Gabriella. "Negotiating Widowhood and Female Agency in Seventeenth-Century Hungary." *The Hungarian Historical Review* 9, no. 4, (2020): 595–623. jstor.org/stable/26984163.

"Értékes kőfaragványokat találtak a borosjenői várfalban" (Valuable stone carvings were found in the Borosjenő castle wall). *Aradi Hirek* (Arad, Romania), October 21, 2019. aradihirek.ro/.

"Evangélikus gyülekezetek, egyházmegyék, kerületek a Dunántúlon" (Evangelical congregations, dioceses, and districts in Transdanubia). *A Reformációtól—Napjainkig*. Szombathely: Western (Transdanubian) Evangelical Church District, 2011.

Farkas, Sándor. *Csepreg mezőváros története: többnyire eredeti adatok alapján* (History of the market town Csepreg: Mostly based on original data). Budapest: Franklin Társulat, 1887.

Fischer, Viktória. "Főúri asszonyok a kora újkori társasági életben" (Noble women in early modern social life). Újkor.hu. November 4, 2020. ujkor.hu/content/fouri-asszonyok-a-kora-ujkori-tarsasagi-eletben.

Fodor, Pál. "Hungary Between East and West: The Ottoman Turkish Legacy." In *More Modoque: Die Wurzeln der europäischen Kulturund deren Rezeption im Orientund Okzident*. Edited by Pál Fodor. Budapest: Autoren, 2013, 399–420.

Gecsényi, Lajos. "Egy kamarai tisztviselő a XVI. században: Nagyváthy Ferenc" (A chamber official in the 16th century: Francis Nagyváthy). *Turul* 3–4 (1999): 77–83.

Gînguță, Alexandra et al. "Genetic Identification of Members of the Prominent Báthory Aristocratic Family." *iScience* 26, no. 10 (October 20, 2023). doi.org/10.1016/j.isci.2023.107911.

Gruia, Ana-Maria. "Healthcare in Cluj in the Sixteenth Century: Overlapping Professions." In *Genius loci: Laszlovszky 60*. Edited by Dóra Mérai et al. Budapest: Archaeolingua Alapítvány, 2018: 168–70.

The Guinness Book of Superlatives. New York: Superlatives, 1956.

Guinness Book of Records. 15th edition. Edited by Norris and Ross McWhirter. London: Superlatives Limited, 1968.

Hetyéssy, Szilvia. "Báthory Erzsébet pere" (The trial of Elizabeth Bathory). *Élet és Irodalom* 24, no. 3 (January 1980): 2.

Horn, Ildikó. "Báthory Gábor belpolitikája" (The domestic policy of Gabriel Bathory). In *Báthory Gábor És Kora*. Edited by Klára Papp et al. Debrecen: University of Debrecen, 2009.

———. "A Fejedelmi Tanács Bethlen Gábor Korában" (The prince's council in the age of Gabriel Bethlen). *Századok* 145, no. 4 (2011): 997–1027.

Hurd-Mead, Kate Campbell. *A History of Women in Medicine*. Haddam, CT: Haddam Press, 1938.

Hussey, Kristin. "'May God Protect Us from Such Drugs and Physicians!': A 17th Century Antimony Cup." Royal College of Physicians, July 27, 2018. history.rcp.ac.uk/blog/may-god-protect-us-such-drugs-and-physicians-17th-century-antimony-cup.

"Iskolánk névadója, Ecsedi Báthori István" (Our school is named after Stephen Bathory of Ecsed). Website of Ecsedi Báthori István Református Általános Iskola és Gimnázium, March 10, 2015. ebirag.hu/?page_id=35.

James, Andrew. "Magyar-British Relations in Elizabethan and Jacobean Times." *Andrew James: The Whole of Human Life Is Here!* (blog), March 7, 2014. chandlerozconsultants.wordpress.com/2014/03/07/magyar-british-relations-in-elizabethan-and-jacobean-times.

Jankovics, József. "Báthory Gábor meggyilkolásának újabb változata: Egy koronatanú elbeszélése alapján" (Another version of the murder of Gabriel Báthory: Based on the narration of a Crown witness). *Lymbus*. Budapest, International Hungarian Studies Association and the Hungarian Academy of Sciences Research Center for the Humanities, 2015: 39–43.

Jedlicska, Pál. *Kiskárpáti emlékek Éleskőtől Vágujhelyig* 2 (Little Carpathian memories from Éleskő to Vágujhely). Eger: Erseki Lyceumi Könyvnyomda, 1891.

Kanacz, Viktor. "Protestáns vagy katolikus volt-e Nádasdy Tamás?" (Was Thomas Nádasdy Protestant or Catholic?). *Evangélikus Élet* 88, no. 11–12 (March 2023): 31.

"Kanizsai Orsolya." *Nádasdy Ferenc Múzeum Sárvár.* March 25, 2013. nadasdy muzeum.hu.

Katona, Imre. "Bűn és bűnhődés Báthory Erzsébet életében" (Crime and punishment in the life of Elizabeth Báthory). *Vasi Szemle—Dunántúli Szemle* 43, no. 4 (1989): 549–62.

———. "Bocskai csapatai Vas megyében" (Bocskai's troops in Vas County). *Vasi Szemle* 27, no. 2 (1973): 274–76.

Kemény, Lajos. "Szepsi Laczkó Máté." *Századok* 43 (1909): 769–72.

Kincses, Katalin Mária. *Tábori sebesültellátás Magyarországon a XVI–XVIII században* (The care of the wounded in Hungarian military camps in the 16th–18th centuries). Budapest: Gondolat Kiadó, 2019.

Klaniczay, Gábor. "Healers in Hungarian Witch Trials." In *Witchcraft and Demonology in Hungary and Transylvania.* Edited by Gábor Klaniczay and Éva Pócs. New York: Palgrave Macmillan, 2017, 111–56.

Köblös, Zsolt and József Kránitz, editors. *A Dunántúli Református Egyházkerület prédikátorai és rektorai I. 1526–1760* (Preachers and rectors of the Transdanubian Reformed Church District. Volume I: 1526–1760). Pápa: Pápai Református Gyűjtemények, 2009.

Kočiš, Jozef. *Alžbeta Báthoryová a palatín Thurzo* (Elizabeth Bathory and Palatine Thurzo). Martin, Czechoslovakia: Osveta, 1984.

———. *Bytčiansky zámok* (Bytča Castle). Martin, Czechoslovakia: Osveta, 1974.

Kohutová, Maria. "Religious Situation in 17th-Century Slovakia: A Case of Southwestern Slovakia." *Human Affairs* 5, 1995: 66–75. doi.org/10.1515/humaff-1995-050108.

Komáromi, Andor, Ed. *Magyarországi boszorkányperek oklevéltára* (Archives of Hungarian witch trials). Budapest: Athenaeum, 1910.

Komáromy, Andras. "Listius Anna Rozina Bünpörehez" (The trial of Anna Rozins Listius). *Magyar Történelmi Tár* 3. Vol 2. Budapest: Magyar Történelmi Társulat, 1897.

Kónya, Peter. "A magyarországi Ágostai hitvallású evangélikus egyház keletkezése" (The origin of the Augustinian Lutheran Church in Hungary). In *Báthory Gábor És Kora*. Edited by Klára Papp et al. Debrecen: University of Debrecen, 2009: 285–92.

Köő, Artúr. "How the Distinctive Clothing of Hungarian Reformed Ministers Took Shape and Changed During the Centuries—Part 1." *Hungarian Conservative*, September 17, 2023. hungarianconservative.com/articles/culture_society/how-the-distinctive-clothing-of-hungarian-reformed-ministers-took-shape-and-changed-during-the-centuries.

Kord, Susanne. *Murderesses in German Writing 1720–1860: Heroines of Horror*. New York: Cambridge University Press, 2009.

Korpás, Zoltán, and János B. Szabó. "'If They Came as a Legation, They Are Many, If They Are Soldiers, They Are Few'—The Military Background of the 1551 Attempt to Unite Hungary." In Ágnes Máté and Teréz Oborni, *Isabella Jagiellon, Queen of Hungary (1539–1559)*. Budapest: Research Centre for the Humanities, 2020.

Koslofsky, Craig. *The Reformation of the Dead: Death and Ritual in Early Modern Germany, 1450–1700*. New York: St. Martin's Press, 2000.

Kovács, Dóra. "Az ecsedi udvar. Szervitori hivatás és kapcsolatrendszer Báthory István famíliájában" ("The Court of Ecsed: Clients and relations in the family of Stephen Báthory"). *Századok* 150, no. 4 (2016): 911–44.

———. "Ecsedi Báthory István levelei Várday Katához (1588–1605)" (Letters from Stephan Bathory of Ecsed to Kata Varday [1588–1605]). *Lymbus*. Budapest: International Hungarian Studies Association and the Hungarian Academy of Sciences Research Center for the Humanities, 2021: 337–98.

Križanová, Eva and Blanka Puškárová. *Hrady, zámky a kaštiele na Slovensku: turistický lexicon* (Castles, chateaux and manor houses in Slovakia: tourist lexicon). Bratislava: Šport, 1990.

Kruppa, Tamas. "Báthory Gábor a forrásokban: propaganda és ellenpropaganda (Gábriel Báthory in the sources: propaganda and counter-propaganda). In

Báthory Gábor És Kora. Edited by Klára Papp et al. Debrecen: University of Debrecen, 2009.

Kubinyi, Miklós. *Thurzó Imre 1598-1621*. Magyar Történeti Életrajzok. Budapest: Hungarian Historical Society, 1888.

Last, István. "Kik voltak az első női főispánok? A vármegyék élén álló nagyasszonyok és emlékezetük" (Who were the first female lord-lieutenants? The women who headed the counties and their legacies). *Újkor.hu*, July 28, 2022. ujkor.hu/content/kik-voltak-az-elso-noi-foispanok-a-varmegyek-elen-allo-nagyasszonyok-es-emlekezetuk.

László, Andor. "Bocskai István fejedelem végrendelete" (The will of Prince Stephen Bocskai). *Erdélyi Múzeum* 83, no. 1 (2021): 54–68.

Leeson, Peter T., and Jacob W. Russ. "Witch Trials." *Economic Journal* 128, no. 613 (August 2018): 2066–2105. doi.org/10.1111/ecoj.12498.

Lenčiš, Štefan. "Historical Personality and Contribution of George III Druget in Zemplén and Ung Counties at the Turn of the 16th and 17th Centuries." *Scientific Bulletin of Uzhhorod University* 43, no. 2 (2020): 103–20.

Lengyel, Tünde. "The Chances for a Provincial Cultural Centre: The Case of Gyorgy Thurzo, Palatine of Hungary." In *A Divided Hungary in Europe: Exchanges, Networks and Representations, 1541–1699*. Vol. 2, *Diplomacy, Information Flow and Cultural Exchange*. Edited by Szymon Brzeziński and Áron Zarnóczki. Newcastle upon Tyne: Cambridge Scholars, 2014.

———. "Everyday Lives of Aristocratic Women in the Early Modern Era." In *A Multiethnic Region and Nation-State in East-Central Europe: Studies in the History of Upper Hungary and Slovakia from the 1600s to the Present*. Edited by László Szarka. New York: Columbia University Press, 2012.

———. "Esettanulmány A Kora Újkori Női Műveltség Kérdéséhez: Elvárások, lehetőségek, határok" (A case study on the question of early modern womens' education: Expectations, opportunities, limits). *Századok* 153 no. 2 (2019): 235–50.

———. "Az írástudatlantól a főispánig: Thurzó Györgyné, coborszentmihályi Czobor Erzsébet" (From illiterate to lord-lieutenant: Mrs. György Thurzó, Erzsébet Czobor of Szentmihály). In *Nők Világa: Művelődés- és társadalomtörténeti tanulmányok*. Edited by Anna Fábri and Gábor Várkanyi. Budapest: Argumentum, 2007: 139–60.

———. "A legrosszabb hírű asszony a magyar történelemben: Báthory Erzsébet gazdasági és közéleti tevékenysége" (The most notorious woman in Hungarian history: Elizabeth Bathory's economic and public activities). In *Báthory Gábor És Kora*. Edited by Klára Papp et al. Debrecen: University of Debrecen, 2009: 53–64.

———. "Nyitra és pozsony megye boszorkányperei a 16–18. Században" (The witch trials of Nyitra and Pozsony counties in the 16th–18th centuries). *Archivum sala—Levéltári évkönyv II*. Edited by István Gaučík. Bratislava: Vágselly Branch of the Slovak State Archives, 2005: 16–28.

———. *Život na šľachtickom dvore: odev, strava, domácnosť, hygiene, voľný čas* (Life at the noble court: clothing, hospitality, hygiene, and leisure time). Bratislava: Slovart, 2016.

Lewis, Margaret Brannan. "Infanticide in Early Modern Germany: The Experience of Augsburg, Memmingen, Ulm, and Nördlingen, 1500–1800." PhD dissertation, University of Virginia, 2012.

Magyary-Kossa, Gyula. *Magyar orvosi emlékek. Értekezések a magyar orvostörténelem köréből* (Hungarian medical memorabilia: Dissertations on Hungarian medical history), vols. 2 and 3. Budapest: A Magyar Orvosi Könyvkiadó Társulat, 1929 and 1931.

Majorossy, Judit, and Katalin Szende. "Hospitals in Medieval and Early Modern Hungary." In *Hospitals and Institutional Care in Medieval and Early Modern Europe*. Edited by Martin Scheutz et al. Munich: Institutionelle Fürsorge in Mittelalter und Früher Neuzeit, 2008.

Masznyik, Endre. "A magyar reformátió eredeti jellemének kérdéséhez" (On the question of the original character of the Hungarian Reformation). *Theologiai Szaklap* 6, no. 3 (1908): 220–26.

Mazzola, Annie. "The Vanishing Children of Paris." *The History Girls* (blog). September 3, 2017. the-history-girls.blogspot.com/2017/09/the-vanishing-children-of-paris-by-anna.html.

McKim, Donald K. "Death, Prayers and Funerals for the Dead in Calvin's Theology." *Calvin Studies* VI. Presented at a Colloquium on Calvin Studies at Davidson College, Davidson, North Carolina, January 1992. foundationrt.org/wp-content/uploads/2016/03/McKim_Death_Funerals.pdf.

McNally, Raymond. *Dracula Was a Woman: In Search of the Blood Countess of Transylvania*. New York: McGraw-Hill, 1983.

Méri, Edina. "A soproni Központi Bányászati Múzeum új állandó kiállítása" (The new permanent exhibition of the Central Mining Museum in Sopron). *Honismeret* 29, no. 1 (February 2001): 97–99.

Mogyorósi, Sándor: "Az északkelet-magyarországi Werwolf-hiedelem interetnikus vonatkozásai" (Interethnic aspects of werewolf belief in northeastern Hungary). *A Herman Ottó Múzeum Évkönyve*, vol. 27. Miskolc, Hungary: Herman Ottó Múzeum, 1989.

Mokos, Gyula. "A dunántúli ág. ev. egyh. megalakulása és 1598-iki törvénykönyve" (The establishment of the Transdanubian branch of the evangelical church and its code of law of 1598). *Protestáns Szemle* 3 (1891): 364–93.

Molnár, Dániel Márton. *A xvi. Századi északkelet-magyarországi főnemesség hivatalviselési, hivatal és birtokszerzési Gyakorlata—losonczy antal és istván pályája* (The practice of holding office, acquiring property, and serving as a nobleman in northeastern Hungary in the 16th-century—the career of Antal and István Losonczy). PhD dissertation, Eötvös Loránd University, 2020.

Molnár, Dávid. "'Many Laughed at the Thought of This Illustrious Young Man Reading Books': About Miklós Báthory's Library and His Cicero-Codex." *Hungarian Historical Review* 8, no. 3 (2019): 573–93.

Molnár, László. "550 éve született Thurzó János, az európai hírű bányavállalkozó" (János Thurzó, the famous mining entrepreneur in Europe, was born 550 years ago). *BÁNYÁSZAT: Bányászati és Kohászati Lapok* 120, no. 4 (1987): 273–75.

Monok, István. "The Nádasdy Courts in Sárvár and Pottendorf and Their Book Culture." In *Blue Blood, Black Ink: Book Collections of Aristocratic Families from 1500 to 1700*. Budapest: National Széchényi Library, 2005.

"Most prolific serial killer (female)." Guinness World Records Limited 2025. https://www.guinnessworldrecords.com/world-records/most-prolific-female-murderer.

Murdock, Graeme. *Calvinism on the Frontier 1600–1660: International Calvinism and the Reformed Church in Hungary and Transylvania*. Oxford University Press, 2000.

Nagy, Iván. "A Losoncziak és Bánffyak nemzedék-rendje" (The Losonczy and Bánffy family trees). *Turul* 1 (1883): 16–25.

———. *Magyarország családai* (The families of Hungary). 12 volumes. Pest: Friebeisz István, 1857–1868.

Nagy, László. *Az erös fekete bég: Nádasdy Ferenc* (Francis Nadasdy: The strong black bey). Budapest: Zrinyi Katonai, 1987.

———. "Erdélyi 'boszorkányperek' a politikai hatalom szolgálatában" (Transylvanian "witch trials" in the service of political power). *Századok* 112, no. 1 (1978): 1097–1141.

———. "Kathay Mihály A Magyar Históriában" (Michael Kathay in Hungarian history). *Valóság* 19 (1976): 93–108.

———. *A rossz hírű Báthoryak* (The infamous Bathorys). 2nd ed. Budapest: Kossuth Könyvkiadó, 1985.

Nagy-Toth, Maria. "A batthyány család gyógyító nagyasszonya" (The healing grandmother of the Batthyány family). In *A Batthyányak évszázadai*, edited by Zoltán Nagy. Scientific conference in Körmend, October 27–29, 2005. Körmend City Municipality, 2006.

"Négyszáz református év" (Four hundred years of the Reformation). Magyarországi Református Egyház (Hungarian Reformed Church), August 28, 2012. reformatus.hu/egyhazunk/hirek/negyszaz-ev/.

Nemeš, Jaroslav. "The Completion of the German Reformation in Hungary: The Disintegration of the Church Unity (1610)." In *Church and Ethnicity in History: First Year of Conference V4 for Doctoral Candidates in Ostrava*. Edited by Vida Beáta. Ostrava, Czech Republic (April 2010): 60–73.

Németh, Ildikó. "Thomas (Hans) Türck soproni disznópásztor boszorkánypere, 1596" (The witch trial of the swineherd Türck in Sopron, 1596). *Soproni Szemle* 62, nos. 1–4 (2008): 170–72.

Németh, Péter, and Eszter Zoltán-Borzován. *Ecsed Vára* (Ecsed Castle). Kisvárda, Hungary: Rétközi Múzeum, 2021.

Nutton, Vivian. *Renaissance Medicine*. London: Routledge, 2022.

Nyakas, Miklós. "Báthory Gábor hajdúpolitikája" (The hajduk policies of Gabriel Bathory). In *Báthory Gábor És Kora*. Edited by Klára Papp et al. Debrecen: University of Debrecen, 2009, 327–36.

Oborni, Teréz. "Báthory Gábor megállapodásai a Magyar Királysággal" (Gabriel Báthory's agreements with the Kingdom of Hungary). In *Báthory Gábor És Kora*. Edited by Klára Papp et al. Debrecen: University of Debrecen, 2009, 111–22.

———. "Georgius Monachus Contra Reginam—Queen Isabella and Her Reign over the Eastern Kingdom of Hungary (1541–1551)." In *Isabella Jagiellon, Queen of Hungary (1539–1559)*. Edited by Ágnes Máté and Teréz Oborni. Budapest: Research Centre for the Humanities, 2020.

Óváry, Lipót. *A MTA történelmi bizottságának oklevélmásolatai* (Copies of documents of the Historical Committee of the Hungarian Academy of Sciences). Vol. 3. Budapest: Athenaeum, 1901.

Pakó, László. "Kényszer vagy erkölcsi romlottság?" (Coercion or moral corruption?). *Korunk* 16, no. 3 (March 2005): 84–93

Pálffy, Géza. *Hungary Between Two Empires 1526–1711*. Bloomington: Indiana University Press, 2021.

Pálvölgyi, Endre. "Aki keres, többnyire talál: Válaszok az olvasók kérdéseire" (Those who seek will usually find: answers to readers' questions). *Könyvtáros* 32, no. 5 (January 5, 1982): 255–58.

Papp, Julia. "Female Body—Male Body: The Valiant Hungarian Women of Eger and Szigetvár from the 16th Century in Historiography, Literature, and Art." *Cogent Arts & Humanities* 3, no. 1 (2016). doi.org/10.1080/233119 83.2016.1147403.

Parsons, Nicholas. "The Reformation in Hungary." *The Hungarian Review* 9, no. 1 (January 4, 2018). hungarianreview.com/article/20180119_the _reformation_in_hungary.

Payr, Sándor. *A Dunántúli Evangélikus Egyházkerület története* (The history of the Transdanubian Evangelical Church District). Vol. I. Sopron, Székely and Co., 1924.

———. *Egyháztörténeti emlékek. Forrásgyüjtemény a dunántúli ág. Hitv. Evang. Egyházkerület történetéhez* (Church history memorabilia: A collection of sources regarding the history of the Transdanubian branch of the Evangelical [Lutheran] Church). Vol I. Sopron: Romwalter Alfréd Könyvnyomdája, 1910. https://mek.oszk.hu/01900/01910/01910.pdf.

———. "Magyari István és Báthory Erzsébet" (Stephen Magyari and Elizabeth Bathory). *Protestáns Szemle* 24, no. 4 (1912): 185–203.

Penrose, Valentine. *The Bloody Countess: Atrocities of Erzsebet Bathory*. London: Calder, 1970.

Peres, Zsuzsanna. "Hitbérkikötések a magyar főúri családok körében a Werbőczy utáni időszakban" (Lease agreements among Hungarian noble families in the post–Werbőczy period). In *A jogi kultúrtörténet és a jogi néprajz új forrásai I-II.: Jogi kultúrtörténeti és jogi néprajzi interdiszciplináris nemzetközi konferencia: Szekszárd, 2017. szeptember 28–29*. Szekszárd, Hungary: PTE Faculty of Cultural Studies, Teacher Training, and Rural Development, 2018, 281–300.

Péter, Katalin. "Báthory Erzsébet—valóság és fantasia" (Erzsébet Báthory—reality and fantasy). *Historia* 31, no. 1 (2009): 25–27.

Péter, Katalin, editor. *Beloved Children: History of Aristocratic Childhood in Hungary in the Early Modern Age*. Budapest: Central European University Press, 2001.

———. "The Golden Age of the Principality (1606–1660)." In *History of Transylvania*. Edited by Gábor Barta et al. Budapest: Akademiai Kiado, 1994: 301–58.

———. "Gabriel Bethlen Stops the War." In *History of Transylvania*, vol. 2. Edited by László Makkai and Zoltán Szász. New York: Columbia University Press, 2002. mek.oszk.hu/03400/03407/html/174.html.

———. *Házasság a régi Magyarországon—16–17. század*. (Marriage in old Hungary—16th–17th centuries). Budapest: L'Harmattan, 2008.

———. "Hungary." In *The Reformation in National Context*. Edited by Robert Scribner et al. Cambridge University Press, 1994: 155–67.

———. "Kanizsay Orsolya (1520–1571)." *Nagy képes millenniumi arcképcsarnok. 100 portré a magyar történelemből*. Edited by Árpád Rácz. Budapest: Rubicon–Aquila, 1999: 67–68.

Poprádi, Janka. *Healers and Lay Medics in Sixteenth-Seventeenth-Century Hungary*. Master's thesis, Central European University History Department, Budapest, June 2008.

"A Protestáns Vallásos Irodalom És Egyházi Szónoklat" (Protestant Religious Literature and Ecclesiastical Oratory). *Magyar Irodalomtörténet*. Vol. 3. Seventeenth Century. Edited by Jenő Pintér. Budapest, 1931.

"The Protestants' Attitudes Towards Death." *Musée Protestant* (Protestant Museum). museeprotestant.org/en/notice/the-protestants-attitude-towards-death.

Rácz, Magdolna D. "Szabolcs-Szatmár-Bereg megye jelentősebb nemesi írói" (Significant noble writers of Szabolcs-Szatmár-Bereg county). *Termés* 3 (2019): 29–27.

Radi, Anita. "Báthory Erzsébet és a négyszáz éves mítosz" (Elizabeth Bathory and the four-hundred-year-old myth). *Múzsa*, September 7, 2019. muzsa.sk/irodalom/bathory-erzsebet-es-a-negyszaz-eves-mitosz.

Rady, Martyn. "Bocskai, Rebellion and Resistance in Early Modern Hungary." In *Resistance, Rebellion and Revolution in Hungary and Central Europe: Commemorating 1956*. Edited by László Péter and Martyn Rady. Budapest: Hungarian Cultural Centre, 2008, 57–75.

———. *Customary Law in Hungary: Courts, Texts, and the Tripartitum*. Oxford University Press, 2015.

Raeburn, Gordon. "The Reformation of Burial in the Protestant Churches." In *A Companion to Death, Burial, and Remembrance in Late Medieval and Early Modern Europe, c. 1300–1700*. Edited by Philip Booth and Elizabeth Tingle. Berlin: Brill, 2020.

Rankin, Alisha. "Becoming an Expert Practitioner: Court Experimentalism and the Medical Skills of Anna of Saxony (1532–1585)." *Isis* 98, no. 1 (2007): 23–53. doi.org/10.1086/512830.

Read, Sara. "Curious Cupping." *Early Modern Medicine* (blog), June 19, 2013. earlymodernmedicine.com/guest-post-curious-cupping.

Reichardt, Gabriella. "A keresztúri uradalom a XVI-XVII. század fordulóján" (The Keresztúr manor at the turn of the 16th and 17th centuries). In *Memoriae commendamus, Studies XI*. Edited by Adrienn Kapitány and Dániel Locsmándi. Budapest: Eötvös College, 2011, 81–101.

Rivière, Lazare. *"Six Hundred Miseries": The Seventeenth Century Womb: Book 15 of "The Practice of Physick."* Translated by Nicholas Culpeper (1678). Edited by John L. Burton. London: RCOG Press, 2005.

Schram, Ferenc. *Magyarorszagi Boszorkanyperek 1529–1768* (Hungarian witch trials 1529–1768). Vol III. Budapest: Akadémiai Kiadó, 1982.

Schulteisz, Emil. "A magyarországi járványok történetéből" (The history of Hungarian epidemics). Budapest, 1964. Reported by Hungarian Institute for the History of Science. mek.oszk.hu/05400/05425/pdf/Schultheisz _Jarvanyok.pdf.

Seitz, Jonathan. "'The Root Is Hidden and the Material Uncertain': The Challenges of Prosecuting Witchcraft in Early Modern Venice." *Renaissance Quarterly* 62, no. 1 (Spring 2009), pp. 102–33. doi.org /10.1086/598373.

"Sigismund Báthory, a Changeable Prince." *Memoria Urbis*. University of Alba Julia. memoriaurbis.apulum.ro/en/story/19.

Sipos, Ferenc. "Keresztnevek egy tiszántúli családban 1498–1798" (First names in a family from Transylvania 1498–1798). *Magyar Névtani Dolgozatok* 142. Budapest: ELTE Magyar Nyelvészeti Tanszékcsoport Névkutató Munkaközössége, 1996.

Smith, Charlie. "A Mercurial Monarch and His Magical Metropolis: Rudolf II's Prague and Its Alchemical Association." In *Central Europe Yearbook* 2 (2020). pubs.lib.umn.edu/index.php/cey/article/view/3043.

Stanonik, Janez. "Captain John Smith in Slovenia." *Slovene Studies* 11, no. 1 (1989): 25–32.

Súpis pamiatok na Slovensku (List of monuments in Slovakia). Volume One: A–J. Bratislava: Obzor, 1967.

Szabó, András Péter, and Matthew Caples. "Betrothal and Wedding, Church Wedding and Nuptials: Reflections on the System of Marriages in Sixteenth- and Seventeenth-Century Hungary." *The Hungarian Historical Review* 3, no. 1 (2014): 3–31. jstor.org/stable/43265189.

Szabó, András. "A Bocskai-felkelés képe a szepességi krónikákban" (The image of the Bocskai uprising in the Spiš chronicles). In *A történelem mint hivatás: A Benda-emlékkonferencia előadásai.* Edited by István Szíjártó. Budapest, Balassi Kiadó, 2015, 45–74.

———. "Női Művelődés A 16. Századi Magyarországon" (Women's education in 16th-century Hungary). In *A Zsoltártól A Rózsaszín Regényig: Fejezetek A Magyar Női Művelődés Történetéből.* Edited by Júlia Papp. Budapest: Petőfi Irodalmi Múzeum, 2014, 71–78.

Szádeczky-Kardoss, Irma. "A Báthory Erzsébet elleni koncepciós eljárás egyes történeti forrásainak értelmezése" (Interpretation of some historical sources from the corrupt proceedings against Elizabeth Báthory). *Levéltári Közlemények.* 65.1-2: 65–87.

———. *Báthory Erzsébet igazsága* (The truth about Elizabeth Báthory). Budapest: Nesztor, 1993.

———. "The Bloody Countess? An Examination of the Life and Trial of Erzsébet Báthory," translated by Lujza Nehrebeczky. Originally published in *Élet és Tudomány* (*Life and Science*), September 2, 2005, and September 9, 2005. notesonhungary.wordpress.com/2014/05/31/the-bloody-countess.

———. "Koncepciós jegyek Báthory Erzsébet ügyében" (Notes on the fabricated case against Elizabeth Báthory). Doctoral thesis, Eötvös Loránd University, September 12, 1994.

———. "Mi az igazság Báthory Erzsébet ügyében?" (What is the truth in the case of Elizabeth Bathory?). *Historia* 8 (1997): 20–22.

Szántai, Gábor. "Count Nádasdy Ferenc, the Strong Black Bey (1555–1604)." *Hungarian History* (blog). hungarianottomanwars.com/essays/count-nadasdy-ferenc-the-strong-black-bey-1555-1604.

———. "The Long War, Part 32: Military Actions in the First Part of 1603." *Hungarian History* (blog). hungarianottomanwars.com/chronologie

/the-fifteen-year-war-series-1591-1606/the-long-war-part-32-military-actions-in-the-first-part-of-1603.

Szatlóczki, Gábor. *Vár a várban. A várak népe és a mezei hadak a 16. század közepén* (Waiting in the castle: The people of the castles and the field armies of the mid-16th century). Szeged, Hungary: Missiles Kiadó, 2016.

Sz. Kristof, Ildiko. "'Charming Sorcerers' or 'Soldiers of Satan'? Witchcraft and Magic in the Eyes of Protestant/Calvinist Preachers in Early Modern Hungary." *Religions* 10, no. 5 (2019). mdpi.com/2077-1444/10/5/328.

———. "Witch Hunting in Hungary." In *Encyclopedia of Witchcraft: The Western Tradition*. Vol 2. Edited by Richard M. Golden. Santa Barbara, CA; Denver, CO; and Oxford, UK: ABC Clio, 2006: 515–520.

Szeghy, Blanka. "Fornicatrices, Scortatrices et Meretrices Diabolares: Disciplining Women in Early Modern Hungarian Towns." *Same Bodies, Different Women: "Other" Women in the Middle Ages and the Early Modern Period*. Edited by Christopher Mielke and Andrea-Bianka Znorovsky. Budapest: Trivent, 2019.

Szeghy, Blanka. "Punishment in Sixteenth-Century Hungarian Towns." In *Friars, Nobles and Burghers—Sermons, Images and Prints: Studies of Culture and Society in Early-Modern Europe*. Edited by Jaroslav Miller and László Kontler. Central European University Press, 2010.

Szentmártoni Szabó, Géza. "Losonczy Anna a források tükrében" (Anna Losonczy in light of the [historical] sources). *Tiszaszentmárton*. Municipality of Tiszaszentmárton, 2014: 63–82.

Szibler, Gabor. "'Az Gyermek Jó és Nagy . . .' A Nádasdy-Gyerekek" ('The child is good and big . . .': The Nadasdy children). Nádasdy Ferenc Múzeum Sárvár, April 25, 2017. nadasdymuzeum.hu/az-gyermek-jo-es-nagy-a-nadasdy-gyerekek-2017-04-25.

Szilady, Jenö. "A Magyarorszagi Tot Protestans Egyhazi Irodalom 1517–1711" (The Protestant congregational literature of Hungary 1517–1711). PhD dissertation, University of Pécs, 1939.

Takáts, Sándor. *Régi magyarország jókedve* (Merrymaking in old Hungary). Budapest: Athenaeum, 1921.

Tamus, Elvira Viktória. *Foreign Influences on Transylvania's Political Elite, 1559–1602.* Master's thesis, Leiden University, 2020.

Teszelszky, Kees, and Márton Zászkaliczky. "Bocskai's Revolt, European Information Networks and Print Culture (Political Propaganda, Diplomacy and News Circulation Between Manuscripts and Prints, 1604-1606)." Presentation. University of Groningen, 2013: 1–12. pure.rug.nl/ws/portalfiles/portal/13912745/Teszelszky_Z_szkaliczky_Presentation_pretext_Wroclaw.pdf.

Theilig, Stephan. "The Change of Imaging the Ottomans in the Context of the Turkish Wars from the 16th to 18th Century." *Cahiers de la Méditerranée* 83 (2011): 61–68. doi.org/10.4000/cdlm.6081.

Thorne, Tony. *Countess Dracula: The Life and Times of Elisabeth Báthory, the Blood Countess.* London: Bloomsbury, 1997.

Thury, Etele. "A csepregi hitvita" (The Csepreg controversy). *Protestáns Szemle* 17, no. 8 (1905): 133–50.

Tiryakioglu, Nevsal Olcen. "The Western Image of Turks from the Middle Ages to the 21st Century: The Myth of 'Terrible Turk' and 'Lustful Turk.'" PhD dissertation, Nottingham Trent University, 2015.

Tóth, Peter G. "'The Bloody Theatre of Europe': The Culture of Pain, Cruelty and Martyrdom in Early Modern Hungary." *Acta Ethnographica Hungarica* 48, nos. 3–4 (2003): 385–96.

Tóth, Peter G., editor. *A magyarorszagi boszorkányperek digitalis adatbazisa* (Digital database of Hungarian witch trials). European Research Council, Project No. 324214. boszorkanykorok.hu/projekt.html.

Tóth, Peter G., and Ildikó Németh. *Soproni Boszorkányperek / Ödenburger Hexenprozesse 1429–1702* (Sopron witch trials 1429–1702, in Hungarian and German). Vol. 3 of *A Magyarországi Boszorkányság Forrásai* (Sources on witchcraft in Hungary). Budapest: Balassi Kiadó, 2011.

Tötösy de Zepetnek, Steven. "Nobilitashungariae: List of Historical Surnames of the Hungarian Nobility." *Library Series, CLCWeb: Comparative Literature and Culture* (2010). docs.lib.purdue.edu/clcweblibrary/nobilitashungariae.

Tradii, Laura. "Cabinets of Curiosities." *Dilettante Army*, Summer 2017. dilet tantearmy.com/articles/cabinets-of-curiosities.

Tusor, Péter. "Dynastic Politics, Diplomacy and the Catholic Church." In *A Divided Hungary in Europe: Exchanges, Networks and Representations 1541–1699*, vol. 2, *Diplomacy, Information Flow and Cultural Exchange*, edited by Szymon Brzeziński and Áron Zarnóczki. Newcastle upon Tyne: Cambridge Scholars, 2014.

Urban, Laszlo. "Sárvár és Csepreg mezővárosok szerepe a polgárias művelődésben a 17. sz.-ban" (The role of the market towns of Sárvár and Csepreg in bourgeois culture in the 17th century). In *A Dunántúl településtörténete I. 1686–1768: Proceedings of the settlement history conference*. Edited by Gábor Farkas. Veszprém, 1976, 304–8.

Vadász, Veronika. "Ecsedi Báthory István végrendelete 1603" (Will of Stephen Bathory of Ecsed, 1603). Master's thesis, University of Szeged, 2002.

———. "Egy prédikátor levelei Bocskaihoz 1605 tavaszán" (A preacher's letters to Bocskai in the spring of 1605). *Aetas—Történettudományi folyóirat* 20, no. 3 (2005): 155–61.

Varga, János, editor. *Magyarország birtokviszonyai a 16. Század közepén* (Land ownership in Hungary in the mid-16th century). Budapest: Akadémiai Kiadó, 1990.

Várkonyi, Gábor. *Báthory Erzsébet: Bűnös Vagy Áldozat?* (Elizabeth Báthory: guilty or victim?). Budapest: Kossuth, 2016.

———. "Hospodárenie—netradicná úloha aristokratickych zien v ranono-vovekom Uhorsku" (Estate management: The unconventional role of noblewomen in early modern Hungary). In *Zena a pravo*. Edited by Tunde Lengyl. Bratislava: Academic Electronic Press, 2004.

———. "A Sárkány Árnyékában—Kultusz és történelem: Báthory Erzsébet életének értelmezései" (In the shadow of the dragon—cult and history: Interpretations of the life of Elizabeth Báthory). *Korunk* 3 (2012): 35–40.

———. "Újabb Források Báthory Erzsébet életéhez" (New sources on the life of Elizabeth Bathory). *Irodalomtörténeti Közlemények* 103, nos. 1–2 (1999). epa.oszk.hu/00000/00001/00008.

Veres, Tünde. "Livestock Keeping at the Regéc Estate as Reflected by 17th Century Sources and Other Rákóczi Estates." *Történeti Tanulmányok* 29 (2021): 52–68.

Viskolcz, Noémi. *A mecenatúra színterei a főúri udvarban Nádasdy Ferenc könyvtára* (Scenes of patronage at the noble court: The library of Francis Nádasdy). University of Szeged Historia Ecclesiastica Hungarica Foundation, 2013.

Wilby, Emma. "Burchard's *Strigae*, the Witches' Sabbath, and Shamanistic Cannibalism in Early Modern Europe." *Magic, Ritual, and Witchcraft* 8, no. 1 (Summer 2013): 18–49. doi.org/10.1353/mrw.2013.0010.

Willumsen, Liv Helene. *The Voices of Women in Witchcraft Trials: Northern Europe.* Milton Park, UK: Routledge, 2022.

Zay, Éva. "Intriguing Carvings Found on the Walls of Borosjenő Castle." *Transylvania Now*, October 25, 2019. transylvanianow.com/intriguing-carvings-found-on-the-walls-of-borosjeno-castle.

Zsupán, Edina. "History of the Library." *Bibliotheca Corvina Virtualis.* National Széchényi Librar. corvina.hu/en/about-corvinas/history/history-of-the-library.

Zubánics, László. *A Múlt Tükrében Elmerengve . . . Északkelet-Magyarország mindennapjai a XVI–XVIII. század fordulóján* (Reflecting on the past . . . Everyday life in northeastern Hungary at the turn of the 16th–18th centuries). Budapest–Ungvár: Intermix Kiadó, 2020.

NOTES

DRAMATIS PERSONAE

5 **her name as "Elizabetth de Batthory":** Elizabeth Bathory to Maria Fugger, August 12, 1593. SB Familienarchiev Pálffy-Daun 8-1-5. Arma I. Lad. 4. Fasc. I. Frust. 5. HHStA. ÖStA.

5 **"Elisabeth comitissa de Bathor":** Elizabeth Bathory to George Pitsch, January 4, 1604. E 185. Box 22. MNL.

PROLOGUE

9 **brightly tiled walls:** Author Tony Thorne viewed these angels and tiles at the museum at Čachtice castle.

11 ***Book of World Records* first appeared, in 1956:** At the time, it appeared under the title *The Guinness Book of Superlatives.*

11 **"63rd Street, Chicago":** *The Guinness Book of Superlatives* (1956), 45.

11 **after being found guilty:** *The Guinness Book of Records* (1968), 201.

12 **"own signature of the Lady":** Testimony of Susanna. E 142. Fasc. 028. No. 19. Page 92. MNL.

12 **1.8 million people:** Palffy, 83.

12 **twenty to twenty-five houses:** Ibid.

12 **150 to 170 people:** Ibid.

12 **by a ten-year-old boy:** Jennet Device in the Pendle witch trials.

13 **"dedicated girl catchers":** Testimony of Lady Barbara. E 142. Fasc. 028. No. 19. Page 66. MNL.

13 **half a castle:** See "1572 dezember 21." Elizabeth had thirty-one thousand gold florins; her uncle purchased the massive Castle Füzér for sixty thousand florins, and her husband's family purchased two castles for a total of eighty-six thousand florins.

13 **weighed over two hundred pounds:** A single Hungarian gold florin weighed 3.51 grams and was close to pure gold (23.57 karats). All dollar comparisons are based on the price per ounce for gold in January 2025 ($86.92/gram).

NOTES

14 **a Hungarian archivist:** Dezső Rexa.

14 **publish his new evidence:** See Thorne, 207, and Benda, "Válasz Hetyéssy Szilviának." (Benda claims that Rexa believed Elizabeth wanted to elope with a coachman; her scandalized family had her arrested to prevent that from happening.)

14 **"Was Elizabeth Báthory Truly":** See Atwal.

15 **scenes were scripted:** For example, Elizabeth I never named James I her heir.

15 **wrapped in funeral shrouds:** Another example: The death of Prince John Sigismund, the son of King John Zápolya, was kept a secret for some time.

CHAPTER 1: A LONG, TERRIBLE YEAR

19 **platters of stuffed capons:** See Lengyel, *Život na šľachtickom*, 143 and 170.

19 **a physician at court:** See Magyary-Kossa, 486: In a 1602 letter to the city of Sopron, Nadasdy confirmed that he could no longer afford a court doctor.

19 **by horse-drawn sleigh:** Thurzo, "Letter 416," January 3, 1604. Vol. 2. 107.

19 **"goes everywhere and wins everywhere":** The Ottoman historian Ibrahim Pecsevi, quoted in Szántai, "Count Nádasdy Ferenc."

19 **Danube into the army camps:** Thurzo: the spread of the plague, see "Letter 412," November 23, 1603. Vol. 2. 103–4; Nadasdy has headed home, see "Letter 413," November 25, 1603. Vol. 2. 104–5.

20 **fourth-most-powerful aristocrat:** Domkovits, 778.

20 **Elizabeth, Countess Bathory:** One example: Elizabeth Bathory to Demeter Napraghy, April 19, 1609. E 204. Bundle 4. MNL.

20 **de rigueur for her station:** See Radi.

20 **sapphires, rubies, or pearls:** See "1572 dezember 21 . . . "

20 **beloved six-year-old Andras:** Francis Nadasdy to Francis Batthyany, January 29, 1603. P 1314: Archivum familiae Batthyany. No. 32007. National Archives of Hungary, Budapest. For other mentions of Andras's short life, see Vadász, *Ecsedi Báthory István*; Szibler, "'Az Gyermek Jó és Nagy' . . ."; Radi; and Laszlo Nagy, *Az erös fekete bég*.

20 **raided by the Turks:** See Szántai, "The Long War."

21 **"sudden illness upon me":** Francis Nadasdy to George Thurzo, January 3, 1604. OK-TK. No. 390. SOBA.

21 **even the moon turned its face:** Historical data about the moon's phases can be found at www.moongiant.com.

NOTES

21 "Jász, Ruthenians and finally Turks": See Oláh, chap. 19.
21 "the star of Europe": Written in 1604 by Francis Vathay, quoted in Fodor, 409.
22 Sforza castles: See Buzás, 368–72.
22 sparkling wine instead of water: See Oláh, chap. 11.
22 "what's more, they are free": Oláh, chap. 5.
22 held before Parliament: The most famous of these was Martin Bylica's demonstration of his astrolabe.
22 "science and discipline": Oláh, chap. 5.
22 silver buckles: Ibid.
22 a little copper leaf: See Zsupán.
22 two vaulted rooms: Oláh, chap. 5.
22 that of the Vatican: See Zsupán.
23 enviable library himself: Nicholas Bathory, Bishop of Vác; see David Molnar, 573, 575, 579–80.
23 Hungary's elite among them: Suleiman the Magnificent recorded this mass execution in his diary.
23 European powerhouse: Palffy, 17.
24 "*From Hungary he's soon away*": This song dates from the 1520s, quoted in Tiryakioglu, 73.
24 "Splitted the babies into two parts": See Theilig, 2.
24 "strongest bulwark of Christendom": See James.
25 paternal grandfather and great-uncle: Elizabeth's grandfather was Andrew Bathory II and her great-uncle was Stephen Bathory III.
25 master of the treasury: See Dániel Márton Molnár, 42. The position was known as *tavernicorum regalium magister* in Latin and in Hungarian as *tárnokmester*.
26 city of Philadelphia today: The Ecsed Swamp was 166 square miles.
26 their ancestral castle of Somlyó: Now known as Șimleu Silvaniei.
26 besieged by his older brother: The siege took place in 1565 at Castle Erdőd, located in what is now Romania.
27 always stayed in the family: See Borbély, "A végvárrendszer . . . ," 173–75.
27 and all kinds of red stones: "Inventory of Klara Bathory's possessions," 1559. Fond familial Bánffy, Seria 2, Subseria 2. Fascicula X, No. 7. ANR, Cluj.
27 The imperial army commandeered: See Daniel Molnar, 47, and Korpás and Szabó, 158. One thousand soldiers were sent to Klara's estate, which was more than one sixth of the invading force.

27 **a remote Gothic tower:** Now Slanec Castle in Slovakia.
28 **distant sixth cousins:** Their great-great-great-great-grandfathers were brothers; George Bathory was descended from Lucas Bathory II, born around 1316; Anna Bathory was descended from Lucas's brother John. For detailed family trees, see Iván Nagy, *Magyarország családai*, vol. 1, 218–28.
28 **the Strong Black Bey:** Laszlo Nagy, *Az erős fekete bég.*
28 **ten thousand local people:** See Szántai, "The Long War."
29 **convinced that God was calling:** Francis Nadasdy to George Thurzo, 3 January 1604. OK-TK. No. 390. SOBA.
29 **a third of Royal Hungary:** Domkovits, 778.

CHAPTER 2: THE FIRST CLUE

31 **"be protected and cared for":** Francis Nadasdy to Francis Batthyany. January 29, 1603. P 1314. No. 32012. MNL. See also Lengyel, "A legrosszabb," 55, and Varkonyi, "Újabb."
31 **townhome in Vienna:** See Varkonyi, "Újabb."
31 **Master of the Horse:** Domkovits, 777.
31 **Knight of the Golden Spur:** He was knighted on June 28, 1598.
31 **lord-lieutenant:** This title is *comes supremus* in Latin and *foispan* in Hungarian.
32 **"warden, guardian and protector":** Francis Nadasdy to George Thurzo, January 3, 1604. OK-TK. No. 390. SOBA.
32 **"things I need for his funeral":** Elizabeth Bathory to George Pitsch, January 4, 1604. E 185. Box 22. MNL.
32 **Francis's family crypt:** In Léka.
32 **$5 million today:** According to calculations made by the imperial court chamber in September 1604, Francis was owed seventeen thousand florins. All dollar comparisons are based on the price per ounce of gold in January 2025 ($86.92/gram).
32 **456 thalers and some odd pfennigs' worth:** One thaler is twenty-five to thirty grams of silver. All dollar comparisons are based on the price per ounce of silver in January 2025 ($0.98/gram).
32 **five-year-old son, Paul:** He was born June 6, 1598.
33 **with a single swing:** Siege of Székesfehérvár, 1543. See Papp.
33 **women even dressed in armor:** Siege of Szigetvár, 1566. See Papp for descriptions of how these women were publicly memorialized.

NOTES

33 **until their sons came of age:** Anna Bathory managed Kraszna and Közép-Szolnok Counties for her son George (see Last and Iván Nagy, *Magyarország családai*, vol. 1, 231). Francis's mother, Ursula Kanizsay, managed Vas and Sopron counties until her death in 1571 (see Péter, "Kanizsay").

33 **behind the guard tower:** Sketch provided by Gabor Szibler of the Ferenc Nadasdy Museum.

34 **when she took ill:** See Varkonyi, "Újabb."

34 **letter to one of his friends:** Francis Nadasdy to Francis Batthyany, January 29, 1603. P 1314. No. 32007. MNL. For more commentary see Radi and Laszlo Nagy, *Az erös fekete bég*, 39–40.

34 **"no foul language":** See Magyari's eulogy for Francis Nadasdy in Payr, *Egyháztörténeti emlékek*, 133–34.

34 **church council on the Nadasdy estates:** See Payr, *Egyháztörténeti emlékek*, 84, and Payr, "Magyari István és Báthory Erzsébet," 188.

34 **the plague was running rampant:** See Agoston, 78.

35 **most people's annual salary:** Examples of salaries: An archbishop's housekeeper earned around twenty-two florins a year, a gardener and his wife twenty, a junior coachman only eight (examples provided by Judit Babcsányi in an email dated July 25, 2023).

35 **"[were] running with blood":** Quoted in "A Protestáns Vallásos . . ."

35 **Hungarian people for their immorality:** See Katona, 553.

36 **a Catholic archbishop had led:** This was Archbishop Paul Tomori.

36 **"pestilence" near and far:** The Chapter of Oradea to Bishop Olah of Erlau, June 27, 1552. LA Ungarn, Ungarisch Akten: Miscellanea 425 No. 61. HHStA. ÖStA.

36 **German and French countesses:** These would include the duchess Elisabeth of Brandenburg, the countesses Barbara von Wetheim and Isabella of Navarre, the princess (and later duchess) Renée of France, and the queens Marguerite of Navarre and Jeanne d'Albret.

36 **off her husband's lands:** See Zay and Szentmártoni Szabó, 64.

36 **Klara closed down a monastery:** These events occurred in 1545 and 1549.

36 **von Beckum sisters-in-law:** Maria and Ursula von Beckum.

37 **"serve to mislead souls":** This excerpt from the 1545 Synod of Erdod is quoted in Barkley, 6, and Kovács, "Az ecsedi udvar," 934.

37 **"performing the sacred service":** See Köő: This was the Debrecen preacher Márton Kálmáncsehi Sánta.

37 **some even ordained women:** These include the preacher Matthias Dévai Biro and many Anabaptist parishes.

38 **reformer mother:** In his will, Elizabeth's brother gave thanks for "my beloved mother, the great Anna Báthory of Somlyó, who raised and brought me up in the confession of faith," quoted in Sipos, 21.

38 **her seventeen-year-old fiancé:** Francis was an orphan himself, his mother, Ursula Kanizsay, having died in the spring of 1571.

38 **its own mills, beehives:** Sárvár Castle Inventory, January 28, 1608. E 156. Fasc. 37. No. 56b. MNL.

38 **goldfish and swans:** Lengyel, *Život na šľachtickom*, 209.

38 **Almonds and figs:** Bobory, 87–88.

38 **orange and lemon trees:** Ibid.

38 **hospital and almshouse:** See "Kanizsai Orsolya."

38 **school and scholars:** Ibid.; also mentioned in Melius, 397.

38 **in the Hungarian language:** John Sylvester's 1541 translation of the New Testament.

38 **Denomination was often dictated:** See Parker.

39 **schoolteachers and preachers:** Csepreg had about three hundred students, which was much smaller than Wittenberg but close to the number of students at Heidelberg University; see Bódi, 46.

39 **convert to the bride's religion:** No evidence of conversion: Lengyel, "A legrosszabb hírű," 62; Elizabeth's father converted: "Iskolánk névadója, Ecsedi Báthori István," plus the examples of George Thurzo's own daughters in Erdélyi, 607.

39 **Francis's mother quoted Calvin:** See Péter, "Hungary," 159.

39 **Catholics among their friends:** Daboczi, 323.

39 **attended the same service:** "Evangélikus gyülekezetek," 7.

39 **unified church district:** See Kónya, 286, and "Négyszáz református év."

39 **once elected bishop:** In 1585, of Sopron and Vas Counties.

39 **death in the nearest river:** Botik, 55–56.

40 **Lutheran churching ceremonies, and Calvinist:** For example, see the service book of the Calvinist bishop Janos Samarjai, described in Barkley, 13–14. A churching ceremony welcomed a woman back to the church after she had recovered from childbirth.

40 **(two of whom died in prison):** Peucer, Schuetze, Stoessel, and Cracow.

40 **chancellor was beheaded:** Nicolaus Krell.

NOTES

40 **Lutheran pastor named John Reczes**: See Mokos, 373: Reczes was known to be "arrogant and violent."

40 **reached with the Ottoman empire**: A peace was negotiated in 1568 and renewed in 1576, 1584, and 1591.

41 **A terrible frost**: Szepsi, 23.

41 **"thieves, fornicators, and murderers"**: Quoted in Masznyik, 224.

41 **Beythe resigned**: Masznyik, 222.

41 **fabricating "fake news"**: Quoted in Thury, 147: *hamis híreket*.

42 **mocking several of the hard-line ministers**: Ibid. No copies of the poem have survived, just the names of the eight pastors it disparaged, most of whom were Lutheran senior clergy.

42 **Reczes demanded all clergy**: In 1593, seventy-eight pastors signed the declaration and a list of their names was published, declaring them the true believers.

42 **five Calvinist ones**: See Köblös, 49, and Murdock, 23.

42 **Calvinist pastors and vice versa**: See Köblös, 51–52; one example: The Diocese of Felsőcsepreg had Lutheran leadership but Calvinist pastors.

42 **began organizing "visitations"**: See Szilady, 48–49. In their letters two preachers, Ponikenus and Lany, discuss the discovery of Czech hymnals in the churches they inspected.

42 **"what books I had!"**: Paul Kincses quoted in Payr, *A Dunántúli*, 632.

42 **threatened, cursed, and slandered**: Bishop Beythe to Francis Nadasdy, January 25, 1598. Archivum generalis Ecclesiae (AGE). I. a. 7 No. 21. EOL.

42 **false criminal charges**: Ibid.

43 **had been hacked off**: See Katona, 553–54.

43 **big Easter holiday**: The letter was written on March 27, 1602; that year Easter was April 7.

43 **"certain wicked woman"**: Michael Zvonaric to George Pythiraeus, March 27, 1602. Archivum generalis Ecclesiae (AGE). I. a. 7 No. 28. EOL.

43 *caro*, **for "flesh"**: *Carnificina illa, carnificam, carnifice*.

43 **meaning of "executioner"**: This was the nickname for the Roman general Gnaeus Pompeius Strabo, and his son Pompey was *adulescentulus carnifex*, the "teenage executioner."

43 **censure or "rebuke"**: *Censuram, admonition*.

43 **until St. Paul's Day**: St. Paul's feast fell on June 29 that year.

NOTES

44 **"a bloodthirsty butcher"**: See "The condemnation of Paul the Instigator, the judgment concerning him, and the order to burn Lutheran books," in Payr, *Egyháztörténeti emlékek*, 13–14.

44 **child-killing werewolf**: In a 1560 letter from Balázs and Ákos Csányi to Francis's father, quoted in Mogyorósi, 287.

44 **defying them altogether**: See Elton, 205.

44 **"the Lord reconciled"**: Testimony of Paul Beod. E 142. Fasc. 028. No. 19. Page 76. MNL.

44 **for over twenty-five years**: Peter Bornemisza, the controversial preacher who had repeated the rumors against Klara, spoke of witches being burned in 1574.

CHAPTER 3: A WEDDING AND A REBELLION

45 **devout and "loving wife"**: Nagy, *Az erös fekete bég*, 275.

45 **nobles from farther afield**: For a list of the people and troops assembled for Francis's funeral march see "Draft of Francis Nadasdy's funeral procession" (Sárvár-Léka, January 11–12). E 185. Bundle 42, last fasc. Folio 133–34. MNL.

45 **eighteen million dollars**: 60,000 florins, or 210,600 grams of gold.

45 **the usual tithe**: The *sedecima*, or one tenth of everyone's income.

46 **"parish, like you do"**: Payr, *A Dunántúli*, 599.

46 **"consolation from him"**: See Magyari's eulogy for Francis Nadasdy in Payr, *Egyháztörténeti emlékek*, 133–34.

46 **"be sure of that"**: See Elizabeth Bathory, Salvus Conductus pro Ecclesiarum Visitatione, January 31, 1605. Quoted in Payr, *Egyháztörténeti emlékek*, 134.

46 **"punishment, believe that"**: Ibid.

46 **"smallest or the biggest"**: John Ponikenus to Elias Lany, January 1, 1611. E 196. Fasc. 7. No. 69. MNL.

47 **puppy misses its mother**: Justine Szambo to Elizabeth Bathory, January 25, 1587. E 185. Box 43. MNL.

47 **about prize greyhounds**: Elizabeth Bathory to Francis Batthyany, January 19, 1605. P 1314. No. 02237. MNL. (Technically "sighthounds," of which greyhounds are the most popular breed.)

47 **"a little bit of profit"**: John Borianszky to Elizabeth Bathory, November 17, 1605. E 185. Box 5. MNL.

47 **an heiress to the Fugger banking fortune**: Baroness Maria Fugger. One of Elizabeth's letters to her, dated August 12, 1593, is preserved in the

Austrian Archives: SB Familienarchiev Pálffy-Daun 8-1-5. Arma I. Lad. 4. Fasc. I Frust. 5. HHStA. ÖStA.

47 **"most devoted friend":** Bishop Zalathnoky of Pécs to Elizabeth Bathory. January 16, 1604. E 185. Box 43. MNL.

47 **other prominent widows:** *Magyar országgyűlési emlékek*, 430.

47 **gambling and shopping excursions:** See Fischer.

47 **Elizabeth came first:** Thurzo, "Letter 288," March 20, 1599. Vol. 1. 287.

48 **"what should happen about this":** Elizabeth Bathory to Archbishop Stephen Szuhay, January 12, 1604. E 185. Box 22. MNL.

49 **make them functional again:** Méri, 98.

49 **the post of Lord High Steward:** Lengyel, "The Chances for a Provincial Cultural Centre," 114.

49 **"Get to know her," he implored:** Thurzo, "Letter 288," March 20, 1599. Vol. 1. 287.

49 **unable to keep food down:** Ibid., and Thurzo, "Letter 289," March 22, 1599. Vol 1. 281–82.

49–50 **"from her earliest childhood":** Quoted in Lengyel, "Esettanulmány," 237, and András Szabó, "Női Művelődés," 73.

50 **beds and candleholders:** See Lengyel, "Az írástudatlantól," 148.

50 **"heart, soul and life":** Elizabeth Czobor to Thurzo, December 27, 1610. OK-TK. No. 106. SOBA.

50 **on his own, as usual:** Lengyel, "Az írástudatlantól," 147.

50 **Thurzo kept her at home:** Lengyel, "Az írástudatlantól," 147.

50 **her "many troubles":** Elizabeth Bathory to Francis Batthyany, February 15, 1604. P 1314. No. 02236. MNL.

50 **reshuffling of the nobles' lodgings:** Thurzo, "Letter 419," March 12, 1604. Vol. 2. 109.

50 **tail of real feathers:** See Tradii.

51 **lead or tin into gold:** Smith, "Mercurial Monarch."

51 **One of her late husband's relations:** Francis's cousin Thomas Nadasdy; see Rady, 144, and Acsady, 19–20.

51 **committing bodily mutilation:** Francis Petheo; see Rady, 144, and Acsady, 19–20.

51 **he was already dead:** Ibid. The noble was Andras Balassa.

51 **accused of usurpation:** George Drugeth of Humenne, Elizabeth's future son-in-law; ibid.

51 **emperor had long coveted:** Trebišov Castle; see Lenčiš, 103–5.

51 protests in 1599 and 1603: Acsady, 20.
52 ejected all Protestant clergy: See András Szabó, "A Bocskai-felkelés."
52 "pay their taxes anymore": Ursula Nadasdy to Elizabeth Bathory, January 18, 1604. In *Nádasdy Tamás nádor családi levelezése*, 16–17.
52 petitioned that they be allowed to keep: The petition was issued March 26, 1604. See *Magyar országgyűlési emlékek*, 472–76.
52 regiment from Alsace: Minutes of the County of Sopron 519 and 520 (April 13, 1604). Jzk. MNL.
52 support an Italian regiment: Minutes of the County of Vas 862 (May 30, 1604). Jzk. MNL.
52 the equivalent of $1.5 million: According to the calculations of the imperial court chamber, Elizabeth was still owed 4,908 florins and 30 krajcár. See Court Chamber calculations, September 1604. Kt. 199 Konv. folio 32r-34v. FHKA. ÖStA.
53 in his thirties: Nicolas Zrinyi IV's exact birth date is unknown, but it is generally assumed to be around 1570–1580. In *Countess Dracula*, Tony Thorne stated that Zrinyi was born later, in 1590 (159).
53 less than ten years: Péter, *Beloved Children*, 11.
53 she began petitioning: Minutes of the County of Sopron 533 (May 3, 1604). Jzk. MNL; see also Reichardt 93.
53 "calamities and difficulties": Minutes of the County of Vas 863 (May 30, 1604). Jzk. MNL.
53 counted among them: Thurzo, "Letter 421," May 10, 1604. Vol. 2. 112.
54 plot of land of their own: Pálffy, 119.
54 "a silver comet star": Astronomer Albin Moller quoted in Boner, 1.
54 portending a new savior: See Eamon.
54 "our dear homeland!": Quoted in Rady, "Bocskai," 11.
55 "food and other necessities": Orava Castle; Thurzo, "Letter 433," November 10, 1604. Vol. 2. 119.
55 young Bathory nephew: Sigmund, who would rule for a time as the prince of Transylvania.
55 also the chief justice: In Hungarian, *országbírója*; in Latin, *judex curiae regiae*.
55 meaning of existence: Rácz, 32.
55 Protestant factions on his estates: Dienes, 188.
56 fortress along with him: "Iskolánk névadója, Ecsedi Báthori István."
56 bodyguard of 150 men: Fifty royal infantry mercenaries and one hundred cavalry soldiers; Kovacs, 949.

56 **courting Stephen Bathory:** Through his pastor; see Vadász, 161.
56 **discussions to paper:** Stephen Bathory went so far as to warn others not to write sensitive material down: "I myself will speak only with Your Grace face-to-face, or I will send a message from . . . an old pious servant of mine." Quoted in Kovács, "Ecsedi Báthory," 340–41.
56 **courier on her estates:** Translation in Thorne, 118.
56 **Stephen's three counties:** Szatmár, Szabolcs, and Somogy.
56 **Bathory had built:** This was done by the Italian commander Giorgio Basta; see Vadasz, 156fn6.
56 **coffins had been broken open:** See Balazs, 44.
57 **send their representatives:** See Rady, "Bocskai," 11; only five of the twenty-seven county assemblies would send representatives.
57 **"[suspicions] have to be eliminated":** Emery Megyery to Elizabeth Bathory, January 24, 1605. E 185. Box 20. MNL.
57 **"Your Ladyship's internal affairs":** Ibid.
57 **"young master" Paul:** Receipt for Elizabeth Bathory from George Pitsch, September 5, 1604. E 185. Box 30, item 520. MNL.
58 **a Calvinist church in the east:** On April 17, 1605, Anna Nadasdy's wedding began in Csepreg and a Parliament was convened in Szerencs.
58 **"Moses of the Hungarians":** See Kálmán Benda, "A kálvini," 327. The declaration was made on April 20, 1605.
58 **gem-encrusted crown:** Bocskai, aware of the optics, wisely refused the physical crown but accepted the Turks' offer of an alliance.
58 **behind the rebellion:** See Dienes, 187.
58 **overriding the wishes of the local people:** The Sopron County council, after a unanimous vote, had petitioned the emperor to appoint Paul Nadasdy as their lord-lieutenant (with someone else, presumably Elizabeth, acting as his regent). See the Minutes of the County of Sopron 534 (May 3, 1604). Jzk. MNL.
58 **Elizabeth's neighbor:** Appointment of Lord Batthyany, May 24, 1605. Familienakten B P 66. Folio 9. FHKA. ÖStA.
58 **reluctantly accepted the appointment:** Domkovits, 782f77.
58 **"Yesterday the Germans came out":** Elizabeth Bathory to Francis Batthyany, June 29, 1605. P 1314. No. 02243. MNL.
59 **captain of a nearby town:** Kőszeg.
59 **Thomas Nadasdy surrendered:** Bariska, 831, and Katona, "Bocskai csapatai Vas megyében," 274.

- 59 **siege of an important city**: This was Paul Nyary, married to Aunt Klara's granddaughter Kate Vardai; for information about the siege, see Pálvölgyi, 257–58.
- 59 **"pious late husband"**: General Basta to Elizabeth Bathory, June 28, 1605. P 1314. No. 2227. MNL.
- 59 **"(I will not have this anymore)"**: Ibid.
- 59 **"settle in the city"**: Elizabeth Bathory to Francis Batthyany, June 30, 1605. P 1314. No. 02244. MNL. For more commentary, see Lengyel, "A legrosszabb hírű," 57, and Nyakas, 98.
- 60 **"condemn my action"**: Thurzo, "Letter 454," July 1, 1605. Vol. 2. 137.
- 60 **letter to Elizabeth from her deputy**: The letter is from Blaise Kisfaludy; it is dated July 17. Although the year is missing, other events described in the letter strongly suggest it was written in 1605.
- 60 **one of her husband's cousins**: Thomas Nadasdy.
- 60 **"undertake anything on her own"**: Blaise Kisfaludy to Elizabeth Bathory, July 17, [year unknown]. E 185. Box 17. MNL.
- 60 **fit of "writhing," died**: Kovács, "Ecsedi Báthory," 340–41.
- 60–61 **although she recovered**: Ibid.
- 61 **rearranging items**: See Németh and Zoltán-Borzován, 54–55.
- 61 **some kind of demonic mischief**: Thurzo, "Letter 484," February 25, 1607. Vol. 2. 175.
- 61 **Elizabeth inherited several properties**: See Stephen Bathory's will in Vadász for a full list of every item and property Elizabeth inherited from her brother.

CHAPTER 4: THE CURIOUS CASE OF MISS MODL

- 63 **harry the locals**: Minutes of the County of Vas 868 (August 23, 1604). Jzk. MNL.
- 63 **"lurk in many places"**: Minutes of the County of Sopron 601 (May 20, 1606). Jzk. MNL.
- 63 **"but to protect us"**: Elizabeth Bathory to Francis Batthyany, August 12, 1605. P 1314. No. 02245. MNL.
- 63 **valuable grazing land**: Minutes of the County of Sopron 601 and 604 (May 20, 1606) and 607 (July 25, 1606). Jzl. MNL.
- 63 **"rise up against them"**: Minutes of the County of Sopron 608 (July 25, 1606). Jzl. MNL.

NOTES

63 **their own harassment:** Minutes of the County of Sopron 593 (May 8, 1606). Jzl. MNL.

64 **"faith and freedoms":** Quoted in Teszelszky, 5.

64 **"self-defense" against an unlawful tyrant:** Quoted in Teszelszky, 9; see also 7–8.

65 **"[mountain] pass for him":** From *Iacobi Franci Historicae Relationis Continvatio* (Magdeburg, 1605), 51. Quoted in Dillon, 66.

65 **he wore German garb:** Sz. Kristof, "Witch-Hunting," 7–8.

65 **bruised and bandaged hands:** Thurzo, "Letter 422," May 31, 1604. Vol 2. 110–11.

65 **430 miles each way:** A more direct route was not possible because she had to avoid the lands occupied by the Turks.

65 **unpredictable autumn weather:** Her brother's funeral was October 9, 1605 (see Balacz, 44, and Szepsi). There is a break in Elizabeth's correspondence that year. She made the trip sometime after September 5 and returned before November 3.

65 **raging plague epidemic:** Schulteisz, 4–5.

66 **to feed their children:** For an example, see Petition of Palkó Hegedűs, April 21, 1586. E 185. Box 14. MNL; mentioned in Lengyel, "A legrosszabb hírű," 59–60.

66 **their wedding feasts:** See Lengyel, "A legrosszabb hírű," 60.

66 **sneaking across the ice:** Minutes of the County of Sopron 573 (January 6, 1605) and 583 (January 24, 1605). Jzl. MNL.

66 **"ruined so freely again":** Elizabeth Bathory to Francis Batthyany, August 12, 1605. P 1314. No. 02245. MNL.

66 **met with the rebel leader:** See Balacz, 44, and Szepsi, 65.

66 **and she was tall:** "of good stature"; see Testimony of Gregory Paztory. E 142. Fasc. 028. No. 19. Page 60. MNL.

66 **serve at the lady's table:** Thorne, 64.

66 **Modl is suspiciously close:** See Koltai, 377.

67 **calling Miss Modl a "whore":** Testimony of Francis Torok and Gregory Paztory. E 142. Fasc. 028. No. 19. Pages 60, 73. MNL.

67 **punishment happened in Vranov:** Testimony of Francis Torok. E 142. Fasc. 028. No. 19. Pages 73. MNL.

67 **back on the estate of Čachtice:** Testimony of Gregory Paztory. E 142. Fasc. 028. No. 19. Page 60. MNL.

67 **simply been flogged:** Testimony of Helen Hernath. E 142. Fasc. 028. No. 19. Page 57. MNL.

67 **"compel them to go everywhere":** Elizabeth Bathory to Francis Batthyany, January 19, 1605. P 1314. No. 02237. MNL.

67 **"securing the servants' salaries":** Emery Megyery to Elizabeth Bathory, January 24, 1605. E 185. Box 20. MNL.

68 **gifted the girls "beautiful skirts":** Interrogation of Katherine Beneczky. E 142. Fasc. 028. No. 19. Page 86. MNL.

68 **"that could be beneficial":** Justine Zambo to Elizabeth Bathory, January 25, 1587. E 185. Box 43. MNL.

68 **offer their assistance:** See László Nagy, *A rossz hírű Báthoryak*, 31.

68 **occupied by Hapsburg troops:** Interrogation of Ficzko. E 142. Fasc. 028. No. 19. Page 79. MNL.

69 **flesh sliced off her backside:** Testimony of Benedict Deseo. E 142. Fasc. 028. No. 19. Page 58–60. MNL.

69 **burned on her abdomen:** Testimony of Adam Szelesthy. E 142. Fasc. 028. No. 19. Page 72. MNL.

69 **had her breasts cut off:** Testimony of Gregory Paztory. E 142. Fasc. 028. No. 19. Page 60. MNL.

69 **"for me," she complained:** Elizabeth Bathory to Francis Nadasdy, February 24, 1595. E 185. Box 22. MNL.

70 **Morgagni-Stewart-Morel syndrome:** See Lengyel, "Az írástudatlantól," 143–45, for a detailed description of Elizabeth Czobor's ailments.

70 **cleanse itself properly:** Lengyel, "Az írástudatlantól," 144.

70 **"hot iron":** See Bullein, 29.

70 **employed the famous Mrs. Zavis:** Lengyel, "Az írástudatlantól," 144.

70 **to supplement them:** Thurzo, "Letter 522," May 7, 1608. Vol 2. 224. See also Lengyel, "Az írástudatlantól," 156.

70 **A Hungarian lady-in-waiting:** Lady Potencia Dersffy.

70 **a German princess:** Sybilla von Anhalt; the pharmacy offered free medical care to the poor.

70 **a Danish princess:** Anna, Electress of Saxony.

70–71 **Lord Batthyany's young wife:** Eva Poppel.

71 **"woman scientist" on the Sárvár estates:** See Várkonyi, "Újabb," and Lengyel, "A legrosszabb hírű," 60.

71 **not Hungarian or Slovak:** See Thorne, 98.

71 **as early as 1595:** Ibid.

NOTES

71 **berated them for their ignorance:** "Letter 91," *Szerelmes Orsikám,* 127.
71 **"the child would be well":** Ibid.
72 **such as France and Italy:** Wyman, 24–26; exceptions were made for the widows of a barber-surgeon, so they might carry on the family business.
72 **to practice medicine:** Since the tenth century; in 1576, Christ's Hospital's resident surgeon-apothecary was a Mrs. Cook, according to Wyman, 29.
72 **and the Netherlands too:** Elizabeth Moulthorne and Elinor Sneshell.
72 **"Jewish woman doctor":** Magyary-Kossa, 33.
72 **woman in "medical science":** See, in Tóth, *A magyarországi boszorkányperek digitalis adatbazisa,* the 1599 case against Mrs. John Nagy and Mrs. Vanda.
73 **"middle of her tooth":** See Thorne, 101.
73 **her baby might be saved:** Nutton, 153.
73 **the noble bled to death:** Megyery-Kossa, 325.
73 **"his head drilled open":** Magyary-Kossa, 306–7.
74 **cutting and cautery:** Pliny the Elder was specifically referring to a doctor named Archagathus of Sparta.
74 **satire against doctors:** The work was by the Byzantine Greek writer Theodore Prodromos.
74 **by an Italian physician:** Julius Caesar Scaliger, sometime around 1530.
74 **with her clothes on:** Testimony of Nicolas Kuzkleba. E 142. Fasc. 028. No. 19. Page 6. MNL.
74 **diarrhea, be kept clean:** See Szádeczky-Kardoss, "The Bloody Countess."
75 **on the way back home:** Testimonies of Adam Szelesthey and Francis Torok. E 142. Fasc. 028. No 19. Page 72–73. MNL.
75 **spread their illness to others:** One such law was passed in Cluj; see Magyary-Kossa, 251.
75 **"needed help from others":** Testimony of Andras Somogy. E 142. Fasc. 028. No. 19. Pages 7–8. MNL.
75 **rather had been "pierced":** *Manus fuisso perforaras;* Testimony of George Lehoczk. E 142. Fasc. 028. No. 19. Page 24. MNL.

CHAPTER 5: SEE YOU IN COURT

77 **"troublemakers to my town":** Elizabeth Bathory to Francis Batthyany, November 4, 1605. P 1314. No. 02249. MNL.
77 **"stay in Sárvár continuously":** Ibid.

78 "this place from danger": Elizabeth Bathory to Matthias II, November 1605. HFU Kt. 199 Konv. folio 97v–99v. FHKA. ÖStA.
78 the famous Captain John Smith: See Stanonik.
78 that siege, in 1603: See Szántai, "The Long War."
79 "possess it for long": Elizabeth Bathory to George Banffy, February 3, 1606. E 185. Box 22. MNL.
79 approached by Mrs. Caspar Banffy: Her maiden name was Katalin (Kate) Petho of Gersei.
79 "rights not to be suffocated": Mrs. Caspar Bánffy to Elizabeth Bathory, September 1, 1606. E 185. Box 2. MNL.
80 Batthyany, to become involved: Varkonyi, "Újabb," and Békefi, 548.
80 begged Elizabeth for help: See Lengyel, "A legrosszabb hírű," 60, and Varkonyi, "Újabb."
81 "the hands of the Lords Banffy": Mrs. Caspar Bánffy to Elizabeth Bathory, September 1, 1606. E 185. Box 2. MNL.
81 moon turned scarlet: March 24, 1606.
82 "pursuit of their religion": "The Peace of Vienna with the Prince of Transylvania," Article 1.
82 The treaty granted amnesty: See Bariska, 832.
82 "before a court and prosecuted": "The Peace of Vienna with the Prince of Transylvania," Article 11.
83 "help and protection," "blood brothers": Quoted in "The Balance Sheet of War."
83 handover to the Bathory women: See Kovács, "Az ecsedi udvar," 947, and Vadász, *Ecsedi Báthory István*, 77.
84 "without food and drink, miserabl[e]": Elizabeth Bathory to Paul Nyary, October 11, 1606. E 185. Box 22. MNL.
84 "occurred in my family": Ibid.
84 piece of real estate: While the case wound its way through the courts, Captain Bay gave the castle to his daughter as a wedding gift; his son-in-law later sold the property. See Kovács, "Az ecsedi udvar," 947.
85 "clothing and other goods": The serfs of Nagyölbő to Elizabeth Bathory, September 6, 1606. E 185. Box 25. MNL.
85 quarter of a million in today's dollars: 800 florins, or 2,808 grams of gold.
85 "we have yet to heal up to this day": The serfs of Ötvösi to Elizabeth Bathory, 1606. E 185. Box 26. MNL.

85 "no serfs at all": Elizabeth Bathory to Francis Batthyany, November 4, 1605. P 1314. No. 02249. MNL.
85 "devastated town": Elizabeth Bathory to Francis Batthyany, August 12, 1605. P 1314. No. 02245. MNL.
85 spend their Christmas holidays: See Varkonyi, "Újabb."
85 then by Bocskai's hajduks: Jedliscka, 538.
85 mark property borders: Minutes of the County of Sopron 690. (August 6, 1608). Jzl. MNL.
85 "the following Wednesday": Minutes of the County of Sopron 629. (December 7, 1606). Jzl. MNL.
86 to a full five years: Lengyel, "A legrosszabb hírű, 58–59.
86 "quite sick again": Elizabeth Bathory to Paul Nyary. October 11, 1606. E 185. Box 22. MNL.
86 from their posts: See Lengyel, "A legrosszabb hírű," 62.
86 provisor of embezzling funds: Minutes of the County of Vas 1163 (June 29, 1609). Jzk. MNL.
86 of the money spent: Ibid.; see also Lengyel, "A legrosszabb hírű, 62.
87 unusually handsome: Based on the recollections of János Szalárdi and János Kemény, quoted in László Nagy, *A rossz hírű Báthoryak,* 121. See also Péter, "Gabriel Bethlen Stops the War."
87 horseshoes in half: László Nagy, *A rossz hírű Báthoryak,* 108.
88 "wisely made his will": Simon Pechy quoted in László Nagy, *Kathay Mihály,* 102. (Some scholars, like Andor László, 57–58, think Nagy reads too much into this phrasing.)
88 it was called dropsy: *Vízkór* or *vizenyő* in Hungarian.
88 looted by Bocskai's hajduks: László Nagy, *Kathay Mihály,* 102.
89 poisoned by the Hapsburgs: Ibid.
89 "them in the future": Szepsi, 98.
89 then serve as *his* chancellor: Ibid.
89 "wedding in a garden": Ibid.
90 "one who did that": Ibid.
90 "in a sheet" for burial: Szepsi, 101.

CHAPTER 6: THE DOSE MAKES THE POISON

91 hereditary Bathory dynasty: See Péter, "The Golden Age," 303–4.
91 contemporary pastor wrote: Szepsi, quoted in Kemény, 770.
91 "customary in this country": Ibid.

NOTES

92 **plague was back again**: See Magyary-Kossa, 312.

92 **neighboring Bars county**: This county bordered Elizabeth's northern estate of Čachtice.

92 **a relative of Elizabeth's**: Paul Nyary, the husband of her cousin, the man to whom she wrote about the loss of Devín Castle.

92 **"Doczy's hospitality and Doczy's cup"**: Szepsi, quoted in Kemény 770.

92 **afoul of religious authorities**: See, for example, the cases of the alleged serial killers Peter Stump, Peter Niers, and Christman Genipperteinga. There had been a recent case of a priest named Dambrovský who poisoned four bishops.

93 **"lips of the public"**: Szepsi, quoted in Kemény, 770.

93 **"send me some"**: Elizabeth Bathory to Francis Nadasdy, February 24, 1595. E 185. Box 22. MNL.

93 **from eastern Transylvania**: See the November 18, 1598, letter in Kovács, "Ecsedi Báthory," 357.

94 **"cow dung water"**: See Frankovith's *Hasznos És Fölötte Szükséges Könyv* (*A Useful and Very Necessary Book*).

94 **"I always felt worse after it"**: Justine Szambo to Elizabeth Bathory, January 25, 1587. E 185. Box 43. MNL.

94 **"godfather of modern chemotherapy"**: Borzelleca, 2.

94 **conditions like scabies and impetigo**: Magyary-Kossa, 7.

95 **which induces vomiting**: Hussey.

95 **personally delivered it instead**: Testimonies of Nicolaus Mazarych, Andras Somogy, and John Zluba. E 142. Fasc. 028. No. 19. Pages 7, 7–8, and 32–33. MNL.

96 **last male Somlyó Bathory too**: He did have a half brother, Andras, who stayed out of politics and moved to Poland.

96 **ensure there was peace**: Oborni, 111.

97 **where witches were burned**: Today a plaque on this spot commemorates Agatha Toott Borlobaschin, the unfortunate healer who, in 1602, became the first person known to be burned as a witch in Bratislava.

97 **they had made him a count**: In 1606; see Lengyel, "The Chances for a Provincial Cultural Centre," 114.

98 ***"your basket with gold"***: 1608 poem by John Rimay, quoted in László Nagy, *A rossz hírű Báthoryak*, 43.

98 **private tutor**: Kubinyi, 5.

98 **rest of the nobility**: See case of Michael Telekessy.

98 **the coronation banquet:** Kubinyi, 8.
98 **lawsuits against him:** See, for example, the "Platthy family" entry in Iván Nagy's *Magyarország családai*.
98 **burned down another neighbor's village:** Thurzo burned down the village of Bodina Kubinyi, owned by the Esterhazy family.
99 **"unprepared to govern":** See Péter, "The Golden Age," 308.
99 **convert back one day soon:** See Horn, "Báthory Gábor belpolitikája."
99 **own family's holdings:** See Nyakas.
100 **clean-shaven:** Lengyel, *Život na šľachtickom*, 62–63.
100 ***"wine have distracted thee":*** Bitskey, 30.
100 **"sacred oracle of Apollo at Delphi":** Caspar Bojthi quoted in László Nagy, *Erdélyi*, 1103.
100 **prince's biological aunt:** The half sister of Gabriel's biological father.

CHAPTER 7: STRAINED RELATIONS

106 **so they could participate:** See Duchoňová, 34, and Takats, 116.
106 **easily consumed six:** Lengyel, *Život na šľachtickom*, 162.
106 **goblet each time:** Takats, 118.
106 **hired from Vienna:** Duchoňová, 33 and 38.
106 **snubbed by whom:** See Takats.
107 **indulged than harshly disciplined:** This is the argument underlying Péter's book *Beloved Children*.
107 **"some small gift":** Paul Nadasdy to Elizabeth Bathory. June 13, 1608. E 185. Box 23. MNL.
107 **"servants respect me greatly":** See Thorne, 117.
107 **"befitting their parents' status":** Last Will and Testament of Elizabeth Bathory. E 148. XX 1610. Fasc. 44. No. 25. MNL.
107 **shop for months:** Takata, 119.
108 **"well-wishing friends":** Elizabeth Bathory to Nicholas Zrinyi, January 3, 1608. E 204. Bundle 30. MNL.
109 **for her dead boy:** Lenčiš, 103–5, and Borbely, 465.
109 **"my head and property":** Lenčiš, 103.
109 **Hapsburgs on her behalf:** Ibid.
110 **Catholicism while in exile:** He did not convert after his wedding, as is claimed by Thorne and others, but rather around 1605 in Prague, and certainly well before 1608. See Lenčiš for more details.
110 **"under strong guard":** See Ronconelli's report 412, in Óváry, 65.

NOTES

110 **"himself king of Hungary"**: See the reports of the envoys d'Appiano d'Aragona and Ronconelli: 411, 412, and 441, in Óváry, 67 and 71.

110 **spirit of the Raven King**: "Sigismund Báthory, a Changeable Prince."

111 **"virgins and other women"**: Thurzo to Andras of Keresztur, March 5, 1610. E 142. Fasc 28. No. 18. MNL.

111 **administered by his wife**: See Fischer and Lengyel, "Esettanulmány," 244–45.

111 **on their future estates**: Monok, 70.

112 **disputes about land borders**: Minutes of the County of Sopron 691 (August 6, 1608). Jzl. MNL.

112 **a disturbance close by**: Szepsi, 125–26.

113 **"kindled against him"**: This account was written in 1624; see Bitskey, 33.

113 **decade after the attack**: Written by Caspar Veres Bojthi, the court historian for Gabriel Bethlen.

113 **much less raped her**: Horn, "Báthory Gábor belpolitikája," 34–36.

113 **explosive placed in his bedroom**: See report 28 by the Venetian ambassador Simon Contarini in Óváry, 69.

113 **Protestant king of his throne**: This claim was made by a Jesuit named Roberto Bellarmino, *Disputationes de controversiis christianae.*

114 **"the shining star"**: Quoted in Bitskey, 30–31.

114 **another Catholic fanatic**: On May 16, 1610; see Kruppa, 38–39.

114 **"secret conspiracy"**: See Szepsi, 125–26.

114 **wrath of the Ottoman Turks**: Oborni, 114.

114 **"enemy to your enemies"**: Oborni, 113.

115 **family's water castle of Ecsed**: See "The Peace of Vienna with the Prince of Transylvania."

115 **calling him a mere "governor"**: Oborni, 113.

115 **make the introduction himself**: Angyel.

115 **refused to hand over the conspirators**: Szepsi, 125–26.

115 **attempt to ease tensions**: Thurzo, "Letter 548," June 7, 1610. Vol. 2. 259.

116 **"held her captive"**: Deposition of Klara Bathory, February 14, 1558. Archívny fond Hodnoverné miesto Spišská Kapitula, oddelenie Autentické protokoly. Protokol nr. 1, fol. 109a, 111b, 112a. ARBSP.

116 **"this [Klara] Bathory"**: Ferdinand I to Anna Pekry, 1553. Héderváry Codex: OSzK. Kézirattár Fol. Lat. 739. Folio 294. NSZL.

116 **"apart from her liberation"** Deposition of Klara Bathory, February 14, 1558. Archívny fond Hodnoverné miesto Spišská Kapitula, oddelenie Autentické protokoly. Protokol nr. 1, fol. 109a, 111b, 112a. ARBSP.

116 **land, money, or title:** All we know about him is that his last name was Bekes or Bekessey; some historians have given him a feasible first name of John.

116 **"capture" of other men's serfs:** Some examples, all from the ANR: Letters of attestation, December 16, 1558. Fasc. X, No. 6; Summons of Anna Pekry, May 16, 1559. Fasc. X, No. 7; and Letters of attestation, September 27, 1559. Fasc. X, No. 7.

116 **accessing his own lands:** Letters of attestation, December 16, 1558. Fasc. X, No. 6. ANR.

117 **appear before the courts:** See Attestation of the delivery of a deed, March 10, 1559. Fasc. J, No. 22; and Summons of Anna Pekry, May 16, 1559. Fasc. X, No. 7. ANR.

117 **on clever technicalities:** *Royal Deputy for Hungary v. the women of the Losonczy family, Lelesz*: Prosecutor's speech, February 2, 1570. Fasc. Y, No. 43. ANR.

117 **"to have intercourse with her":** Forgách, 40.

118 **widow Helen Hernath:** Court documents identify her as "previously widow of the late John Ungvary, then of the late John Zalay." Other documents refer to her as Mrs. Szalay.

118 **"within one or two or three weeks":** Deposition of Helen Hernath, August 22, 1610. Vasvár-Szombathely County Court. XII.a.23 No. 124. VVL. MNL.

119 **"fully and publicly exonerated":** Ibid.

119 **Most Illustrious Prince:** Oborni, 115.

119 **"side become suspicious":** Quoted in Oborni, 117. These instructions, given to the imperial envoy Cesare Gallo, were dated October 17, 1610.

CHAPTER 8: THE PREACHER OF ČACHTICE

121 **"of both sexes":** Thurzo to Moses Cziraky, March 5, 1610. E 142. Fasc. 28. No. 18. MNL.

121 **two girls with injured hands:** Testimony of Andras Somogy, 7–8. E 142. Fasc. 028. No. 19. MNL.

121–22 **girl being flogged:** Testimony of Francis Torok, 72–73. E 142. Fasc. 028. No. 19. MNL.

122 **seen a girl faint:** Testimony of Adam Szelesthey, 72. E 142. Fasc. 028. No. 19. MNL. (Francis Bornemisza was another potential eyewitness, who claimed he saw girls hanging from their hair from the lattices of the castle windows, but he could not remember how many girls, what they looked like, or when the event took place.)

122 **"point of absurdity":** See Rady, 126; this questionnaire was the *De eo utrum (Deutrum).*

122 **now called Nové Mesto nad Váhom:** At the time, it was known as Vag-Ujhely.

122 **around one thousand adults:** There were two hundred houses, according to Jedliscka, 532.

123 **hour and a half's walk:** Jedliscka, 499.

123 **gardens, and vineyard:** From the 1645 description of the castle captain Paul Kardoš. See "Čachtice" in *Súpis pamiatok na Slovensku*, 254–57, and Križanová, 63.

125 **"behalf of the dead":** Quoted in Koslofsky, 86.

125 **pastor being present:** Koslofsky, 87

125 **"beasts, like dogs":** Quoted in Koslofsky, 91.

125 **"without any honor":** Quoted in Koslofsky, 91.

125 **singing at burials:** See "The Protestants' Attitudes Towards Death"; Barkley, 15; and McKim, 93.

125 **in an unmarked grave:** See "The Protestants' Attitudes Towards Death," and Raeburn, 166.

126 **"knowledge of the pastor":** Quoted in Koslofsky, 91.

126 **village's Lutheran pastor:** Zachary Gasparides.

126 **"both places are my possessions":** Testimony of John Ponikenus. E 142. Fasc. 028. No. 19. Pages 38–39. MNL.

127 **"they supposedly died":** Testimonies of Michael Fabri. E 142. Fasc. 028. No. 19. Pages 15 and 18. MNL.

127 **"in the early dawn":** Testimony of George Mladych. E 142. Fasc. 028. No. 19. Pages 20–21. MNL.

128 **torturing over a hundred virgins:** Testimony of Thomas Zima. E 142. Fasc. 028. No. 19. Page 92. MNL.

128 **alleged death toll:** Testimony of Stephen Raczyczenus. E 142. Fasc. 028. No. 19. Page 4. MNL.

128 **all of their clothing:** See Koltai, 575–77.

128 **attendant or two:** Lengyel, "Esettanulmány," 244–45.

129 newspapers and broadsides: Lengyel, "The Chances for a Provincial Cultural Centre," 124.
129 over 140 children: *Warhafftige und erschreckliche beschreibung*, 3.
129 "sickness comes on her": Quoted in Thorne, 235.
130 "40 pikemen, and 15 carriages": See Lengyel, "The Chances for a Provincial Cultural Centre," 121.
131 "superstitious instruments": Sz. Kristof, "Charming Sorcerers."
131 had been overcharged: See Testimonies 21 and 23 in Schram, 234–35.
131 "wrestle" with his wife: See Testimony 1 in Schram, 228.
132 "Farmer's Wife from Myjava": See Thorne, for example.
132 chickens and dairy cows: Veres, 61–63.
132 with their cheese: Testimony of John Kadlwecz. E 142. Fasc. 028. No. 19. Page 27. MNL.
132 knowledge of local herbs: Szadeczky-Kardoss, "Mi az igazság Báthory Erzsébet ügyében?" 20–21.
132 preparations for her lady: Ponikenus, in his letter to Lany, mentions she prepared herbal baths for the Countess.
132 "fingernail poison": Szádeczky-Kardoss, "The Bloody Countess?"
133 large library at Sárvár: This was Frankovith's *Hasznos És Fölötte Szükséges Könyv* (*A Useful and Very Necessary Book*).
134 from the Nagyvathys' properties: They had a manor in the same county and a house just outside of Bratislava; see Gecsényi, 78–80, and the "Nagyvathy family" entry in Iván Nagy, *Magyarország családai*.
134 died of the plague instead: Testimony of Francis Torok. E 142. Fasc. 028. No. 19. Pages 72–73. MNL.

CHAPTER 9: THE MYSTERIOUS WILL

138 resembled his father, Francis: A portrait of Paul can be found in the Historical Picture Gallery of the Hungarian National Museum in Budapest.
138 her castle of Léka: Minutes of the County of Vas 1200 (May 15, 1609). Jzk. MNL.
138 bandits in the area: See Lengyel, "A legrosszabb hírű," 62.
138 son of the local shoemaker: Payr, *A Dunántúli Evangélikus*, section IIf.
139 pastors of major estates: Ibid. For more on elites studying abroad, see Tamus, 33.
139 Shoemaker of Sárvár: Ibid.

139 "noble wisdom," "bell-ringer": Ibid.
139 to avoid gossip: Testimony of Michael Zvonarics. E 142. Fasc. 028. No. 19. Pages 71–72. MNL.
140 from the very beginning: See Payr, "Magyari István és Báthory Erzsébet."
140 administering the family estates: Péter, *Beloved Children*, 113.
140 make money for themselves: Péter, *Beloved Children*, 114.
140 commissioners on another project: Minutes of the County of Vas 1142 (March 18, 1609). Jzk. MNL.
141 supervised any prisoners: See Szatlóczki.
141 prominent Hungarian scholar: Gabor Varkonyi.
142 would be close to $250,000: George Thurzo to Adam Szelestey. January 27, 1612. E 204. Bundle 46. MNL.
142 allowed to attend Parliament: Minutes of the County of Vas 1339 (February 9, 1613). Jzk. MNL.
142 or "Elisabeth comitissa de Bathor": Elizabeth Bathory to Archbishop Náprághy. February 19, 1609. E 204. Bundle 4. MNL.
143 "quite sick again": Elizabeth Bathory to Paul Nyary. October 11, 1606. E 185. Box 22. MNL.
143 wine, and a new dress: Declaration of Klara Bathory. April 6, 1570. P 47. III 42 No. 5. MNL.
144 "all my castles": Last Will and Testament of Elizabeth Bathory. E 148. XX 1610. Fasc. 44. No. 25. MNL.
144 earlier, at eighteen or so: See Péter, *Beloved Children*, 101, 103.
144 "until my death": See, for example, Craft, *Infamous Lady*, 284. Thorne has a different variation on 154: "I desire only to be allowed to keep for my lifetime my wedding dress and jewels."
144 morning gift, in German: See Peres, 281.
144 moved to another manor: Varkonyi, "Újabb."
145 sentimental importance to her: Ibid.
145 throughout Royal Hungary: See Kónya, 289.
146 elections be held: Elias Lany to Thurzo, "Letter 114," November 19, 1611. *A Thurzó-Levéltár Protestáns Egyháztörténeti Iratai*, 128–29.
146 refusing to attend services: See Nemeš, 66.
146 defect to the Calvinists: See Kónya, 290.
146 administrators to enter: Elias Lany to Thurzo, "Letter 106," March 18, 1611. *A Thurzó-Levéltár Protestáns Egyháztörténeti Iratai*, 117–19.

146 **"like a dog!":** John Ponikenus to Elias Lany, January 1, 1611. E 196. Fasc. 7. No. 69. MNL.
146 **trying to duel again:** See Lengyel, "A legrosszabb hírű," 60–61, and Thorne, 135–36.
147 **"from you and your servants":** Elizabeth Bathory to Thurzo, October 20, 1610. II-B/24. OK-TK. SOBA.
147 **one of Elizabeth's servants:** Testimony of Gregory Testimony. E 142. Fasc. 028. No. 19. Page 60. MNL.
148 **prepare the case:** See Rady, 127–28.

CHAPTER 10: THE RAID

149 **been troubling him since summer:** Magyary-Kossa, 350.
149 **another, less biased source:** *Adatok Csejthe Történetéhez* (Chronicle of Castle Čachtice).
150 **part of her estate:** See Jedliscka, 507, for a list of the villages associated with the Čachtice estate.
150 **others still in quarantine:** Quarantine was a well-known practice. Even Thurzo's own nanny made use of it: See Lengyel, *Az írástudatlantól*, 145.
150 **"were circulating about her":** Testimony of Nicolas Baroseus. E 142. Fasc. 028. No. 19. Page 31. MNL.
151 **were all capital offenses:** Tripartitum II, chapter 42.5, in Bak, 1514.
151 **committing a capital offense:** Tripartitum I, chapter 9, in Bak, 1384–85.
151 **mutilation of the body:** Tripartitum II, chapters 42 and 75, in Bak, 1514, 1538.
151 **carried out in a cart:** Testimony of George Kubanovich, Martin Waychko, and Martinus Lofaak. E 142. Fasc. 028. No. 19. Pages 34–35, 77. MNL.
152 **examine the surviving girls:** Testimony of Andras Pryderowyth. E 142. Fasc. 028. No. 19. Page 35. MNL.
152 **small village near Trenčín:** The village of Dubmicza.
152 **"pair of shears":** Testimony of Martin Waychko. E 142. Fasc. 028. No. 19. Page 34. MNL.
153 **One historian:** Irma Szádeczky-Kardoss.
153 **"lips of the public":** Szepsi, quoted in Kemény, 770.
153 **"that damned woman":** Thurzo, "Letter 584," December 30, 1610. Vol 2. 300.
153 **"heavy guard":** Ibid.

154 **in her new prison:** Ibid.

154 **trailed by two pastors:** Zachary Gasparides from Podolie and Nicolas Baroseus from Vrbové.

154 **"You priests are the cause":** John Ponikenus to Elias Lany, January 1, 1611. E 196. Fasc. 7. No. 69. MNL.

154 **"You ungodly and malicious priests":** Testimony of Nicolas Baroseus. E 142. Fasc. 028. No. 19. Page 31. MNL.

155 **"never named you":** John Ponikenus to Elias Lany, January 1, 1611. E 196. Fasc. 7. No. 69. MNL.

155 **"you are my enemies?"** Testimony of Nicolas Baroseus. E 142. Fasc. 028. No. 19. Page 31. MNL.

155 **in the first Book of Samuel:** See I Samuel 28.7. This name is derived from "Pythia," the name of the high priestess at Delphi. More recent translations of the Bible call this woman the Witch of Endor.

155 **"*this world innocent!*":** Elias Lany to Thurzo, "Letter 116," February 27, 1612. *A Thurzó-Levéltár Protestáns Egyháztörténeti Iratai*, 132–33.

156 **"fire or otherwise?":** Testimony of Nicolas Baroseus. E 142. Fasc. 028. No. 19. Page 31. MNL.

156 **"not obliged to tell you":** John Ponikenus to Elias Lany, January 1, 1611. E 196. Fasc. 7. No. 69. MNL.

156 **"[legal] case" instead:** Ibid.

157 **diocese of Čachtice:** See Csepregi's list of pastors and parishes.

157 **three other pastors:** Gasparides, and Baroseus, along with the pastor of Kostol'any, Michael Fabri.

157 **pastor of Beckov:** Testimony of George Kromholcius. E 142. Fasc. 028. No. 19. Page 42. MNL.

157 **their "trusted assistant":** Thurzo, "Letter 570," December 30, 1610. Vol. 2. 284.

157 **"according to my judgment":** John Ponikenus to Elias Lany, January 1, 1611. E 196. Fasc. 7. No. 69. MNL.

158 **"roasted flesh then allowed to be served":** Matthias to Thurzo, January 14, 1611. E 196. Fasc. 8. No. 7. MNL.

CHAPTER 11: THE SERVANTS' TRIAL

161 **the upcoming action:** Testimony of Benedict Deseo. E 142. Fasc. 028. No. 19. Pages 58–60. MNL.

161 **"force of arms"**: Quoted in Várkonyi, *Báthory Erzsébet*, 38.
161 **allegiance to King Matthias II**: László Nagy, *A rossz hírű Báthoryak*, 45. Even Thomas, the Nadasdy cousin who had joined the Bocskai rebellion, was accused of treason and of being in league with Gabriel Bathory and his hajduks.
161 **the "grave mark" of treason**: Nicolas Zrinyi to George Thurzo, December 17, 1610. OK-TK. No. 682. SOBA.
162 **"this [process] . . . publicly"**: Ibid.
162 **children's "guardian and protector"**: Francis Nadasdy to George Thurzo, January 3, 1604. OK-TK. No. 390. SOBA.
162 **pardon one year later**: See Komáromy, 627.
163 **independent judges and jurors**: Jedliscka, 538.
163 **account of Johannes Junius**: Junius.
164 **"poor man all my life"**: Philipp Puchler; see Toth and Nemeth, 157.
164 **"south of Poland"**: Interrogation of Helena Jo. E 142. Fasc. 028. No. 19. Pages 81–84. MNL.
165 **"wall [was] washed"**: Ibid.
166 **"needle, in the carriage"**: Interrogation of Ficzko. E 142. Fasc. 028. No. 19. Pages 77–81. MNL.
166 **at the town house**: Located on Augustinerstraße 12.
166 **fourteen "beautiful skirts"**: Interrogation of Katherine Beneczky. E 142. Fasc. 028. No. 19. Pages 86–87. MNL.
167 **"with students"**: Interrogation of Helena Jo. E 142. Fasc. 028. No. 19. Pages 81–84. MNL.
167 **"with other servants"**: These answers are compiled from these each servant's answer to the seventh question.
168 **"as long as they both lived"**: Interrogation of Katherine Beneczky. E 142. Fasc. 028. No. 19. Pages 86–87. MNL.
169 **visiting with her husband**: See Szádeczky-Kardoss, "Mi az igazság Báthory Erzsébet ügyében?" 21.
170 **three English queens**: Anne Boleyn, Joan of Navarre, and Elizabeth Woodville. For more information, see Gemma Hollman's *Royal Witches: Witchcraft and Nobility in Fifteenth Century England* (New York: Pegasus Books, 2020).
170 **accused in their lifetimes**: Elizabeth's aunt Margot Majlath and her mother-in-law Ursula Kanizsay.
170 **angels via a crystal**: Bornemissza, *Ördögi Kísértetekről*, 1022–23.

171 **"bald coachman"**: Stephen Kocis, who had served the Nadasdy family for a long time; he had also been the coachman for Elizabeth's deceased mother-in-law.

172 **"recruit and lure"**: This was the fourth question listed on all four servants' interrogations.

173 **of his 964 victims**: Case of Christman Genipperteinga; see Herber, 1.

173 **"causing her the utmost pain"**: Testimony of Anna, widow Gonczy. E 142. Fasc. 028. No. 19. Page 94. MNL.

174 **"alive on the fire"**: Judgment of the Bytča Tribunal. E 142. Fasc. 028. No. 19. Pages 94–97. MNL.

174 **"guilt may be determined"**: Ibid.

174 **cross-examined in court**: See the 1561 case of Matthias Forintos in Tóth, *A magyarországi boszorkányperek digitalis*.

175 **ended up dead**: Testimony of John Kadlwecz. E 142. Fasc. 028. No. 19. Page 27. MNL.

175 **"Bytča as a witch"**: See *Adatok Csejthe Történetéhez* (Chronicle of Castle Čachtice). In other records there is a mention of a "Mrs. Simon" burned in the area around this time, who may have been the unnamed "woman scientist" of Tokorcs, but could have just as easily been another unfortunate village healer.

CHAPTER 12: HER DAY IN COURT

178 **"goodwill toward me and my sisters"**: Paul Nadasdy to Thurzo, February 23, 1611. OK-TK No. 391. SOBA.

178 **"Lordship's letter (which we keep secret)"**: Ibid.

178 **"said Royal Majesty"**: Thurzo to Andras of Keresztur, March 5, 1610. E 142. Fasc 28. No 18. MNL.

178 **"innocent virgins and women"**: Matthias to Thurzo, January 14, 1611. E 196. Fasc. 8. No. 7. MNL.

179 **even, in a tower**: This assumption seems to spring from the mistranslation of a phrase used by Ponikenus, who wrote that Elizabeth was "enclosed by a wall," a reference to the wall surrounding Castle Čachtice itself.

179 **female contemporaries suffered**: Anna of Saxony, for example, after her affair with Jan Rubens (father of the famous painter) had the windows of her room walled up; her only connection to the outside world was a small slit in the iron grille placed over her door, through which food was passed.

NOTES

179 **northeast of Royal Hungary:** Keresztúr, in Abauj county.
180 **"circumstances of the deaths":** Matthias to Thurzo, January 14, 1611. E 196. Fasc. 8. No. 7. MNL.
181 **"immediate response":** Matthias to Thurzo, February 26, 1611. E 196. Fasc. 8. No. 40. MNL.
181 **"ears of your Benevolent Majesty":** Thurzo to Matthias, March 30, 1611. Von Elsburg, 262–3.
182 **"had written it himself":** Bitskey, 32.
182 **their leader was a secret Muslim:** Bitskey, 32.
182 **"be favored by any Christian":** Matthias to Thurzo, "Letter 112," August 31, 1611. *A Thurzó-Levéltár Protestáns Egyháztörténeti Iratai.* 126–7.
182 **ran through the eastern part:** Borbély, 17.
182 **Anna had . . . the treasury forced open:** See Thorne, 189: He states that Thurzo's wife took the jewels. However, in an email conversation Thorne clarified that this was a translation error and the text does refer to Elizabeth's daughter Anna.
183 **"a little annoyed":** Quoted in Cziraki, 324.
183 **"pretext of religion":** Matthias to Thurzo, "Letter 112," August 31, 1611. *A Thurzó-Levéltár Protestáns Egyháztörténeti Iratai*, 126–27.
183 **enemy of Royal Hungary:** Minutes of the County of Vas 1271–1273 (September 8, 1611). Jzk. MNL.
184 **subject of widespread ridicule:** Angyal.
184 **"silently neglected":** Hungarian Court Chamber to Matthias II, December 18, 1613. HFU Kt. 244, folio. 79–85. FHKA. ÖStA.
185 **"*several* decent women and innocent girls":** Ibid (emphasis mine).
185 **"with a sufficient bail?":** Matthias to Thurzo, January 24, 1613. E 142. Fasc. 28. No. 18. MNL.
185 **called in his legal experts:** Legal opinion of Ladislaus Pethi, February. 8, 1613. HFU Kt. 244, folio. 79–85. FHKA. ÖStA.
186 **testify against the Countess:** Of the 225, 118 knew nothing or had only heard the vaguest rumors, and another 70 reported only hearsay. See also Appendix.
186 **Pastor Ponikenus testified:** Testimony of John Ponikenus. E 142. Fasc. 028. No. 19. Pages 38–39. MNL.
186 **with burning candles:** See Read.
186 **died at Elizabeth's finishing school:** Testimony of Anna, widow Szelesthey. E 142. Fasc. 028. No. 19. Pages 57–58. MNL.

186 **deceased girls to 6:** In addition to the maid Doricza, whose body was found during the raid, the following girls from the lower nobility were said to have died under the Countess's care: the unnamed ten-year-old daughter of Anna and Stephen Gonczy; Anna Ztubyczay, sister of Caspar Ztubyczay; Elizabeth Bardy, daughter of Dorothy and Francis Bardy; Suzska Zelesthey, daughter of Anna and John Zelesthey; and Kata Birinyi, niece of John Deseo, the warden of Keresztúr Castle.

186 **"after a lot of torture":** Testimony of Benedict Deseo. E 142. Fasc. 028. No. 19. Pages 58–60. MNL.

187 **peasant woman called Chiglei:** Interrogation of Helena Jo. E 142. Fasc. 028. No. 19. Page 81–84. MNL.

187 **Dorothy both referred to her:** Albeit it was by her husband's name, as Mrs. John Szalay.

187 **"they would be killed":** Interrogation of Helena Jo. E 142. Fasc. 028. No. 19. Page 81–84. MNL.

187 **just flogged and chained:** Testimony of Helen Hernath. E 142. Fasc. 028. No. 19. Page 57. MNL.

187 **by the washerwoman Katherine:** By her husband's name: "the wife of Michael Kardos."

188 **"Those whores were lying":** Testimony of Anna Velikey. E 142. Fasc. 028. No. 19. Page 30. MNL.

188 **niece of another employee:** The niece of the castellan of Vrbové.

188 **"the golden nation reigns":** "Letter 100," *A Thurzó-levéltár egyháztörténeti iratai*, 109fn2.

CHAPTER 13: THE LAST BATHORY

189 **"untidy mop of hair":** Péter, "Gabriel Bethlen Stops the War."

189 **easy to overlook:** Ibid.

189 **payment was sent late:** László Nagy, *A rossz hírű Báthoryak*, 136.

190 **three Bathory princes:** Sigmund, Andrew, Gabriel.

190 **"plotting against us":** This letter from September 14, 1612, is quoted in László Nagy, *A rossz hírű Báthoryak*, 136.

190 **"begging for mercy":** Ibid.

191 **key supporter of the prince:** László Nagy, *Erdélyi*, 1101.

191 **courted by Thurzo:** Michael Dengeleghy, the commander of Lippa Castle.

NOTES

191 **had been forced to flee:** See László Nagy, *A rossz hírű Báthoryak*, 137, and László Nagy, *Erdélyi*, 1102.
191 **his imminent arrest:** László Nagy, *Erdélyi*, 1102–3.
192 **avenge his dishonored wife:** László Nagy, *A rossz hírű Báthoryak*, 123.
192 **"freely elected him":** Péter, "Gabriel Bethlen Stops the War," fn22.
192 **actually be of use:** László Nagy, *A rossz hírű Báthoryak*, 137.
193 **four hajduk captains he knew well:** Captains John Szilasy, Gregory Ladányi, John Basa, and Blaise Zámbó. According to László Nagy, *A rossz hírű Báthoryak*, 104–8, Szilasy was a former miller's boy; Ladányi was a nobleman who had joined the outlaws; and Zámbó was a war hero. (Basa is mentioned in some accounts but not others.)
193 **"friends and supporters":** Quoted in László Nagy, *A rossz hírű Báthoryak*, 106.
193 **helped plot the assassination:** Jankovics, 40.
194 **his infantry captain:** Balázs Nagy.
194 **stronghold of Ecsed:** Jankovics, 40.
194 **"good news" to the Hapsburg court:** Jankovics, 39.
194 **organized the assassination:** Barsony, 24.
194 **facing frequent death threats:** Barsony, 24.
194 **too many plots against him:** László Nagy, *Erdélyi*, 1109.
195 **"protector of Transylvania":** Bitsky, 29, and Szepsi, 145.
195 **expansion of Transylvanian territory:** Bitsky, 32.
195 **"good deeds for us":** László Nagy, *Erdélyi*, 1108.
195 **"higher than Olympus":** Quoted in Bitskey, 33.
195 **as a holy martyr:** László Nagy, *Erdélyi*, 1108.
195 **"with a handkerchief":** Szepsi, 145.
195 **"who had killed him":** Letter from János Ivánczy, Grand Prelate of Győr, to Demeter. Napraghy, former bishop and chancellor of Transylvania, quoted in Kruppa, 38–39.
196 **"many Hungarian warriors":** Anonymous Transylvanian poem, quoted in László Nagy, *A rossz hírű Báthoryak*, 106.
196 **sister, aunt, and cousin:** See Horn, "A Fejedelmi Tanács," 1007–9.
196 **fought back and won:** Castle Huszti; see László Nagy, *Erdélyi*, 1108.
197 **"charming witchcraft":** This phrasing refers to the casting of charms; see László Nagy, *A rossz hírű Báthoryak*, 111.
197 **just ten years old:** László Nagy, *Erdélyi*, 1119.
197 **since mysteriously disappeared:** Ibid.

197 **sentence was declared:** Ibid.
198 **"Lord George of Humenne":** Declaration of Elizabeth Bathory, July 31, 1614. Quoted in von Elsburg, 268–69.
198 **"not retire for the night?":** Stanislas Thurzo to Thurzo, August 25, 1614. OK-TK. Sign. II-T/22. SOBA.

EPILOGUE

199 **Thurzo's secretary:** George Zavodszky.
199 **which, translated, reads:** Copied from Juvenal's *Satires*, Satire 10, lines 112–13: *Ad generum Deceris, sine caede et sanguine, pauci Descendant Reges, et sicca morte Tyranni.*
199 **"descend to the underworld":** More literally, "to Ceres's son-in-law," i.e., Pluto.
199 **"few tyrants die a dry death":** Závodszky, quoted in "Ecsedi Báthori Ersebet," 57–60.
199–200 **"fain die a dry death":** *The Tempest*, I.i.72.
200 **"black silk cover":** See Jedlicska, 468, which cites the inventory in the Čachtice parish book.
200 **"buried in the Čachtice church":** *Adatok Csejthe Történetéhez* (Chronicle of Castle Čachtice).
200 **beyond his position as pastor:** He served as a pastor until 1627 (and died in 1630). Thorne claims that Ponikenus was promoted, but this stems from a mix-up with a different pastor with a similar name.
200 **desecrated the communion host:** Testimony of Stephen Vaghy. E 142. Fasc. 028. No 19. Page 74. MNL.
201 **accused him of being Anna's lover:** László Nagy, *Erdélyi*, 1123.
201 **most of her jewels:** Thorne, 243–44.
201 **arrested for a third time:** László Nagy, *Erdélyi*, 1126.
201 **"the guilty shall be burned":** László Nagy, *Erdélyi*, 1126.
202 **"blood-sucking prince":** László Nagy, *Erdélyi*, 1128f12.
202 **"serve his country and people":** The preacher Peter Alvinczi, quoted in Bitskey, 34.
202 **"no smell either":** The memoirist Francis Nagy Szabó, quoted in László Nagy, *A rossz hírű Báthoryak*, 107.
202 **"and a wretch too":** László Nagy, *Erdélyi*, 1128.

NOTES

202 **victim just seven years old:** See Burr.
203 **at the stake as witches:** Lengyel, "Nyitra és pozsony," 22, and Schram, 228–54.
203 **lord-lieutenant for some time:** See Lengyel, "Az írástudatlantól," 157.
203 **would not pay for a tutor:** Lengyel, "Esettanulmány," 242.
203 **struggled with reading and writing:** Lengyel, "Esettanulmány," 57.
203 **a year after her mother:** August 13, 1615.
204 **Bathory family estates:** Zubánics, 36–37.
204 **imprisonment, for some time:** Zubánics, 52–53.
204 **would suffer from epilepsy:** Correspondence about Paul Nadasdy's injury, October 1616. Hoffinanz-Ungarn No. 112. Fol. 39–46. FHKA. ÖStA.
204 **testimony against his mother:** Paul Nadasdy and Barbara Cziraky were married on June 19, 1617. See Paul Nadasdy wedding, June 19, 1617. Hoffinanz-Ungarn No. 113. Fol. 13–16. FHKA. ÖStA.
204 **his old friend Cziraky:** See Dominkovits, 784.
204 **stature and political influence:** Dominkovits, 782.
205 **captured and convicted of treason:** This occurred in 1671.
205 **"condemned without an interrogation":** Quoted in László Nagy, *A rossz hírű Báthoryak*, 39.
205 **"the points of the interrogation":** Testimony of Pastor Nicolas Baroseus. E 142. Fasc. 028. No 19. Page 31. MNL.
205 **"stood by these":** Ibid.
205 **a low-ranking nobleman:** Lord Carl David of the village of Turčiansky Peter.
206 **for the great Bathory family:** See Turóczi, 188.
206 **blood to appear eternally young:** See Turóczi, 190–91.
207 **vampirism in the Hapsburg lands:** Between 1725 and 1734.
207 **"bled from all their limbs":** See Mazzola.
207 **emerging field of psychopathology:** Elizabeth is "Gräfin B." (Countess B.) in Wagner's 1796 work.
208 **the Countess's Court inn:** Grofkin Dvor.
209 **older sister were werewolves:** See the 1595 case against Folkt and Hendrika Dirks.
209 **shape-shifted into bears:** See the 1633 case of Kanti Hans and his wife.
209 **hearts of unborn babies:** See the 1589 case of Peter Stubbe (aka Stump).

209 **stricken from the record:** For example, the 1971 *Guinness Book of Records*, 370, mentioned a "cannibalistic cave-dwelling family in Galloway, Scotland in the early 17th century," which has since been acknowledged to be pure fiction.

209 **"impossible to separate fact from fiction":** See *Guinness's* 2025 online entry for "Most prolific serial killer (female)."

ELIZABETH BATHORY: FACT VS. FICTION

289 **commander was Stephen Bathory V:** He lived from 1430 to 1493.

290 **"overpowered and deflowered her":** Letter of protest: Elizabeth Bathory v. Ladislaus Bende, November 4, 1609. ETL HH Liber 11 210v–211r. EPL.

290 **entries into the nobility:** See Iván Nagy, *Magyarország családai*.

291 **after a fall from a horse:** Correspondence about Paul Nadasdy's injury, October 1616. Hoffinanz-Ungarn No. 112. Fol. 39–46. FHKA. ÖStA.

293 **Čachtice was excavated:** On July 7, 1938; see Branecky, 192–94.

293 **no excavation has yet been planned:** See the theories of the Slovak writer Viliam Apfel and the Czech YouTubers Researchers (@Researchers-cz).

IMAGE CREDITS

p. 20   Wikimedia Commons

p. 26   Gottfried Prixner, *Das ehmals gedrückte, vom Türken berückte, nun trefflich erquickte Königreich Hungarn*, Frankfurt, 1688: Gottfried Prixner flhc jdb23/Alamy

p. 48   Franz Hogenberg, View of Bratislava from the south, 1588: Collection of Bratislava City Gallery

p. 49   Aegidius Sadeler II, Portrait of George Thurzo, 1607: Sepia Times/Universal Images Group via Getty Images

p. 54   Wilhelm Dilich, *Ungarische Chronica*, Kassel, 1600: Early and Rare Printed Books Department, National Széchényi Library

p. 72   Cornelis Dusart, *The Cupper*, Holland, 1690: Heritage Art/Heritage Images via Getty Images

p. 111   Dominicus Custos, *Atrium heroicum*, Augsburg, 1600–1602: Fine Art Images/Heritage Images/Getty Images

p. 112   Reprinted in *Magyar művelődéstörténet* Vol 3. Edited by Sándor Domanovszky. Budapest: Magyar Történelmi Társulat, 1939–1942: General Collection, National Széchényi Library

p. 125   Johann Eberlin von Günzburg, *Das Lob der Pfarrer*, Zürich, 1521: Zentralbibliothek Zürich

p. 143   Elizabeth Bathory to Demeter Napraghy, April 19, 1609 (HU-MNL-OL-E 204): National Archives of Hungary, Budapest

p. 143   Last Will and Testament of Elizabeth Bathory, 1610 (HU-MNL-OL-E 148-44.-25.-6): National Archives of Hungary, Budapest

p. 190   Aegidius Sadeler II, Portrait of Gabriel Bethlen, 1620: Penta Springs Limited/Alamy

p. 203   Jörg Merckel, *Hexenverbrennung in Derenburg am Harz*, Nuremburg, 1555: ullstein bild/ullstein bild via Getty Images

IMAGE CREDITS

PLATE SECTION

p. 1   Copy of a 1585 portrait, painted in 1869 by J. Valentínyi for the Zay noble family: Zoom Historical/Alamy

p. 2   Copy of a 1585 portrait, artist unknown: The History Collection/Alamy

p. 3   Portrait of Elisabeth Báthory, TK Festménygyűjtemény, ltsz. 53.6: Hungarian National Museum, Public Collection Centre

p. 4   Portrait of Gabriel Báthory, Nr. Inv. 436/997: National Library of Romania—Batthyaneum Library, Alba Iulia

p. 4   *Kaiser Matthias (1557–1619) als Erzherzog, mit Stab, Kniestück* by Lucas I. van Valckenborch: The Picture Art Collection/Alamy

p. 5   *Arx Sárvár ad Orientaen* by Matthias Greischer, circa 1680. TK Grafikai Gyűjtemény, ltsz. T.4622: Hungarian National Museum, Public Collection Centre

p. 5   Courtesy of Nate Miles

p. 6   Trenčín Museum—Čachtice branch

p. 6   Cs 105: Csejte; Báthory vár; Báthory Erzsébet 1570–1614, postcard. National Széchényi Library—Map, Poster and Small Print Collection

p. 7   Courtesy of Nate Miles

p. 7   Courtesy of Nate Miles

p. 8   Courtesy of Nate Miles

p. 8   Courtesy of Nate Miles

INDEX

Note: page numbers in italics refer to figures.

Abaffy, Nicolas, 192, 194
accusations, unfounded,
   seventeenth-century
   penalties for, 92–93
Anabaptists, 37
Andreas of Keresztúr, 122
antimony, medical use of,
   94–95
Banffy, George (aristocrat)
   Bathory's lawsuit to regain
      Lendava lands, 79, 147
   family of, 7
   seizure of Bathory's Lendava
      lands, 78–79, 81
   seizure of Mrs. Caspar
      Banffy's lands, 79–80
Banffy, Mrs. Caspar (sister-
   in-law of George Banffy),
   7, 79–81
Baroseus, Nicolas (Lutheran
   pastor), 8
   visit to imprisoned Bathory
      to gain confession,
      154–56, 157
   warning of Bathory about
      rumors, 150
Basta, Giorgio, 59
Bathory, Anna (adopted child
   of Stephen Bathory)
   adoption of, 87
   Bethlen's plan to kill, 201
   Bethlen's trials of, 197,
      201
   family of, 6
   as heir to Gabriel Bathory,
      196
   land holdings in 1610, *2–3*
   loss of property in Bethlen's
      prosecution, 201–2
   small estate granted by
      Royal Hungary to, 202
Bathory, Anna (mother of
   Elizabeth Bathory), 36, 37
Bathory, Elizabeth (Countess
   Bathory)
   adultery accusations
      against, 117–18
   ailments afflicting, 69, 86,
      143
   appearance, 20
   Bocskai and, 66
   and brother's funeral, 66, 68
   burial site of, 200, 292–93
   castles, current uses of, 208
   childhood of, 38
   children of, 6
      care for, 106–7
      and child mortality rate,
         69
      and division of her
         property, 162
      oldest son, death of, 20, 34
   commanding manner in
      public affairs, 78–79
   commoners and women
      seeking her assistance,
      79–80
   control of family lands after
      husband's death, 29, 47
   and daughter's marriage,
      cost of, 52, 57–58
   death of, 198, 199–200
   epilepsy, rumors of, 291
   family's support
      of Protestant
      Reformation, 36
   fifty-man personal guard
      of, 77–78, 149
   final decree on distribution
      of her property, 198
   funeral of, 200
   government funds owed to
      husband, 32, 52, 78, 180
   husband's funeral,
      arrangements for, 32
   illegitimate child, rumors
      of, 290
   illustrious family of, 20
   investigations of
      corruption on her
      estates, enemies made
      by, 86–87, 141–42
   lands seized by Banffy,
      77–78, 81
   marriage to Francis
      Nadasdy, 38, 39, 47, 144
   as moderate Calvinist, 38
   parents of, 27–28
   popularity during
      husband's life, 47
   pride in daughters' successful
      marriages, 107

INDEX

Bathory (cont'd)
   property inherited from her brother, 61, 83
   as related to both Bathory family branches, 27–28
   as religious enemy, in Thurzo's view, 199–200
   reputation for good treatment of servants, 65–66, 67–68
   reputation for political savvy and influence, 79–80
   reputation for rectitude, 79–80
   servants attacked, 146–47
   signature of, 142, 143
   as son's regent after husband's death, 32–33
   stationing of Catholic mercenaries on estates of, 52, 53
   tenuous position after husband's death, 33
   travel to ancestral home to bury brother, 65–66, 75
   troubles of early seventeenth century, 20–21
   true horror of her story as mundane human evil, 209–10
   wealth and privilege of, 13
   wealth of, after death of brother, 61
   will made by, 142–44
      as defense against seizure of her property, 143–44
      retention of Čachtice castle as personal residence, 144
      as signal of her retirement, 144
      transfer of properties to children, 143–44
   See also investigation of Elizabeth Bathory; legend of Elizabeth Bathory's crimes

Bathory, Gabriel (adopted child of Stephen Bathory)
   adoption of, 87
   assassination attempts against, 112–15
   Bathory's close relationship with, 88
   Bethlen's insincere celebration of, 202
   campaign to defame character of, 99–101, 113
   as candidate to Transylvanian throne, 87–91
   corpse of, as uncorrupted, 202
   death by assassination, 192–96
   family of, 6
   impact of death on Bathorys, 195–96
   Kate Iffiu and, 100
   as last male Bathory, 96, 196
   lying in state at Ecsed, 195
   marriage to Anna Horvath, as political liability, 99–100
   negotiations with Matthias II over sovereignty, 114–15, 119
   overthrow by Bethlen, 192
   murder while assembling counterattack, 192–93
   public backlash against murder of, 194–95
   Royal Hungary's token support and, 192
   as ruler of Transylvania betrayal by Gabriel Bethlen, 190–92
   and Hapsburgs' ambition to seize Transylvania, 101
   Hapsburgs' efforts to overthrow, 181–82
   renegotiation of Peace of Vienna with Royal Hungary, 114–15
   secret alliance with Royal Hungary against Turks, 184
   struggle to balance factions, 99
   service in Bocskai's rebel army, 88
   as strong, handsome, and valorous, 87–88

Bathory, Klara (aunt of Elizabeth Bathory)
   and civil war in Hungary, 27
   family of, 6
   imprisonment by Hapsburgs, 59, 115–16, 143
   inclusion in popular book about crimes of, 200
   and Protestant Reformation, 36
   slur campaign against, 116–17
   ties to Drugeth family, 108

Bathory, Sigmund (cousin of Elizabeth Bathory), 111
   arrest for conspiring to become king of Hungary, 110, 111, 115
   death of, 199
   political career of, 110–11
   release from prison, 184

Bathory, Stephen V, 289

Bathory, Stephen XIII (brother of Elizabeth Bathory)
   adopted children of, 6, 87
   avoidance of 1604 Parliament, 55–56
   and Bocskai's revolt, 55–56, 57, 59, 60–61
   character and career of, 55
   family of, 6
   funeral and burial, 66, 68
   Calvinist upbringing, 38

INDEX

property of, inherited by
  Bathory, 61, 83
suspicious death of, 60–61
ties to Drugeth family, 108
Bathory family
  at Battle of Mohács, 25
  Bocskai's revolt and,
    55–56, 59
  and civil war in Hungary,
    25–27
  cousin charged with treason
    by Rudolf II, 51, 59
  and division of Hungary, 27
  land holdings, in 1610, 2–3
  power and influence of, 27
  prominence in Hungarian
    history, 22–23
  targeting of, 199
Batthyany, Francis (Elizabeth
  Bathory's neighbor), 7
  assistance to Bathory in
    legal matters, 80
  and Bathory's hiring of
    guards, 77
  Bathory's titles given to, 58
  and Bocskai's revolt, 59
  command of Hapsburg
    troops near Bathory's
    castle, 63, 85
  Francis Nadasdy's deathbed
    letter to, 31
  wife of, as woman
    scientist, 70–71
Bende, Ladislaus, 290
Beneczky, Katherine
  (washerwoman), 7
  accusations against other
    servants, 169
  arrest and initial torture
    of, 154
  confession under torture,
    164–65, 166–67, 168,
    169–70, 174
  and new pretrial
    depositions, 187
  ties to Zvonarics, and
    lighter sentence, 174

Bethlen, Gabriel, 7, *190*
  betrayal of Gabrial
    Bathory, 190–92
  death of wife, 201–2
  flight to Ottoman Empire,
    lies about, 190–92
  installation as ruler of
    Transylvania, 192
  Machiavellian scheming
    as adviser to Gabriel
    Bathory, 189–90
  and murder of Gabriel
    Bathory, 194
  as ruler of Transylvania
    Bathory women as threat
      to, 196
    celebration of Gabriel
      Bathory, to appease his
      supporters, 202
    charging of Bathory
      women with incest and
      witchcraft, 197, 201–2
    designs on Bathory lands,
      196–97, 201–2
    and return of Gabriel
      Bathory's enemies, 197
    shaky grip on power, 201
Beythe, Stephen (Protestant
  bishop), 8
  and bitter conflict between
    Lutherans and
    Calvinists, 41–42, 128
  Magyari and, 41–42, 45–46
  mixed religious practices
    of his flock, 39–40
  as Nadasdy family friend, 39
  religious tolerance of,
    39–40
  on Zvonarics, 139
blood bath
  origin of legends of, 206–7
  as term, 12
Bocskai, Stephen (Protestant
  Lord), 7
  death of, 87
  Hungarian reunification as
    goal of, 83

and Peace of Vienna,
  82–83
as prince of Transylvania,
  82, 87
at Stephen Bathory's
  funeral, 66
support for Bathory's land
  rights, 68
and throne of Transylvania,
  struggle over, 87–91
murder of key Gabriel
  Bathory supporter,
  89–90, 93
Parliament's appointment
  of Rakoczi, 91
politically motivated
  rumors of poison as
  Bocskai's cause of
  death, 88–90
Bocskai's revolt against
  Rudolf II, 54–61
  Bathory's difficult position
    in, 55–58, 59, 60
  Bathory's help for peasants'
    rebuilding after, 85–86
  Bathory's lands lost or
    damaged in, 58, 83–85
  Bathory's public support of
    Rudolf II, 68
  comet appearing during, 54
  death of Stephen Bathory
    and, 60–61
  German-Hungarian
    tensions and, 64
  groups joining revolt, 54
  and growing opposition to
    absolute monarchy, 64
  liberation of Hungary as
    goal, 54
  lingering tensions
    following, 83–84
  nobles, 60
  Parliament of 1605 and, 57
  peace agreement ending,
    81–83
  propaganda campaigns to
    sway public, 64–65

INDEX

Bocskai's revolt (*cont'd*)
  rebels' crowning of
    Bocskai as King of
    Hungary, 58
  religious overtones of
    conflict, 64
  Rudolf II's stripping of
    Bathory's titles, 58
  Rudolf II's suspicions
    about Bathory family,
    55–56
  and spread of disease, 69
  theft and violence by
    Hapsburg soldiers,
    63, 85
  threats against Bathory, 59
  Thurzo and, 55
  Turkish incursions during,
    63
Bratislava, capital at, 47, 48
burial practices, Lutheran-
  Calvinist dispute over,
  124–26, 127, 133, 167
  and Bathory's dispute with
    pastor Ponikenus,
    124–27
  as likely reason for
    accusations of secret
    burial by Bathory, 127,
    133, 167
Čachtice castle
  as Bathory's marriage gift
    from her husband,
    39, 144
  Bathory's retirement to,
    144–45
  described, 123
  enemies of Bathory
    surrounding, 144–45
  healers residing at, 71
  house built for daughter
    and her husband at,
    108–9
  and legend of Miss Modl,
    67
  as modern tourist
    attraction, 11, 208

  and war-torn countryside,
    60, 85
  wedding of Bathory's
    daughter Kate at,
    105–6
  See also imprisonment of
    Bathory; Ponikenus,
    John (Lutheran pastor
    of Čachtice); raid on
    Bathory's castle at
    Čachtice
Calvin, John, 37–38, 125
Calvinist Church
  dispute over burial
    practices, 124–26, 127,
    133, 167
  establishment of, 37–38
  religious tensions with
    Lutherans, 40–42
Catholics
  anti-Protestant violence of
    early sixteenth century,
    113–14
  See also Counter-
    Reformation
Counter-Reformation, 37
  and anti-Protestant
    violence, 113–14
  success of in Hungary, 206
Cziraky, Moses, 140, 158,
  186, 204
Czobor, Elizabeth (wife of
  George Thurzo), 7
  children of, 70
  chronic illness of, 70
  later life of, 203
  married life of, 49–50, 291
  Thurzo's efforts to make
    Bathory's acquaintance
    and, 49–50
Darvulia, Anna (court
  midwife and healer), 6
  accused servants' efforts to
    blame, 171
  common people's mistrust
    of, 71
  death of, 131–32, 153

  as possibly the "*carnifex*"
    disciplined by local
    pastor, 74
  as woman scientist at
    Bathory's court, 71
  work as barber-surgeon as
    likely source of torture
    accusations against,
    72–73
Defenestration of Prague,
  Second, 201
Deseo, Benedict, 186
Devín Castle (Bratislava),
  Bathory's loss of, 83–84
Doczy, Andreas (lord-
  lieutenant)
  accusers' spread of rumors
    about, 153
  trial for alleged poisoning
    spree, 92–93, 145
Doricza (maid of Elizabeth
  Bathory's)
  display of corpse to public,
    151–52, 172–73
  as one of small number of
    verified deaths, 292
  as only body recovered in
    investigation, 151
  Thurzo's lies about, 173, 180
  Thurzo's likely wounding
    of body, 152
  witnesses to her illness, 154
Drugeth, George (Count of
  Humenne, husband of
  Kate Nadasdy)
  Bathory's enthusiasm
    about daughter's
    marriage to, 108–9
  character of, 109–10
  and division of Bathory's
    properties, 162, 198
  efforts to exploit Bathory's
    imprisonment, 179,
    182–83
  enemies' near-successful
    effort to strip him of
    land and titles, 109, 162

INDEX

family of, 6
family ties to Bathory
   family, 108
as Hapsburg ally against
   Gabriel Bathory, 119,
   182
lands of, 108
and Transylvania-Royal
   Hungary border
   dispute, 115
Drugeth, Valentine, of
   Humenne
as candidate for
   Transylvanian throne,
   87–91
as cousin of George
   Drugeth, 7
death of, 92
Drugeth, John (son of Katalin
   Nadasdy), 204
eclipse of March 1606, 81
Ecsed water-castle, 26, *26*
and Bathory family Ecsed
   branch, 27, 55, 83, 87,
   96, 196
Bathory's childhood in,
   26, 38
and Gabriel Bathory, 87,
   194, 195
seizure by Transylvanian
   government, 201–2
Stephen Bathory and,
   56–57, 60–61, 68
Transylvania-Royal
   Hungary conflict and,
   115, 119
Eger, siege of, 33
female healers
at Bathory's court, painful
   treatments by, and
   torture rumors, 72–75,
   152–53, 187
burning of three, on
   Thurzo estates, 131, 203
targeting by Lutheran
   Church, 131–32
See also Darvulia, Anna;

Myjava, Mistress of;
   Szentes, Dorothy
Ferdinand I (Holy Roman
   Emperor), 7, 25
finishing school
on Bathory's estate, alleged
   crimes at, 111–12,
   118–19, 128
as common at aristocrats'
   homes, 111
students at, as
   prepubescent girls, 111
typical number of students,
   128
Fugger banking family, 47, 49
Gasparides, Zachary
   (Lutheran pastor of
   Podolie), 8
funeral for girl performed at
   Bathory's request, 126
visit to imprisoned
   Bathory to gain
   confession, 154–56
Giczy, Andrew, 192–94
Gonczy, Anna (local
   noblewoman), testimony
   on death of her daughter,
   173
Guinness Book of World Records,
   on Elizabeth Bathory's
   murders, 11, 12, 14, 209
Gutenberg, Johannes, 35–36
hajduks, 54, *54*
and Bathory's
   imprisonment, 156
and Bocskai's revolt, 54,
   60, 68
and Gabriel Bathory's
   seizure of Transylvanian
   throne, 95–96, 99
and murder of Gabriel
   Bathory, 193, 194, 195
murder of Katai, 90, 93
postwar rampaging by, 96
public's fear of, 63, 64
and struggle for
   Transylvania throne

after Bocskai's death, 88
theft and violence by, 85
and Transylvania-Royal
   Hungary border
   dispute, 114–15, 119
Hapsburg family, 7
back salary owed to
   Bathory's husband, 32,
   52, 78, 180
and civil war in Hungary,
   25–27
conquest of Transylvania,
   206
and Counter-
   Reformation, 206
and growing opposition to
   absolute monarchy, 64
interbreeding in, 28, 64
See also Ferdinand I (Holy
   Roman Emperor);
   Matthias II (King of
   Hungary); Rudolf
   II (Holy Roman
   Emperor)
Helen (coachman's widow),
   171–72, 173
Helena Jo (nanny to
   Elizabeth Bathory's
   children), 6
accusations against others,
   187
arrest and initial torture
   of, 154
confession under torture,
   164–66, 167, 174
execution of, 174–75
Hernath, Lady Helen
   (noblewoman in
   Elizabeth Bathory's
   court), 6
death of daughter, 173
interview in Bathory
   investigation, 187
testimony concerning
   death of her daughter,
   118–19, 130, 142, 145,
   151, 187

INDEX

Horvath, Lady Anna, 99–100
Hungary
  Battle of Mohács, trauma of, 23, 24, 25
  civil war after death of Louis II, 25–26
  division into Royal Hungary and Transylvanian state, 27
  Ottoman attacks on, 23–24, 41–42
  prominence of Bathory family in, 22–23
  prosperity under Matthias the Just, 21–22
Iffiu, Kate (cousin of Elizabeth Bathory)
  family of, 6
  influence on Gabriel Bathory, 100
  rumored affair with Gabriel Bathory, 100
  and Transylvania-Royal Hungary border dispute, 115
  wealth of, 196
  as wife of John Imreffy, 100
imprisonment of Bathory
  after raid on Bathory's castle, 153
  Bathory's hope for support from powerful friends, 156–57
  Bathory's spurning of Lutheran pastors as enemies, 153–54
  correspondence and visitors allowed during, 179
  Lutheran pastors' effort to gain confession, 154–56
  petitioning of Matthias II from, for fair trial, 179
  son forbidding to visit, 177
  son-in-law's efforts to exploit, 182–83

as total immurement, in legend only, 10, 179
Imreffy, John, 100, 115
interrogation of Bathory's servants under torture, 162–73
  accusations against noblewomen linked to Bathory, 172
  blaming of dead or departed servants, 171
  blaming of other servants, 169–70, 171–72
  confessions about disposal of bodies, 167–69
  details mirroring true-crime broadsheets, 170
  fantastical crimes confessed to, 209
  initial arrest and torture, 153–54
  interrogators' limited interest in evidence, 170
  locating alleged torture chamber as goal of, 165–66
  locating of bodies as goal of, 167–69
  and necessity of confessing to interrogators' charges, 163–64, 169, 171
  testimony denying Bathory's involvement, 168
  transfer to Thurzo's family seat for, 162–63
  types of torture used, 164
  vague, conflicting, or absurd details in, 164–67, 169–70
investigation of Elizabeth Bathory
  accusations against noblewomen linked to Bathory, 172
  accusations of secret

burials as likely part of Lutheran-Calvinist dispute, 127, 133, 167
allegations leading to, as dubious, 111–12
allegations of treason, 158, 170, 171
allegations of witchcraft, 157–59, 170–71, 179, 200
alleged tortures in urban Vienna, 166
arrests of servants and healers, 153–54
and attacks on her servants, 146–47
Bathory's awareness of, 77, 115
Bathory's claims of innocence, 15–16
Bathory's early efforts to address accusations, 118–19, 142–44, 145
Bathory's interrogation, limited evidence of, 205
Bathory's reliance on support of friends, 145
child trafficking ring, accusations of, 13, 172
correspondence on wicked "*carnifex*" in Bathory's household, 43–45, 74–75
as corrupt, 14
evidence
  first set of depositions, 121–22, 292
  second set of depositions, 133, 292
  third set of depositions (servants' confessions), 163–72, 185, 292
  fourth set of depositions, 181, 185–86, 292
  fifth set of depositions, 181, 186–87, 292

280

INDEX

failure to interview obvious witnesses, 187
failure to locate any bodies, 169
and flight, Bathory's decision against, 147–48
Hapsburgs' concurrent efforts to overthrow Gabriel Bathory, 181–82, 183–84
interview of supposed noble accomplices, 187–88
leading questions addressed to witnesses, 122
and loss of legal case over Lendava lands, 147
Matthias II's concerns about handling of, 178, 179
murder accusations' initial lack of traction, 127
nearby murderous countess possibly confused with Bathory, 129–30
opening of, by Palatine Thurzo, 111
parallels to slur campaign against Klara Bathory, 116–17, 143–44
Ponikenus's wild accusations, 122–23, 157–59, 171, 179, 200
and punishment, 161–62
range of horrific charges, 200
recent published stories of female serial killers and, 129
records on Bathory's defense, as missing, 205
servants' confessions under torture, 155–56
small group of Lutheran pastors active in, 157
small number of accusers, 201
Thurzo's biased account to Matthias II, 178–79

victims, alleged
actual confirmed deaths, and causes, 173, 186, 292
conflicting stories about, 188
as mostly never identified or verified, 134–35, 292
witnesses
conflicting details given by, 134
confusing of medical treatments with torture, 72–75, 132–33, 152–53, 187
cronies of Red Megyery as, 140–42
general unreliability in sixteenth and seventeenth centuries, 12–13
hearsay evidence taken as fact, 12
number of, 8, 291–92
outrageous claims by, 12–13
Thurzo's control over many, 142
See also imprisonment of Bathory; interrogation of Bathory's servants under torture; Matthias II (King of Hungary), and Bathory investigation; Ponikenus, John (Lutheran pastor); raid on Bathory's castle
Junius, Johannes (mayor of Bamberg), confessions under torture, 163–64, 171
Justine (maid of Elizabeth Bathory), 68, 94
Katai, Michael, murder of, 89–90, 93
Kendi, Stephen (chancellor of Transylvania), 112–13

Kisfaludy, Blaise, 80
Kornis, Balthazar, 113
Lany, Elias (Lutheran bishop)
and burning of local witch, 155
election to Lutheran governing board, 130–31, 145–46
and investigation of Bathory, 157–58, 163
as mentor to Ponikenus, 8, 128, 130
as personal pastor to Thurzo, 8, 128, 130
legend of Elizabeth Bathory's crimes, 9–11
appeal to scholars and crime buffs, 14
and Bathory's loss of Devín Castle, 84
blood baths stories, origin of, 206–7
as Central European tourist attraction, 207–8
claimed number of victims, 10, 12
cruelty of entitled elite as common moral drawn from, 13
curious lack of discussion of, after her death, 200–201
as dubious and inaccurate, 12–13
early elements of, 77
early popularization of, 205–7
evolution into popular culture phenomenon, 207
Guinness Book of World Records on, 11, 12, 14, 209
investigators with doubts about, 14
local lords benefiting from damage to Bathory, 81

legend of Elizabeth (*cont'd*)
    modern fascination with, 11–12
    motive, dubious theories on, 14–15
    peasants' postwar return to her lands as evidence against, 86
    sloppy research and translation in, 15
    and tales about theft of children for their blood throughout history, 15, 207
    and vampire legends, 207, 289
    war, disease, and religious strife as larger context of, 75
    See also Modl, Miss, legend of
Listius, Anna Rozina (Countess)
    murders by, 129, 135
    pardon of, 162
    public's possible confusion of Bathory with, 129–30
Little Ice Age, 41, 92
Louis II (King of Hungary), 23, 25
Louis XV (king of France), 207
Luther, Martin, 35, 37, 40, 125
Lutheran Church
    campaign against aggressive medical care, 131–32
    Council of 1610, 130–31
    dispute over burial practices, 124–26, 127, 133, 167
    establishment of, 37
    religious tensions with Calvinists, 40–42
    uprising against Council of 1610, 145–46
Lutheran pastors, 8
    small group persecuting Bathory, 122–23, 157
        visit to Bathory before raid, 150
        visit to Bathory under arrest, 153–56
Magyari, Stephen (Lutheran pastor of Sárvár), 8
    anti-swearing campaign, 34–35, 46
    Bathory's grudging support of, 46
    On the Causes of the Decay of Our Country, 43
    church council on Nadasdy estates, 34–35
    comfortable living in Francis Nadasdy's employment, 45–46
    correspondence on wicked "*carnifex*" in Bathory's household, 43–45, 74–75
    and Francis Nadasdy's funeral, 34, 45–46
    long association with Nadasdy family, 35
    on moral rot in Hungary, 43, 130
    strong anti-Catholic and anti-Calvinist views, 45
    as successor to Reczes, 42
    traumatic service as army pastor, 35
    on Turkish attacks as God's punishment, 35
Matthias II (King of Hungary)
    ambition of, 97
    and Bathory investigation
        allegations of treason and, 158, 170, 171
        Bathory's petitions for fair trial, 179
        criticism of Thurzo's handling of, 178, 179, 185
        decision to proceed with trial, 184–85
        demands to review evidence from, 179–81
        hopes for financial profit from, 180, 185
        order for speedy trial, 179, 181
        Thurzo's delay in notifying king of, 178
        Thurzo's selective, sensationalized account of, 178–79
        Thurzo's stalling in delivery of evidence, 180–81
    as brother of Rudolf II, 7
    elevation to Holy Roman Emperor, 184
    governing style of, 97
    invasion of Transylvania as concurrent with investigation of Elizabeth Bathory, 181–82
        defeat, and subsequent peace, 183–84
        implications for Bathory investigation, 183, 184
        Thurzo's opposition to, 183
    negotiation of peace with Turks and Bocskai's rebels, 82
    seizure of Royal Hungary throne, 96–97
    subjugation of Transylvania as goal of, 114–15
Matthias the Just (King of Hungary and Croatia), 21–22, 97, 289
medical care in Bathory's time, 69–73
    barber-surgeons, 70, 72–73, 73, 166
    at Bathory's court
        heavy use of antimony, 95
        as likely fatal in some cases, 95

282

INDEX

painful treatments, and torture rumors, 72–75, 152–53, 187
types of healers, 70–72
and witchcraft allegations, 186
cannons and muskets in war and, 73
common people's suspicions about foreign healers, 71
as dangerous and unregulated, 73
doctors, 70, 71, 72
high rate of illness and, 69
high-quality care provided to Bathory's servants, 68
Lutheran Church's campaign against, 131–32
Paracelsus's research and, 94
unregulated substances in, 93–95
women scientists in, 70–71
Megyery, Emery "Red" (nobleman in Elizabeth Bathory's court)
Bathory's investigation into staff corruption as threat to, 141–42
and division of Bathory's properties, 162
exploitation of Bathory's imprisonment, 182–83
and investigation of Bathory, 165
knowledge of Bathory's impending arrest, 145, 161
as likely working against Bathory, 140–41
and Parliament, 57
and Paul Nadasdy, guardianship of, 6, 138, 204

and Paul Nadasdy's submission to Thurzo, 177–78
real estate wealth acquired by, 139–40
son educated beside Paul Nadasdy, 140
warnings to Bathory about Bocskai's revolt, 57, 67
Modl, Miss, legend of damage to Bathory's reputation from, 84
early seventeenth-century medicine and, 69, 74
likely political motives of, 68
mundane event likely at core of, 67
similarity to contemporary folktales, 67
as supposed victim of Bathory, 66–67
testimony on, 67, 68–69, 186
witness's debunking of, 187
Mohács, Battle of
deaths in, and women in male roles, 32–33
disastrous losses in, 23, 25
and Protestant Reformation, 36, 37
as wound to Hungarian psyche, 24
Myjava, Mistress of (*majorosné* of Bathory's farms and herbalist)
as Bathory's trusted companion, 7, 132
confession under torture, 174
execution of, 174
herbal baths for Bathory, 143
other servants' accusations against, 171
targeting by Lutheran Church for healing

practices, 132
witchcraft accusations against, 158–59, 171, 175
Nadasdy, Andras (child of Elizabeth Bathory), 20, 34, 71
Nadasdy, Anna (child of Elizabeth Bathory)
Bathory's correspondence with, 107
death of, 203
engagement party, 52–53
family jewels removed by, 182–83
family of, 6
marriage of, 53, 107–8
Nadasdy, Francis (Count of Nádasd and Fogarasföld, husband of Elizabeth Bathory)
appearance, 19–20, 20
battles against Turkish invaders, 28, 42
"Black Lord," nickname of, 28
as celebrated warrior, 19
children of, 6
death of oldest son, 34
final letters asking protection for his family, 31–32
funeral of, 32, 33–35, 124
honors from Hapsburgs, 31
illness and death of, 19–21, 28–29
large amount owed by Hapsburgs to, 32, 52, 78, 180
life of, 19
and local religious conflict, 41–42, 44
as Master of the Horse at Parliament, 48
troubles of early seventeenth century, 20–21

283

INDEX

Nadasdy, Francis III (son of Paul Nadasdy), conviction for treason, 204–5
Nadasdy, Katalin "Kate" (child of Elizabeth Bathory)
- accused as accomplice of Bathory, 172
- children of, 203–4
- family of, 6
- fight to recapture the Bathory family estates, 204
- marriage celebration, 105–6

Nadasdy, Paul (child of Elizabeth Bathory)
- Bathory's efforts to guide, 138
- Bathory's opposition to guardians for, 140
- and epilepsy, 204, 291
- family of, 6
- full control of property delayed until age twenty-four, 138
- guardians of, as working against Bathory, 138–42, 144
- letter submitting to Thurzo, 177–78
- life of, 204
- Megyery as guardian of, 6, 138, 204
- seat in Parliament, at age twelve, 137–38
- son of, 204–5
- and trauma of Bathory case, 177

Nadasdy, Thomas (cousin of Elizabeth Bathory), 51, 59, 193

Nadasdy family
- lands owned by, 38–39
- religious affiliation of, 39

Ottoman Empire
- attacks on Hungary, 23–24, 41–42
- and Bethlen's installation on Transylvanian throne, 23–24
- and Bocskai's revolt, 58
- expulsion from Hungarian lands, 206
- Hapsburg's negotiation of peace with, 82
- incursions during Bocskai's revolt, 63, 78
- reputation for brutality, 24

Parliament
- Bathory's attendance as issue in, 57–58
- Bathory's attendance with husband, 47
- Bathory's decision not to attend after husband's death, 48, 50
- Bathory's popularity at, 47
- and Bocskai's revolt, 57
- Paul Nadasdy seat in, at age twelve, 137–38
- unrest against Rudolf II at, 50–52

Peace of Vienna, 82, 87, 97, 130

ongoing border clashes following, 110, 114

Transylvania-Royal Hungary renegotiation of, 114–15

Ponikenus, John (Lutheran pastor of Čachtice), 8
- access to Palatine Thurzo, 128–29
- account of attack by devils sent by Bathory, 159
- accusations of witchcraft and treason against Bathory, 157–59, 171, 179, 200
- Bathory's confrontation of, for attacks on her, 154–55
- and burning of local witch, 155
- complaints about support for Bathory, 156–57
- dispute with Bathory over burial practices, 124–27
- as ethnic Slovak unable to speak Hungarian, 123–24, 154
- at Francis Nadasdy's funeral, 124
- influence over witnesses, 127–28
- and Lutheran campaign against female healers, 131–32
- and Lutheran unrest after council of 1610, 146
- number of murders attributed to Bathory, 128, 141
- as pastor in Bathory's town of Čachtice, 123
- poem written for Bathory's trial, 188
- resentment of Bathory's avoidance, 126
- as source of murder allegations against Bathory, 122–23, 127, 128
- spread of accusations against Bathory, 128–29
- stalled career of, 200
- and strong language of bitter Lutheran-Calvinist dispute, 128
- testimony on Bathory under oath, 186
- visit to imprisoned Bathory to gain confession, 154–56
- Zvonarics's collaboration with, 139

printing press, and bitter conflict between Lutherans and Calvinists, 41

INDEX

Protestant Church, early schism into denominations and sects, 37–38
Protestant Reformation, 35–42
 doctrinal issues in, 37
 noblewomen as crucial early supporters, 36
 origins of, 35–36
 printing presses and, 35–36
 spread in Hungary, 36, 37
 violent suppression by Catholic Church, 36–37
"Pythonissa," burned as witch, 155–56
raid on Bathory's castle at Čachtice, 149–54
 arrests of servants and healers, 153–54
 Bathory's detainment following, 153
 court documents' lies and errors, 173–74
 doctor's examination of girls in infirmary, 151, 187
 failure to discover bodies or torture chamber, 150
 illegality of, 150–51
 Lutheran pastors visiting Bathory prior to, 150
 sick girls and single body found in infirmary, 150
 Thurzo's care to spread rumors about, 153
 Thurzo's claim to have interrupted torture session, 149–51
 Thurzo's mutilation and public display of dead infirmary patient, 151–52
 witnesses to sick girls, before raid, 150, 154
Rakoczi, Sigmund, 91, 96
Reczes, John (Lutheran pastor), 8, 40, 41–42, 128

religious tensions of Bathory's time
 and accusations of Calvinist practices, 43–45
 at Bathory's husband's funeral, 34–35
 Bathory's religious tolerance and, 46
 conflict between Lutherans and Calvinists, 40–42
 exacerbation by war and poor crops, 41
 Francis Nadasdy's efforts to calm, 41, 44
 Thurzo's Lutheran Council of 1610 and, 145–46
 See also Protestant Reformation
Royal Hungary
 Archduke Matthias seizure of throne, 96–97
 religious freedom gained in Peace of Vienna, 82, 130
 See also Matthias II (King of Hungary)
Rudolf II (Holy Roman Emperor), 7
 confiscations of Protestant church property, 52
 death of, 184
 Hapsburgs' reigning-in of, 82
 nobles' complaints about land seizures, 51–52
 profligate spending, and need for funds, 50–51
 seizure of "traitors'" assets to raise funds, 51
 stationing of Catholic mercenaries on Protestant estates, 52, 53
 throne of Royal Hungary wrested from, 96
 and unrest in Parliament, 50
 See also Bocskai's revolt against Rudolf II

Sara (servant), testimony against Bathory, 173
Sárvár Castle
 Bathory's private guard at, 77–78
 Bathory's turnover to son Paul, 144
 described, 38
 as Francis Nadasdy's ancestral home, 38
 Hapsburg troops stationed at, 52, 53, 59, 85
 healers at, 71
 library at, 93, 133
 religious turmoil in region of, 41–42, 44
 See also Magyari, Stephen (Lutheran pastor of Sárvár)
serial killers
 Guinness Book of World Records on, 13
 typical profile of, 13
 See also Listius, Anna Rozina (Countess)
servants of Elizabeth Bathory, 6
 and local tensions before Bathory's arrest, 168–69
 punishment of, 174–75
 as supposed accomplices in her murders, 10
 See also interrogation of Bathory's servants under torture; trial of Bathory's servants
Sittkey, Gabriel, 134, 164
Sittkey girls, as supposed victims, 134, 165
Smith, John, 24, 78
Suleiman the Magnificent, 23–24
Susanna (servant), evidence against Bathory, 12, 173
Szelestey, Adam, 142

285

INDEX

Szentes, Dorothy (court midwife and healer), 7
  accusations against others, 187
  accusations by other servants against, 168, 169
  arrest and torture of, 153–54
  confession under torture, 164–65, 167, 174
  execution of, 174–75
Szigetvár, Battle of, 53
Szilvasy, Jacob, testimony of, 186
Tatay, Caspar, 146–47
Tepes, Vlad (Vlad the Impaler), 289
Thirty Years' War, 201
Thurzo, Emery (son of George Thurzo), 98, 203
Thurzo, George (palatine of Hungary), 49
  admiration for Bathory, 47
  at Anna Bathory's engagement party, 53
  Bathory's servants' trials, rigging of, 162–63
  Bethen and, 190–91
  and Bocskai's revolt, 55, 60
  burning of witches / female healers, 131, 203
  children, lives of, 203
  on danger of travel, 65
  death of, 203
  and division of Bathory's properties, 162
  efforts to make Bathory's acquaintance, 49–50
  elevation to Count, 97
  family of, 7
  Francis Nadasdy's deathbed letter to, 31–32
  grooming of son, 98
  and Hapsburgs' campaign against Bathory, 118, 128–29, 137
  and Hapsburgs' campaign against Gabriel Bathory, 114, 115, 119, 137
  and invasion of Transylvania, 183
  and investigation of Bathory, 111, 121
  and Lutheran Church council, 130–31, 145–46
  married life of, 291
  medical care at court of, 73
  motives for accusing Bathory, 162
  and murder of Gabriel Bathory, 194
  as nouveau riche social climber, 48–49
  as Palatine of Royal Hungary, 97–98
  at Parliament, 50
  relative convicted of serial murders, 129–30
  renegotiation of Peace of Vienna, 114–15
  shifting of blame to Bathory's healers, 157
  on Stephen Bathory's death, 61
  unchecked ambition, enemies made by, 97–98
  See also raid on Bathory's castle; trial of Bathory
time period of Bathory murders
  belief in witchcraft, 12, 15, 44, 155
  high rate of illness in, 69
  new printing technology, and spread of rumors, 15
  notable events of 1610, 105
  notable people and scientific discoveries, 15
  political tensions, and fights among servants, 146–47
  routine confessions to fantastical crimes under torture, 208–9
  Turks' attacks on Hungary and, 28
  women's wartime adoption of men's roles, 32–33
  See also medical care in Bathory's time; religious tensions of Bathory's time
Tokorcs, woman scientist of (village healer)
  appeal to Bathory for help against vandals, 80
  as foster mother, 7
  Ponikenus' accusation of witchcraft against, 158
  targeted by Lutheran Church for healing practices, 131–32
Torok, Kate (cousin of Elizabeth Bathory)
  Bethlen's accusations against, 191
  family of, 6
  lands seized by Bethlen government, 196, 197
  wealth of, 196
Transylvania
  absorption by Hapsburg Empire, 206
  Bocskai's rule in, 82, 87
  Gabriel Bathory's seizing of throne, 95–96
  and Hungarian civil war, 25
  Parliament's appointment of Rakoczi to throne of, 91
  postwar deaths, numerous causes of, 92
  public panic over poison, after Bocskai's death, 91–92
  separation from Royal Hungary, 27
  Sigmund Bathory's periods of rule in, 110

INDEX

struggle for throne after Bocskai's death, 87–91
See also Bathory, Gabriel; Bethlen, Gabriel; Bocskai, Stephen; Matthias II
trial of Bathory's servants
  court judgment, lies and errors in, 173–74
  execution of witnesses, as highly irregular, 174, 178
  testimony mirroring true-crime broadsheets, 173
  Thurzo's rigging of, 162–63, 174
  unindicted servants' testimony, 173
  witnesses at, 172–73
trial of Elizabeth Bathory
  Bathory's death prior to, 198
  as contrary to fact, 15–16
  evidence on, finally delivered to crown, 185
  in legend, 10
  preparations for, 184–85
  and reduced number of supposed victims, 184–85
  Thurzo's efforts to avoid, 178, 180–81
Turoczi, Laszlo, 205–7, 208
Ujvary, John aka Ficzko (footman to Elizabeth Bathory), 6
  accusations against Bathory and other servants, 170–72

arrest and initial torture of, 154
attack on, 147
confession under torture, 164–65, 166, 167, 170–72
execution of, 174–75
Vaghy, Stephen, 170
vampires, and legend of Elizabeth Bathory, 207, 289
Velikey, Lady Anna (noblewoman in Elizabeth Bathory's court), 6, 187–88
witchcraft
  accusations against Bathory, 157–59, 170–71, 179, 200
  accusations against foreign women of high rank, 170
  Bathory women charged with, by Bethlen, 197, 201–2
  belief in, in Bathory's time, 12, 15, 44, 155
  burning of witches, 44, 131, 164–65, 175, 203, 203, 209
  increase in trials for, during Thirty Years' War, 202
Wittenberg University, religious conflict at, 40
women
  adultery or incest allegations as tool against, 100–101, 117–18

as doctors, 72
exploitation by men, as norm in Bathory's time, 79
women scientists in medical care, 70–71
Zápolya, John, 25–27
Zrinyi, Count Nicolas (husband of Anna Nadasdy), 6
  abandonment of support for Bathory, after threats, 161, 162
  advanced notice of Bathory's arrest, 161
  and division of Bathory's properties, 161, 162
  engagement party, 53
  as good husband and friend of Bathory, 107–8
  marriage to Bathory's daughter, 53, 58
  and Transylvania-Royal Hungary border dispute, 115
Zvonarics, Michael (pastor), 8
  background and rise to Lutheran leadership, 138–39
  as guardian of Paul Nadasdy, 138, 139
  and investigation of Bathory, 165
  as likely working against Bathory's interests, 139
  testimony against Bathory, 139, 157

A NOTE ON THE AUTHOR

SHELLEY PUHAK is a critically acclaimed poet and writer whose work has appeared in the *Atlantic, Smithsonian, Virginia Quarterly Review*, and elsewhere. Her essays have been included in *Best American Travel Writing* and selected as Notables in four consecutive editions of *Best American Essays*. She is the author of the national bestseller *The Dark Queens* and three award-winning books of poetry. She lives in Maryland.

ELIZABETH BATHORY: FACT VS. FICTION

This appendix is designed to address and debunk the many inaccuracies circulating in print and online about Elizabeth Bathory's life.

Is there any link between Elizabeth Bathory and Dracula?

Beginning the 1980s, following a resurgence of vampire themes in popular culture, a series of books and films began to appear with titles like *Dracula Was a Woman* and *Countess Dracula*, exploring a possible connection between Countess Bathory and Count Dracula. Most notably, Raymond McNally, a scholar of both eastern European history and horror films, argued that Bram Stoker's *Dracula* was inspired by the Blood Countess legend. (While unlikely—there is no mention of Elizabeth Bathory in the detailed notes Stoker kept while writing his novel—it is still possible that Stoker encountered a mention of the Countess in a folklore book he read at the time.)

As for a link between the two historical figures, only the most tangential exists.

Vlad Tepes, or Vlad the Impaler, was born more than 125 years before Elizabeth Bathory. His life, however, is intertwined with Hungarian history—Vlad Tepes was alternately an ally and an enemy of the great Hungarian king Matthias I, also known as the Raven King.

The Raven King's top commander was Stephen Bathory V. During two military campaigns, Vlad Tepes and Stephen Bathory fought alongside one another. There were many Stephen Bathorys in the family (it was a popular name!), but this specific one had no children, so he is not a direct ancestor of Elizabeth Bathory.

Did Elizabeth Bathory have an illegitimate child?

It is often claimed that, before her marriage at age fifteen, the Countess had some sort of relationship that resulted in a pregnancy.

This story is derived from a court deposition dated November 4, 1609, in which a girl named Elizabeth Bathory accuses a young nobleman of raping and impregnating her. The girl testifies that Ladislaus Bende "attacked her in the dark, stopped her mouth (so she couldn't shout), overpowered and deflowered her." When she became pregnant, the Bende boy begged her not to tell his parents and began "searching through his father's books to find a remedy with which he could end a pregnancy." He encouraged her to eat hemp seeds to cause an abortion, but she refused (even had she done so, the seeds would have done nothing). Eventually the Bende parents discovered the pregnancy and their son's role in it. To avoid a scandal, the girl was sent to a country house to give birth, and then, once "the bastard" was one week old, sent to live with her widowed mother. This paperwork was the opening salvo in her attempt to collect child support.

This first-person account is fascinating for the glimpse it gives of how the courts handled cases of sexual assault, of how abortions were attempted and pregnancies concealed, but it has nothing to do with Countess Elizabeth Bathory. The testimony is given by a young, unmarried girl; in 1609 Countess Elizabeth Bathory was a forty-nine-year-old widow. This girl lists her parents as free commoners and describes working for eight years as a domestic servant in the Bende household. The Bendes were recent entries into the nobility, not an established old family. They were the sort of family that might serve at the court of the Bathory family, but it is unconceivable to think of *any* woman in the noble Bathory family toiling for years as a Bende housemaid.

It is curious that this commoner has the same last name as an illustrious noble family, but there are several plausible explanations: The girl's father (one Paul Bathory) could have been descended from a former Bathory serf who adopted the ancient family's name. Alternately, the last name could simply indicate that the family hailed from one of the many towns with Bator (the Hungarian word for "brave") in their names.

Did Elizabeth Bathory have epilepsy?

It has been claimed that Elizabeth suffered from bouts of temporary psychosis, induced by epileptic fits. While there are records of many illnesses and injuries endured by the Bathory family, there is not a single record of the Countess having anything remotely resembling a seizure. The rumors of epilepsy likely started from a mistranslation or misreading of source texts. There *was* epilepsy in the Bathory family, but it was experienced by Elizabeth's son, Paul, well after his mother's death. This was no hereditary condition; it was the result of a severe head injury after a fall from a horse.

Was George Thurzo in love with Elizabeth Bathory?

Some argue that George Thurzo was in love with Elizabeth Bathory and angry that she had once turned down his marriage proposal. While there certainly *were* women who found themselves accused of witchcraft or other crimes for turning down a suitor, in this case that seems highly unlikely.

Thurzo was seven years younger than Elizabeth Bathory; the Countess had already been married for ten years when Thurzo first went looking for a wife. After his first wife died in childbirth, Thurzo sought a second wife. It would have been unthinkable for Thurzo to propose marriage to an older married woman; Thurzo was a devout Lutheran and also a notorious prude. While Thurzo once admired the Countess, he preferred more subservient women, pursuing the much younger Elizabeth Czobor. The personal letters between Thurzo and his second wife are unusually affectionate and the two seem to have shared a strong bond.

How many people testified against Elizabeth Bathory?

A total of 303 witnesses testified in Elizabeth Bathory's case (one man testified twice).

There were five rounds of depositions: two while the Countess was being investigated, one more during the trial of her servants, and two more afterward, in preparation for her trial. Many of those who testified did not actually give evidence against Elizabeth Bathory. For example, the largest round of depositions was the fourth, during which 225 people were interviewed. More than 80 percent of these people did not offer testimony against her (118 either said they knew nothing or had only heard the vaguest rumors, and another 70 reported only hearsay). Some people testified only after they had been named as accomplices, under threat of being arrested themselves.

How many deaths have actually been linked to Elizabeth Bathory?

There are six possible victims. One was Doricza, a commoner maid whose body was found in the Čachtice infirmary. The others were girls from the lower nobility who were confirmed to have died while at the court of Elizabeth Bathory, although most of their families did not think their deaths were the result of ill-treatment or murder. These girls were: the unnamed ten-year-old daughter of Anna and Stephen Gonczy; Anna Ztubyczay, sister of Caspar Ztubyczay; Elizabeth Bardy, daughter of Dorothy and Francis Bardy; Suzska Zelesthey, daughter of Anna and John Zelesthey; and Kata Birinyi, niece of John Deseo, the warden of Keresztúr Castle.

There are many secondhand allegations about the deaths of other noble girls. In all of these instances, either the witness could not provide basic identifying information about the girl (such as her first name) or the family never confirmed whether they indeed had a daughter who had died while under the Countess's care.

Is it true that no one knows where Elizabeth Bathory is buried?

Yes. While other Bathorys are buried in some of Europe's most illustrious churches, from St. Vitus's Cathedral in Prague to Wawel Cathedral in Kraków, it is unclear where the Countess's remains lie today.

Contemporary documents tell us she was buried in Čachtice; they just don't indicate exactly *where* she was buried. Most elite nobles were buried in the crypt underneath the church itself. However, in 1938, when the crypt at Čachtice was excavated, no Bathory coffin was found. The absence of the Countess's remains was explained away by local folklore, which claimed villagers had been so outraged by the burial that they had demanded she be dug up and moved.

If the Countess was indeed reburied elsewhere, the most logical location would be alongside her brother and nephew in the Bathory crypt close to her childhood home of Ecsed. However, when excavations were undertaken, no obvious signs of the Countess's remains could be found there either. Another possibility is that she was reburied alongside her husband, Francis, in his family crypt at Léka (now Burg Lockenhaus in Austria).

More recently, a Czech reporter has returned to the Čachtice church with underground radar and claims to have found a very promising undisturbed cavern under the church's altar that may contain human remains, although no excavation has yet been planned.

Also Available from Shelley Puhak
The Dark Queens

The remarkable, little-known story of two trailblazing women in the Early Middle Ages who wielded immense power, only to be vilified for daring to rule.

Brunhild was a foreign princess, raised to be married off for the sake of alliance-building. Her sister-in-law Fredegund started out as a lowly palace slave. And yet—in sixth-century Merovingian France, where women were excluded from noble succession and royal politics was a blood sport—these two iron-willed strategists reigned over vast realms, changing the face of Europe.

The two queens commanded armies and negotiated with kings and popes. They formed coalitions and broke them, mothered children and lost them. They fought a decades-long civil war—against each other. With ingenuity and skill, they battled to stay alive in the game of statecraft, and in the process laid the foundations of what would one day be Charlemagne's empire. Yet after the queens' deaths—one gentle, the other horrific—their stories were rewritten, their names consigned to slander and legend.

In *The Dark Queens*, award-winning writer Shelley Puhak sets the record straight. She resurrects two very real women in all their complexity, painting a richly detailed portrait of an unfamiliar time and striking at the roots of some of our culture's stubbornest myths about female power. *The Dark Queens* offers proof that the relationships between women can transform the world.

"Powerful feminist history . . . sweeping and detailed." —*USA Today*

"A lyrical and astute assessment of the political maneuvers, battlefield strategies, and resilience of medieval queens . . . A deeply fascinating portrait of the early Middle Ages that vigorously reclaims two powerhouse women from obscurity."
—*Publishers Weekly* (starred review)